D1629597

Sidesplitter

Sidesplitter

How to be From Two Worlds at Once

PHIL WANG

HODDER studio

First published in Great Britain in 2021 by Hodder Studio
An Hachette UK company

1

A CIP catalogue record for this title is available from the British Library

Hardback ISBN 9781529350272
Trade Paperback ISBN 9781529350289
eBook ISBN 9781529350296

Typeset in Bembo MT by Hewer Text UK Ltd, Edinburgh
Printed and bound in Great Britain by Clays Ltd, Elcograf S.p.A.

Hodder & Stoughton policy is to use papers that are natural, renewable and recyclable products and made from wood grown in sustainable forests. The logging and manufacturing processes are expected to conform to the environmental regulations of the country of origin.

Hodder & Stoughton Ltd
Carmelite House
50 Victoria Embankment
London EC4Y 0DZ

www.hodder-studio.com

Contents

To Mum, Dad, Aimée, Anna, Rose,
the Wangs, and the Pipers.

Introduction

Hey. It's me. Phil Wang.

Now, I just want to say: This book is not a memoir.

Although there is a lot of stuff about me and my life. But, again, it is not a memoir. It makes my skin crawl to think I've written a memoir. First of all – it makes me sound old. Very old. So old that I've decided that everything worth mentioning about my life has already happened, and that I'm near enough to the end of it that it's appropriate to write a retrospective of my time on this planet. What is a memoir, after all, if not a eulogy you can sell? It also makes me sound very old to use a French word like 'memoir' when I could just use the modern term for a book about your life: 'paper blog'. It makes me sound *old*.

Secondly, there are already too many of them. I swear there are more memoirs today than there are people alive. We're now at a point where memoirs are being written by the *children* of famous people about the experience of simply growing up the child of someone who has *also written a memoir*. I wouldn't write a memoir for the same reason I wouldn't start an alternative milk business or an online clothing brand – it's a saturated market. Do subscribe to one of my podcasts, though.

Thirdly, I don't consider myself to have lived a life worth writing a book about. I haven't escaped a gulag or won the Ballon d'Or (yet). I have not overcome some great adversity or revolutionised an industry. Memoirs should be the preserve of Nobel Prize winners, civil-rights heroes, and the occasional golfer. A memoir is an inherently arrogant thing to write, which is fine if you're Malala, but not if you're me – a man whose greatest challenge at the moment is that his fridge is too noisy.

I would only go so far as to say that, being half British and half Malaysian, my *circumstances* are noteworthy. One might even say, interesting. My parents. My heritage. My cultural identity. And as the mixed-race, multicultural experience is becoming more and more common with each subsequent generation of our human species, my observations about that aspect of my life are, I think, worth writing a book about. I hope.

So, this is not a memoir.

What follows instead are ten themed chapters, each on an aspect of life that is affected by my being mixed-race and from two countries at once. They are: FAMILY – aw; WORDS – which technically describes all the chapters, but this one is specifically about language; FOOD – delish; RACE – hoo boy; COMEDY – in which I lay out my defence of a racist old sitcom; LOVE – cute; HISTORY – which is about the British Empire and will, I'm sure, make me popular with *everyone*; ASSIMILATION – which is about the difficulties of feeling truly British and my issue with having an issue with cultural appropriation; NATURE – yuck; and HOME – in which I try to make you cry. In each I talk about how being mixed-race can complicate these facets of one's life, all of which might have been simpler had I been born either completely British or entirely Malaysian. And I illustrate the points I make with relevant stories of my own experience living as me, Phil Wang.

But it is not a memoir.

So where are you from? I mean *really* from? No. I mean, where are you *originally* from? As in, where are your *parents* from?

Now, I don't know about you (how could I?!), but having a British mother and a Chinese Malaysian father, I have been asked some form of that question my whole life, looking and sounding neither like I exactly fit in Asia nor Europe.

Am I British or Malaysian? In cricket, do I support England or Malaysia? Trick question – I don't watch cricket. And also, I don't think Malaysia fields a good enough team to play England. And even if they did, I wouldn't know because, again, I don't watch cricket.

It's a question I often ask myself. And to be honest, I'm not so sure of the answer. I live in the UK now but grew up in Malaysia until the age of sixteen. In a year's time I will have spent exactly half of my life in each country. Maybe I will know then. Once I have given each place an equal shot. Or maybe the process of writing this book will bring me clarity. This book that is not a memoir. Just a collection of personal stories from my and my family's lives about ten different themes, told by me from my perspective.

OK, it's part memoir. *Part.* But I'm a stand-up comedian and most stand-up is a kind of running memoir. It's about something that's happened to you recently, or a weird conversation you had, or a tub of jelly you saw fall on someone, or some thought that came to mind. So fine. Part memoir.

But mainly, this is a book about being mixed, about belonging, about having two sides of yourself that don't always harmonise. Maybe you are mixed, maybe you aren't. Both are cool with me. Perhaps you have been asked the question yourself. *Where are you REALLY from?* Perhaps from time to time, you ask it *of* yourself. Or, perhaps, you have never been asked it at all. Also fine. Whatever your situation is, I just hope you enjoy this book, to be honest. A collection of humorous essays about the mixed-race experience, and part *(part!)* memoir.

A Note on Ethnicity

Before we start, I should just clarify the distinctions between Chinese, Malaysian, and Chinese Malaysian. In my stand-up I predominantly refer to myself as Chinese. Which is true. My father's father was from China, but moved to Malaysia where he had my Dad. This makes Dad Chinese Malaysian. Chinese is the ethnicity, Malaysian is the nationality. My father's mother was a native of Borneo (the Malaysian part), a member of the Kadazan-Dusun people. I don't talk about them so much in my stand-up. Not for a lack of affection, of course. But you can imagine they are a little harder to do stand-up comedy about. Not so many widely known reference points about the Kadazan-Dusun people of North Borneo to play off (yet!). And again, Kadazan-Dusun (sometimes referred to as just 'Kadazan' or just 'Dusun') is an ethnicity of its own and is not part of the 'Malaysian ethnicity' because there is no such thing. However, Malay people, who make up a large part of Malaysia's population *are* an ethnic group. And this is where confusion often arises.

I'm glad we've cleared that up.

Enjoy!

FAMILY

A Murder of Teens

I could do nothing but watch as a gang of teenagers had a good old laugh at me for going to the cinema with my mum. At seventeen, I was a teenager too, of course, but they were younger. Fifteen or so. Children, in comparison, and occupying those years in which teenagers are especially feral. I forget what film Mother and I (I find it funny to call her that) had come to the Odeon in Bath to watch, but I know what those teens had come to see: a 6 foot 1 Eurasian virgin chowing down on Skittles outside Screen 2, staring blankly into the middle distance pretending not to notice them as he waited for his mum to return from the ladies'. And they were *loving* it.

The lead child, who looked like a sort of middle-class Beavis – a mushroom of sandy curls on his head, and an overbite of cruel teeth – was leading the laughs. Boy, he was really going at it. Pointing at my sullen face and wheezing with laughter like he really was a cartoon character, sprawled over a sofa, arm wrapped around his shaking middle, holding in his splitting sides. And his pals, perched around him like crows, followed suit.

Now, I don't have a very good memory, which is not really ideal for a book that I have now accepted is part memoir – I have a terrible memoir-y, I find it hard to re-memoir things – but I remember this well. The memory is clear for two reasons. First of all: it was very embarrassing, and my bastard brain is such that while the happy memories of my life all blur into one indecipherable and formless fog so that no one event can be retrieved with any real clarity, every indignity, disappointment and humiliation I have ever suffered is preserved in crystal-clear high-definition, lest I ever allow myself a moment's inner peace. And secondly, Beavis and his cawing murder of teens were a powerful representation of a different culture of family that I would have to understand now that I was in the UK. A culture in which the family is life's mere starting point, and those who hold onto it beyond their childhood years are social failures. Babies who can't stand on their own two feet. The family is a nest to be flown; a chrysalis to emerge from and leave behind once you become a fully formed individual, ready to go out into the world and ridicule Skittle-loving, mother-escorting immigrants in cineplexes with your mates.

This was a stark change for me. I had only just moved to England from Malaysia where I had grown up, and where the attitudes about family couldn't have been more different. In Asia your family *is* your social life. Which sounds sad now that I type it out. But I swear it is true. I hung out with my extended family all the time and, with my father being one of eight siblings, believe me when I say my family was *extended*. Although Dad sadly lost a sister in childhood, I was still left with five uncles, an aunt, four more aunts by marriage, and ten cousins. The regularity of the many Chinese festivals alone meant I saw these people by a rough estimate . . . 1,593 times a year. Chinese New Year (we just call it New Year), Lantern Festival, Qingming Festival (pronounced 'ching ming'), Moon Cake Festival. Not to mention – thanks to Malaysia's position directly on the equator – the hottest Christmases the Devil's ever known. These were large, bustling, cheerful affairs – long tables covered in food, boxed juices of lychee, chrysanthemum, winter melon and sugarcane, and houses full of voices: the strained exasperated stories of uncles, the giggling conspiracy of aunts, and the excited, playful camaraderie of children and teens at the kids' table.

These dinners were the focal points of my young calendar, and in between I would hang out with my cousins at sleepovers, at kung fu class, in shopping malls and, yes, at the cineplex.

Fighting with My Family

That's not to say that peace always reigned. My family fought regularly. Physically. Fists flew. Bodies were slammed to the ground. Limbs were twisted. But that's martial arts for you. My entire family learnt *Shorinji Kempo* – a Japanese variation of Chinese Shaolin kung fu. Every Saturday night, I – along with my two sisters and 163 cousins – would be driven to the dojo run by my uncle David, where we would suit up in our white *gi*, strap on our belts, and punch, block, and yelp in time, like an army of prepubescent North Koreans in an adorable military parade.

Kempo, as we called it, was a glue that held this large family together. My father, his brothers, and his sister are all black belts. Uncle David (yes, I will keep saying 'uncle' – there's this weird custom in Asia called *respect for our elders*) set up

Malaysia's first *Kempo* club, and within one generation it became a family tradition, with all members silently expected to take it up as a matter of initiation. Some families have christenings, others bat mitzvahs. In mine, we put on some ill-fitting cloth and kick our uncle in the stomach. Even now, at the rare opportunities that our even larger, globally dispersed family has to convene, the men will be found in the corner after dinner discussing the best defensive stances, putting each other in painful holds to demonstrate a weak point to the others, in the way most families discuss sport or share the latest gossip. Mine is a family of men who communicate primarily through arm locks. It's probably why my cousins and I were all so well behaved as kids. It's a much scarier proposition to get in trouble with your parents when they all have black belts.

I also have a black belt now, but through no small amount of nepotism. Before leaving Malaysia, it was agreed that Uncle David would take me on for a one-on-one crash course to acquire my black belt before I moved to England and left the dojo behind. What followed was a week of intensive daily training of about forty-five minutes a day. I was honoured to receive my belt at our final lesson – Uncle David collecting it from his office drawer and handing it to me, crackling in its clear plastic wrapping – a beautiful and ancient ceremony. However, staying to watch that evening's regular weekend class, and confronted with the technique and discipline of the other (real) black belts (and even a couple of *brown* belts), I was made plainly aware that I was not nearly good enough to have it. But such are the perks of being nephew to the king. The martial arts world is rife with this kind of abject corruption, I'm afraid to tell you. One can only imagine what unearned garments have been flung at the feet of Jaycee Chan* or Ayako Fujitani.† It turns out that in kung fu, it is more about who you know than how you throw.

I still have my *gi*. It is folded away in our family home‡ in Bath – waiting for me, like a superhero's cape, should my public ever need me to misremember the Japanese name for 'sideways hand chop'. It is now little more than a relic – another piece of memorabilia amongst the many dispersed and dusty items that make up the scattered museum of one's childhood.

The last time I put it on was over a decade ago and for only one day. My father had ambitions of starting a *Kempo* school of his own in Bath. A way to get involved in the community and take out some long-held frustrations with White people at the same time. Our local church kindly lent him a room and let him put up notices for any parishioners who might be interested in learning the way of the fist (non-sexual). Father asked me to help with the first lesson as his assistant and I jumped at the chance to prove myself worthy of a black belt that I was beginning to feel I had 'earned' about as much as Prince Charles 'earned' the Duchy of Cornwall.

The first person to arrive at the class was a very nice young Polish woman named Zuzanna. She poked her head through the door to find my father and me stood at attention in full

* Jackie Chan's son.

† Steven Seagal's daughter. Hey, I guess if she ever joins the navy, she would be a Seagal Sea Gal . . . Look, you try writing a book.

‡ My British friends would call this their 'parents' house'. Which I've always found a peculiar and sad name for the house you grew up in. Of course, your parents *bought* it (as a baby you were hardly in a position to put down a deposit), but in the spiritual sense it is yours too, isn't it?

kung fu garb, like a pair of Asian beefeaters tasked with guarding an empty church hall.

'Is this the kung fu class?' Zuzanna asked.

Looking back, I wish I had said 'No'. Just to see how she would have processed that: an old man and his tall son stood alone in a bare room in fighting gear just watching a door in silence.

She came in and waited with us for more students to arrive. She quickly proved herself to be our best student, because she quickly proved herself to be our only student. No one else turned up. It turns out that Christian pensioners aren't all that interested in learning how to fly-kick, so we began the class with Zuzanna alone. A class, I just want to make clear, that had twice the number of teachers as students.

It was an introductory lesson so there weren't many moves Zuzanna could do without my father and me first demonstrating, usually on her. You have to get a feel for the impact of the strikes and the pressure of the arm holds, so Dad and I took turns lightly punching and kicking Zuzanna – who, by the way, was wearing her regular clothes – and twisting her wrists so that she would have to slowly fall to the ground to relieve the pain.

'See? See how that hurts?' my father would instruct.

'Yes,' Zuzanna would politely reply as she calmly folded to the floor.

Only when the class ended did I realise that to an outsider looking in, our session could be seen one of two ways. One: two kung fu black belts from the Far East had given a new disciple a private lesson in our mystical ways for free. Or two: a man and his son spent an hour together very slowly beating a woman up in a place of worship. I want to reiterate that it was all done carefully and gently, and that she was not injured in any way. But if you'd filmed our lesson and sped up the footage, it would have looked horrific. Incredibly, she seemed happy with the experience. She thanked us, picked up her bag and left, soothing her new Chinese burns (we just call them burns).

My father wasn't welcomed back to teach there again after that. And not because news had spread of him and his child attacking an EU national in a space usually reserved for meetings about biscuits. You see, Shaolin kung fu is associated with the teachings of Buddha, and a couple of purists in the church's congregation felt there was only space in their belief system for one jolly fat man, and that spot was taken by a certain Saint Nick. A man who has firmly secured his place in the Christian tradition with a great deal of – let's face it – bribery. How could you *not* love someone who not only brings you presents, but puts pressure on all your friends and family to buy you presents too? To the contrary, Buddha instructs his followers to *renounce* their material possessions, and have *fewer* things. Which, if you think about it, makes Buddha the Anti-Santa – a veritable PR death sentence.

Dad moved his class to the nearby hospital where my mother was working as a doctor, and for a very sweet year both my parents worked in the same building. Father beating people up, then sending them upstairs to Mum for treatment, before she sent them back down to Dad to get beaten up all over again. The circle of life.

Zuzanna came back, incredibly. This time with a friend. And as I had at this point returned to university, Dad found that it was now he who was outnumbered in the lessons two-to-one. The tables had turned. The beater-upper had become the beater-uppee. And that is called karma. Another philosophy presumably not allowed at church.

A Wang is Born

Technically, I met the non-Wang side of the family first. I was born in the North Staffordshire Maternity Hospital in Stoke-on-Trent, my mother's hometown. The singer Robbie Williams (of 'Angels' fame and 'Party Like a Russian' disgrace) was born in the same hospital.*

Mother was back in the UK to finish her medical training and had gained a diploma in Tropical Medicine† and Hygiene‡ because she likes her medicine like she likes her men. She had timed it so perfectly that I arrived almost concurrently with her graduation, and should really have been handed to her along with her diploma in the maternity ward. Mother wearing nothing but a mortarboard hat, and me a red bow tight around my fat naked waist.

The reality was much less cute. I subjected Mother to a fourteen-hour labour having already been ten days past my due date. Had I been milk I would have been poured down the drain, no sniff needed. Dad was there too, having taken five weeks off work to come over from Malaysia. Five weeks I had significantly eaten into with my tardiness.

* I once mentioned this fact onstage and a woman in the audience was so impressed that she audibly yelped with excitement, despite the two births being sixteen years apart and my having never even met Robbie Williams. It was the first thing she had reacted to the entire show, which – considering we were about thirty minutes in by that point – was not a promising indication of how well it was going.

† Ooh la la!

‡ Ew.

By some incredible coincidence, I was delivered by a Malaysian doctor, Dr Vijay Menon, who happened to be working at that hospital in Stoke. So even though mum had flown back to the UK to give birth, I was still delivered by a Malaysian. Mum just couldn't escape them. Vijay must have been a great source of comfort for Dad. A familiar accent in a strange land can be a calming thing. And I like to imagine them shooting the breeze, reminiscing about *nasi goreng* and equatorial humidity, while my mother heaved and sweated and swore.

When I finally decided to knock on the door of life, I was so hefty that Vijay had to pull me out by the head with forceps (you know, like a farm animal). I came out at a hulking 9 pounds and 8 ounces (the average in the UK is 7 and a half pounds; in Malaysia, even less), and inheriting a touch of macrocephaly meant I had a large head (even for a big baby) that was rock-hard to boot. To be honest, Mum's first steps after that were more deserving of applause than mine.

However, I wasn't in great shape. A theme that would continue into adulthood. For one, I was grunting. Probably because I had some excellent new observational material on the birth canal but didn't yet possess the language skills to do it justice. Also, I had blue lips and blue patches on my back – never a good colour for a baby. It turned out these were something called Mongolian blue spots – temporary birth marks common with Chinese newborns. Mongolians are never good news if you are Chinese. If they aren't invading your northern borders, they're turning your babies into the aliens in *Avatar*.

I was put in an incubator in a room mainly reserved for premature babies, so I stuck out like a sore thumb among the tiniest, wrinkliest infants Staffordshire had to offer. If that sore thumb was also huge and Asian. So as not to completely sever the tie between mother and child while I was in there, Mother was handed a photo of me to hold on to. A Polaroid. Because it was the nineties.

I felt better once I vomited for the first time – a technique I would go on to employ to great effect in my late teens and early twenties – and I sprang to life the fun-loving vagabond you read before you today.

I was swapped back with the Polaroid, and that's when I first met my parents, Madeleine Piper and Benny Wang (nice couple!). I was the spitting image of my father, which was fortunate. I think it's good to get that question out of the way as early as possible.

I was then taken to a semi-detached house on a hill in Weston Coyney in Stoke, where I met my mother's parents. Gordon (Grandad) was a tall moustachioed working-class Derby man, and Ginette (Granny) was an exuberant, warm French woman from Le Mans – a wonderful cook who laughed a lot and put every room she entered at ease. She smelled the way grandmothers do. A smell immediately retrievable from memory for the rest of your life. A smell that caresses the sinuses and puts you to sleep. A loving chloroform.

Dad always got on with them both, calling them 'Mum' and 'Dad' from the moment he and Mother married, words he hadn't been able to say for a decade. It must have got the kind of strange looks that my sisters and I still get whenever we walk around town with our own mother – a seemingly unrelated White lady who has either calmly abducted us or is our tour guide.

Now, I'd like to say that 'Philip' was the result of some arduous and thoughtful search for the perfect name for my parents' first child. It is Greek for 'lover of horses'*. Perhaps my folks thought their son would take life by the reins; galloping across the world conquering everything in his path, atop the mighty stallion of his talent and conviction.

What actually happened was that my parents pulled my name out of a hat. The deadline to register me was fast approaching but Mother couldn't decide what to call me. Which is understandable. Naming a baby is difficult. Babies don't suit any names. They're babies. Blobs. And it's strange to name a blob. If you pointed at a baby and said, 'That looks like a Meredith', people would rightly assume you were nuts. Meredith is an adult person's name. Not a baby's name. The only names that suit a baby are silly ones like Squeezy, or Fatlump, or Ian. Because babies are silly blobs. Regardless, people were getting tired of saying '*It's* done a poo again', so I needed a name and fast. In an attempt to break our impasse, my father, ever the pragmatist (and probably losing patience), wrote some names on pieces of paper, grabbed Grandad's flat cap, threw them in, and Mother fished 'Philip' out at random. Like a game of charades. Though I hope to God she didn't start acting out 'lover of horses' in front of her family.

I've always found this a valuable story. Whenever I catch myself being arrogant or self-important in adulthood, I remind myself that I am but a loose piece of paper, a servant of chance,

* Imagine being so into horses in Ancient Greece that everyone knew you as *the horse lover*. It would be nice to believe that it was passed down through a long line of celebrated equestrians. But let's be honest. I think we all know where it came from. What filthy act and subsequent awful rumour created this name. And I think we all know what a sick, sick bastard that first Philip was. Funny thing is, I, Philip Wang, think horses are gross, and wouldn't have sex with one in a million years. Not in a million years.

and I was one bad bit of stitching and a loose label away from being named 'Dunn & Co. Hats'.

My parents flew me to Malaysia three weeks after I was born. Dad's five weeks of leave had run out, what with me being such a womb potato, so I was on a plane before I had even seen a month of ground life.

In transit at Kuala Lumpur International Airport, we were intercepted by three Chinese women who cooed over me (what can I say, I've always had it) and asked how old I was. 'Three weeks,' Mother told them. They were horrified.

'Three weeks?! Oh no, no, no, no.'

In Chinese tradition, neither the mother nor the baby is meant to leave the house for the first month*. *Zuò yuè zi* – 'sitting the month'. The idea is to protect mother and child from the dangerous and unhealthy elements of the outside world by making them live like a pair of stoners for four weeks. Their immune systems need to build, goes the theory. Dad didn't even want mum to have a *bath*, as tradition demands that the mother shouldn't wash her hair lest she catch a chill. Though he might have made that one up to try and secure himself a little more personal bathroom time.

Had I been at full capacity I would have informed the ladies that I had been born a week late. Add that to my three weeks on the outside and all in all I had done my time. But again my articulation failed me and I said, 'Geh gehhhh wada' or something equally hack.

* A Chinese custom unknowingly adhered to by every mother who had a baby in a COVID-19 lockdown. Congratulations, all your kids are going to be great at maths.

My folks had married in the UK, but were now building a life together in Sabah – a state on the northern tip of the island of Borneo, and a part of Malaysia.* After they'd got me back there, Mother continued to receive unsolicited Chinese child-rearing advice and traditional remedies. Asian people are not afraid to tell you you're messing up your kid in a way that would be considered rude and none of their business in the West. The mothers on my dad's side of the family very much viewed Mum as a clueless White woman who was going to get this baby *wrong*. But never fear – they were there to help. They were committed to making sure Mother raised me right, but it didn't always work. One of my aunts came over with drunken chicken – chicken cooked in rice wine – for Mum to eat to protect her from the chilling effects of cold winds. But the rice wine got into Mother's milk and gave me a rash, giving my aunts the impression that I really was a demon. Or at the very least, not into Chinese food. Which is the same thing. Though in my defence, turning red from a drop of alcohol was surely the most Chinese thing I could have done.

British baby care, on the other hand, is very different. The British do not sit the month. No months get sat. Parents parade their babies around town as soon as they can – down the park; at the pub. They invite friends over to meet it (as if it has anything interesting to say), exposing it to as many germs as possible to build up its tolerance to future disease, and drink

* It's a bit confusing. Malaysia is a country split into two halves by the South China Sea. Half is a peninsula poking out from under Thailand, and the other half is across the sea on Borneo. Borneo is the third largest island in the world after Greenland – which isn't green, it's all ice – and New Guinea – which isn't new, it's fucking ancient. So Borneo is the world's largest island that isn't named after a lie.

booze around it so that the fumes get into its nose and through its skin and into its bloodstream, all to build up its alcohol tolerance in preparation for future messy nights out. Meanwhile, my mother's breast milk still gets me absolutely wasted.

Not Quite Noon

Some people ask me where I got my funny bones from. Other people ask me where I got the nerve to think I'm funny. To the first group I'd have to say my grandad. To the second group I'd have to say your mum's house last night.

Grandad was the first joke teller I ever met. He always had a few saved up to delight us with each time we visited. I don't know where he got them from, but he seemed to have a vast mental library from which he could pluck a gag to suit almost any subject that came up. I didn't always laugh because I didn't always understand them. But I was in awe of jokes as an idea. Sentences created just to elicit laughter. What a fantastic thing for humans to do.

Grandad was my first conception of what a funny person was. In Mother's stories of his younger days, Grandad was a kind of slapstick figure, often set against the rather serious backdrop of the mid-twentieth century. During the Second World War, for example, he broke his leg just when everyone was called up for duty. Never one to slack, he hobbled on his crutches for five miles to sign up for the Fleet Air Arm. He wanted to help land planes by learning semaphore – that code with the small flags. Upon arrival, however, he discovered in the entrance tests that he was colour-blind – had been his whole life – making him unsuitable for what was quite a colour-based job. He was rejected. So, he just turned around and hobbled all the way back home.

Eventually, he began assisting the airborne effort in Research and Development instead, working at the Rolls Royce factory in Derby, testing Frank Whittle's crazy new invention – the jet engine.

Grandad was a smart man, but his starting point in life near the lower end of Britain's class structure meant he was never able to see his full potential through. Nevertheless, he had a natural technical aptitude, which made him an asset on the home front. Mother has unearthed an old photograph for me that shows Grandad sat at a table littered with tea mugs. Four other young men stand around the table chatting. One of the bystanders has put his left foot up on the table, bringing his knee uncomfortably close to his chin. On the back of the photo, Grandad has written 'Waiting for the "boffins" to give us the next test instructions.'* Little did he know then that in decades to come, a certain grandson of his would go to Cambridge University to study the engineering degree that he should have been able to, and work in Whittle's Laboratory where Frank first proposed his world-changing invention, because that particular grandson would be very clever. What a clever grandson that grandson would be†.

Granny was a kind and clever woman. If Grandad was held back by class, then Granny was held back by her sex, with

* Reading the note now, I'm astonished to see his handwriting looks identical to mine – terrible. But bad in the exact same ways. It is genuinely like reading something I've written. Eerie. He never taught me to write or anything, and I never read his handwriting before I learnt to write myself, so this must be pure natural inheritance. It's astonishing how our genetics can tie us together across generations; across time. It's even more astonishing that after thirty years on this planet I have still never learnt how not to write like a chicken having a seizure.

† I'm talking about me. I am the grandson.

aspirations and talents beyond what the times allowed a woman. She was very French but also very nice if you can imagine such a thing. She pronounced the word *salt* 'sohwt', which I always thought was just wonderful. She came to Britain after the war with an organisation that sent Europeans over to help bring in the British crops. Bloody Europeans. Coming over here, making us eat our vegetables.* She found the Scottish farmers friendlier than those she encountered south of the border, but must have acquired a taste for rudeness (or 'our world-famous sense of humour' as the English call it) because she decided to stay, and took a job as a French assistant at a school in Nottingham. Meanwhile, my grandfather was in Shardlow, single, and eager to learn French. A French friend of his hung out occasionally with a few other French people at an ice rink in Nottingham, and invited him to join, where he met French Granny, and where – I presume – they Frenched.

Granny passed away when I was fourteen, and being on the other side of the world most of the time, I never got to know her as well as I'd wanted to. And although Grandad lived on a further fifteen years, by which time I had moved to the UK, I never got to know him as well as I should have. Life's other commitments can distance you even when geography doesn't. And before I knew it, it was 2019 and I had no grandparents left.

I have never met my father's parents. He lost his mother in his late teens, and his father in his twenties, before any of my

* Some things never change, including the peculiarly British reticence to feed ourselves. European workers still make up the backbone of the Britain's harvesting operation. The economic and political self-harm of the UK's decision to leave the European Union will force us to reap what we've sown, but unfortunately not in the literal sense.

generation were born. So among myself, my sisters and my cousins, our grandparents exist as a kind of abstract legend.

The Wangs refer to our grandfather as Gong Gong and our grandmother as Po Po (pronounced 'paw paw' like a tiger's hand, not 'poe poe' like she's American police). The Chinese language employs a complex tree of unique names for each member of your family in relation to you. For example, what you call your grandmother on your dad's side is different to what you call your grandmother on your mum's side*, and each of your uncles and aunts has a different name depending on their position in age among their siblings. Although I am aware that to many readers 'Gong Gong' and 'Po Po' sound like two panda bears at Edinburgh Zoo, I assure you they weren't. Pandas have to be cajoled by teams of zoologists into reproducing. And as I said, my father was born one of eight.

Gong Gong's name was Wang Yap Kong (Chinese names begin with the surname) and Po Po's was Sanoh binti Lukim (Sanoh, daughter of Lukim†).Him a Chinese communist on the run, finding peace in a new land as the town barber, her an orphan of the Kadazan-Dusun people of North Borneo. Their marriage was a point of disapproval among the local Chinese émigrés, who stuck to marrying their own, and referred to my father and his half-caste siblings as 'eleven o'clock' – not quite noon. Not quite Chinese. Not quite right. Mixed-race

* Your dad's mum is *pó po* and your mum's mum is *wài pó*. Literally 'grandmother' and 'grandmother from the outside' respectively. You think mother-in-law jokes are problematic? Try 'mother-in-exile'!

† Sanoh's adoptive father Lukim was a master fighter, with the strength of three men. At least according to family legend. One advantage of coming from somewhere with no reliable record keeping is that myth takes its place, which, whether true or not, is always more fun.

families are an aberration everywhere, it seems. And though I grew up assuming my father was of a simpler background than myself – completely Malaysian, and ethnically plain old Chinese – it turns out we are more similar than I'd thought.

There is only one picture of my Asian grandparents – a black-and-white photograph from the sixties. It's a little blurry, and their skin glows fluorescent with overexposure. But you can make out Yap Kong's steeliness and Sanoh's alert eyes and soft beauty. Perhaps that softness is just the blur. For my entire life, this one photograph and a handful of stories have been all I've known of them.

Still, Gong Gong and Po Po were a lingering presence throughout our childhoods. Especially on the day of the Qingming Festival, or to use its more to-the-point English name, Tomb-Sweeping Day. Each year the family makes its trip to my grandparents' cemetery – a rather haunting, chaotic graveyard improvised into the slopes of a roadside hill, so crowded with gravestones that it is hard to imagine fitting all those coffins in together at once. None of the tranquillity of an English graveyard here. It's a nightmarish scene, hiking up an overpopulated city of the dead in the equatorial heat, careful not to step into any collapsed graves, nodding grimly at the other families as you pass, tending to their own, sun beating down on you while traffic growls angrily and apathetically from below. The objective is to burn paper offerings and clear the area around Gong Gong and Po Po's graves, which are adorned with their two polished faces, each taken from that old familiar photograph. To make this monolithic grave-mountain all the more bizarre, it is also wrapped around an enormous fire station at the foot of the hill, which I have never seen anyone go in or out of. I imagine because no one has ever agreed to take a job there.

But creepy or not, macabre though it may be, every year the pilgrimage must be made. The dead must be remembered. It is the responsibility of Gong Gong and Po Po's children – my father and his siblings – to remember and observe the numerous Chinese festivals each year, including Qingming, for which it is their humble duty to gather the family at Yap Kong and Sanoh's graves to honour them and tidy their resting place.

One year, they let it slide. People were busy or tired or simply not bothered, and my father and Uncle David and the rest let Qingming pass without gathering the family, leaving the graves unattended. The following night, Dad had a dream: trapped at home as it thundered with rain, he heard a tapping coming from somewhere in the house. Tap, tap, tap it went, though he could not see where from. He searched through the house for the source of the sound. Following the tapping through the din of the downpour outside, he eventually came to a window, where he found his parents looking in, soaking and cold, saying nothing. Just tap, tap, tapping on the glass. The family never missed one again.

White Families Be Like

British families, specifically those who have been British for a few generations, are usually less close to their extended family. The nuclear family is important – parents and siblings – but the extended family – your aunts, uncles, cousins – are relative acquaintances, only seen once a year or so around the holidays. Even though it was only every other year that we flew to England to see Granny and Grandad, I saw them infinitely more often than Gong Gong and Po Po. But to be fair to GG and PP, they did suffer the quite devastating handicap of being dead. Pretty difficult keeping up contact time with the old grandson when you're busy making sure a fire station is well and truly unsellable.

I have British cousins. A good bunch, all. But I was never able to form the close, friendly relationships that I had with my Malaysian ones. In part this was of course to do with our having grown up on different sides of the globe to one another. But in observing their interactions with each other, I get the impression there was less intimacy to be had there, anyway. They care about each other, and like each other, but for the most part live their own lives.

Many extended families in the UK that I have observed seem so unfamiliar with each other, they may as well not be related. An attitude that is practically encoded in the law. It is, after all, legal to marry your cousin in the UK. Your *first* cousin. Not just your second cousin or third cousin. Your *first* cousin. Your uncle's daughter. Your aunt's son. And although it isn't particularly common to meet such a couple in the UK – a couple who, let's say, have *too* much in common – that it is still enshrined in law that every Briton has a God-given right to bang their cuz says a lot about the cultural lack of closeness within extended families.

It is illegal to marry your cousin in China. You can't do it, no matter how estranged or sexy they are. Genetically speaking, British cousins are as related to each other as Chinese cousins are. But culturally, Chinese cousins are closer, and their romantic and sexual union all the more perverse. If anything, the Chinese take it too far. Not only is it illegal to marry your cousin, for many centuries in China it was illegal to marry anyone *with the same surname*, at times even punishable by death, so close-knit is the extended Chinese family unit. It is now no longer illegal, but still very much frowned upon, just to be on the safe side. My family would never accept me marrying another Wang*. I have fortunately not fallen in love with any Wangs, which – considering it is the most common surname in the world – is some pretty lucky going. I am very happy to be a Wang, but there is no doubt that it has ruled out of my sexual remit literally *millions* of excellent candidates. But we all make sacrifices.

In contrast, the Queen of England, Elizabeth II – the British head of state, and as head of the Church, implied moral example to the nation – married her third cousin, Prince Philip†. They were blood relatives. Which probably explains why Charles has those ears. And why Andrew is . . . well, you know.

The idea of furrowing your own path is very important to the British. To stand on your own two feet; to pay your own way; to be your own person. The sanctity of the individual is central to much of European philosophy and values. A continent of small states with big identities, the arc of European history could be seen as one long journey towards the distinct and powerful self. From the Magna Carta and the Renaissance, to the French Revolution and the spread of Western democracy, the story of Europe (and of Britain and of the wider Western world) is the story of the individual, the individual's personal freedoms, and the right of each person to shape the

* Sorry, Vera!

† In this case, considering the Queen's fondness for racing thoroughbreds, 'Philip' is Greek for 'lover of lover of horses'.

world in their image of what is right and good and build their ideal life.

The Chinese, in contrast, have always had a deep sense of the greater good; of putting aside personal gratification in service to your wider society, and to know and accept your place in it. Confucian philosophy, which underpins Chinese culture to this day, declares that to live well is to honour the hierarchies in life: to honour your parents, your leaders, and (arcanely) if you are a wife, your husband. In contrast to the French Revolution, China's Cultural Revolution strove to *reduce* the role and rights of the individual and bring the largest collective society on Earth together under the control of a *leading* collective, China's Communist Party.

Wealth has a part to play too. In general, the less money in the bank, the stronger the family unit must be. Without financial security, people make up the shortfall by looking after each other. So, we have on the one hand the family-led cultures of Asia's developing nations, and on the other, the individual-oriented wealthy societies of Europe, enriched largely by their imperial conquest of the former.

This certainly carries water in the Chinese example. Considered a developing nation until as recently as the eighties, China's rapid economic rise has not given its family culture time to change. Although it has meant more young people have left their ancestral countryside communities to take part in China's exciting new megacities, the successes of this new generation of pioneering cosmopolitans are shared back home as the successes of their families.

Similarly, in the UK, working-class families are generally closer and more involved in the extended family than those higher up the class ladder. Working-class communities are closer-knit in general. Housing was built around centres of industry, and there grew interlocking communities of neighbours with jobs in those industries. Unionisation and the labour movements strengthened these ties further.

The middle classes (to which I belong) are more individually minded (as I now am), focus on their own children (as I will when I have children), expend time, energy, and money to give their children every edge they can over their competition (as I will), so that they may build on their parents' achievements and continue their ascent up the socio-economic mountain once they have shuffled off this mortal coil (I'll see the rest of you parents at the Thunderdome, motherfuckers).

Finally, at the very top of British society, upper-class families are essentially all strangers to each other, bound by a name, a crest, and a real-estate portfolio. After all, what need is there to get to know your sister when you've each got a wing of the house to yourself?

In the traditional British upper classes, the sooner you're off your mother's teat the better, and it's a sign of weakness if you have any need for her after your first step. Ideally your family could afford a wet nurse and you never had to sully your mother's teat in the first place. In aristocratic circles, children are treated as individuals with their own responsibilities the moment they are born, it seems. No sooner have they left the womb and met their parents than they are sent packing to fend for themselves at boarding school, where they are prepared in a still-imperial militaristic environment not just for academia, but also, it seems, for some impending invasion of the British Isles, by assailants unknown in any aspect except that their weaknesses are Latin and a solid scrum.

The British Empire was built on, among other desires, an itch to leave home. Over the ensuing four centuries, the riches of the colonies promised rewards of wealth and adventure for those who ventured out on their own. And now, after Brexit – the newest manifestation of that old buccaneering itch – the UK finds itself adrift, paddling headstrong towards a destination unknown, shooting at shadows, separated from a family across the Channel it was desperate to leave for reasons it either can't express or doesn't know. We are an island nation obsessed with legacy, but forgetful of where we've come from, what we've done, who we did it to, and who we did it with. We didn't do it with anyone, we tell ourselves. Whether it's building the Empire, or winning the Second World War. We went it alone. With stiff upper lip. The British bulldog. The feisty, resourceful scrapper. These lonely isles. This God-anointed nation. This country's memory is about as good as mine.

A Murder of Teens II

Perhaps all of that is why those teens were having such a laugh at me in that Odeon. 'Look at him!' Beavis the ringleader thought, 'He's a full-grown seventeen-year-old adult and he is still part of a family who he loves and who love him! Hahaha. What a loser! Not like us on our sofa. Five strong and independent post-family individuals who need each other desperately. Oh God we need each other. I don't know what I'd do without these guys. I didn't use to need them. I had something else once. I had other people who cared about me to spend time with. But I had to get away from them. I don't know why. I was just supposed to. It's better this way.

Isn't it? Yes, of course it is. It's better this way. I miss my mum.'*

I am glad that I grew up with all those noisy family dinners. I am glad that I grew up punching my uncles, and laughing with my cousins. And I am glad I went to see that evidently forgettable movie with my mother. Even if it did attract the unforgettable ridicule of some teens. I was brought up with the Malaysian family spirit, and it has made me the man I am today. A Wang with a claim to the name, and a strong tie to the people who share it.

You have an entire life to go it alone and only a few years at the beginning to spend with your family. Very soon, sooner than you think, it'll be too late, and all you have left of them is a thin anthology of half-remembered interactions; a fading photograph; ghosts in the rain, tapping at your window.

* I want to be clear that I hold no animosity towards those teens. It's an awkward time of your life, with so much to prove, and we all behaved in ways we now regret. Their laughs hurt me at the time, but in the years since, I have gained a greater sense of perspective. Although I do hope they all failed to get into their first-choice universities. The worst thing that can happen to anyone.

WORDS

English Rose

I don't know if you've noticed, but this book has been written in the language of *English*. My own English, in fact. What's that? My English is very good? Why thank you. You're impressed? Well . . . yes, I guess it is quite impressive, isn't it? Oh, please you're making me blush now. Thank you. No, you're right. It is quite incredible. I didn't even grow up here and . . . yes, you're right, it is very sophisticated considering I grew up in Southeast Asia, and . . . yes, it is better than a lot of native English speakers, you're right, I . . . well, I wouldn't say it makes me a *hero*, per se, but certainly an . . . yes, an inspiration to children and adults alike, yes, I'd agree with that. Yes. Thank you. No, thank you. No, thank *you*.

When I had just moved to the UK, a classmate at school told me with wide-eyed astonishment that my English was 'awesome'. I didn't really know how to react. It was a compliment, of course. But a compliment based on a patronising assumption – the assumption that I wouldn't be able to speak English because of my surname, where I was from, how I looked, and, I guess, how my English sounded. I was tempted to tell him that English was, in fact, my first language. Always had been. Even in Malaysia. The English language is pretty popular the world over, it turns out. Despite humble beginnings, it has managed to spread all over the planet like rock 'n' roll or a terrible virus. In some cases, adopted by choice, in other cases, not so much choice involved. Nevertheless, the English language has proved so successful that there are now, in fact, more English speakers *outside* of England (its home country) than in it. If an English person were to speak English to an Indian person in India (a country with an estimated 125 million English speakers – more than double England's population), statistically speaking, that Indian person would be entitled to say, 'Wow! Your English is amazing. And there are hardly any English speakers from England!'

I didn't say all that to my classmate, of course – I was still desperate to make friends at the time – so I just replied, 'Oh yessee thankee you very muchum. Me is ah so happy you likey my words. I extremely to like England weather and fish or chips.' And reader, I married that man.

The British are notorious monoglots. *Monoglot* is a great word that means 'a person who only speaks one language' and is also the sound of a bucket of custard being poured down a shower drain. I also speak, with lower levels of competence, Mandarin and Malay. Which I guess makes me a 'triglot'. Although that's nothing compared to some. I have a friend who speaks *five* languages, including Elvish as devised by J. R. R. Tolkien, which makes him a 'loser'.

Most kids in Malaysia grow up learning at least two languages: English and Malay. If you went to Chinese school, which I did for a spell, then you learn Mandarin too. As a result, most Malaysians know at least two languages, and many know more.

Chinese Malaysians often know two or three other dialects of Chinese (Cantonese, Hakka, Hokkien etc.) on top of Mandarin, English and Malay. Being multilingual is not notable in Malaysia, but the norm.

The UK is a different story indeed. Two thirds of Brits don't speak any language at all apart from English. And half of *them* only know the phrases 'Oi oi!' and 'Get it down yer'. It is a sad state of affairs. The result, I suppose, of being an island at the edge of a continent. When everyone on your piece of land speaks the same language, why learn anything else? Because it's not as if polyglotism (the ability to speak numerous languages, although it sounds like 'being greedy at an orgy') is uniquely Asian or non-White. Just over the channel in Western Europe are some of the most multilingual people on earth. Pretty much every Dutch adult or Scandinavian baby speaks English well enough to hold a press conference, while the average Brit's grasp of French only just about equips them to ask for a swimming pool of bread in the small library, but little else.

I sometimes wonder if the 'unbreakable German code' in the Second World War that stumped British military intelligence for so long was just *German*, and Alan Turing was more prepared to invent the computer to decipher what the Nazis were talking about than take one evening class in elementary Deutsch. What do people say about the importance of winning The War? 'If it wasn't for my grandfather, we'd all be speaking German!' Oh no! Not a second language! The Holocaust was one thing, but it wasn't until Churchill heard about Hitler's plan for fortnightly oral exams that he knew that monster had to be stopped.

I don't mean to be unfair to the English. It is not merely the result of disinterest or a Little England mentality that so few speak another tongue. The English are unlucky, in a sense. England is not an environment conducive to learning and maintaining a second language. Even the closely neighbouring nations of Scotland, Wales, Northern Ireland and the Republic of Ireland, each have their own Celtic languages to enjoy – a smorgasbord of throat-clearing noises developed over centuries of interrupting each other's stories. But in poor England there is rarely any opportunity to practise any other language aside from English. And there is never any need. Unless you yourself are from an immigrant household, odds are English will get you anywhere you want to go to in your day-to-day life. The reason Europeans are good at English is that they have to be. There is so much English *there*. In their menus, in their histories, in the film and television they receive. And this is the case even further afield. Malaysians were taught English as subjects of the Empire, and then, after the British left, were encouraged to keep going with it to keep up with the modern English-speaking world that the Empire left behind. Perhaps this was the true purpose of the British Empire – to make the rest of the world speak English so that the British would never have to learn another language again, no matter where they went on holiday.* The British Empire, the global cultural domination of twentieth-century America, Hollywood, and now the Internet, have made the pidgin tongue of a rainy island of monoglots the world's unofficial official language.

The English are victims of their own success. English has taken over the earth so effectively that they have little impetus to learn anything else. It is a double-edged sword. On one

* Don't you think it's rather convenient that the British Empire just 'ended' but only after all the hotels had been built? Wake up, sheeple!

edge, many English people will never know the joy of another tongue, the shared humanity revealed by the similarities and shared histories of the speech of our species. On the other edge, though, is the luxury of not *having* to learn another language. The assumption that *someone* will be able to understand you wherever on earth you are. The English are expert at enjoying this luxury, safe in the knowledge that their trips abroad need not be encumbered by a phrasebook or dictionary. They'll know English in Bratislava. They'll know English in Phnom Penh. And if they don't at first, that's fine. We'll just speak it slower, louder, and more angrily. That will remind them that they, in fact, *do* know English, and have merely forgotten for a moment, in the meaningless, desperate chaos of their foreign lives.

The Brown of Accents

But that is not to say that all English is created equal. Even when I am speaking technically perfect English in the UK, I do not fit in. Because of my damn accent. There I was in Malaysia as a boy, thinking I was Little Lord Fauntleroy with my clipped syllables and the regal roundness of my pronunciations, only to move to the UK and discover that to actual British people, I sounded like a bloody Yank. A bloody Yank, I tell you.

I once performed in Belfast (is that British? I don't know, let's fight about it for years) early on in my stand-up career to one of the most terrifying audiences I've ever encountered. The Northern Irish have a reputation for being intimidating, and on this – my first visit to the country – I found out why. This particular comedy club was notorious for being hard on any act who wasn't Irish of some kind, Northern or Republic. If your set wasn't about the differences between Catholics and Protestants, you were in trouble. After the local host of the show brought the house down with some stuff about what pots Proddies have in their kitchen, he announced me as the first guest act of the night.

The name 'Wang' got a worryingly muted response (that usually gets *something*), and when I showed my face the air was instantly filled with the collective disappointment of a room of people who were now absolutely sure that I had nothing at all on the Sacraments. The first face I saw in full was a man stood so close to the raised stage that it looked like he was wearing it as a bib. He had an expression that I can only describe as the opposite of a smile, and for the entire duration of my walk to the front of the stage, he stared me down with one enormous black eye – an injury apparently so regular and casual for him that he had still come to the theatre. I braved the final few steps, and half expecting a trap door to open out from under me, said 'Hello' into the microphone, and the entire room got up and went to the bar. All except for the man with the black eye, who – to his credit – stayed and watched my entire set. Now that I think about it, he might have been dead.

Outside after the show, a cheery man who had been in the audience tried to comfort me with a statement that is a source of pride only in these bastard islands: 'We're a difficult crowd, aren't we?' I said that they were all fine, really, and that I was just happy to see a new place. He wished me a pleasant stay in Belfast and signed off with – in an exaggerated American accent – 'Well howdy!' for my benefit. He thought I was American. After listening to me speak for twenty minutes, he thought I was American. I was tempted to point out that *howdy* is actually 'hello' and not suitable as a sign-off (it isn't like a Texan 'aloha') but that would have just made me look more American. I simply returned the 'howdy' and returned to my hotel. Probably better to be assumed American than English here, I supposed.

My accent is the product of a mysterious phenomenon known among those of us afflicted as the International School Accent. The International School Accent is held by anyone who has attended an international school at any point in their life. And what is peculiar about the International School Accent is that no matter where in the world that international school is – whether it's in Brunei, Thailand, Nigeria, or Mexico – the accent is identical: American. A kind of generic American accent. A *coastal* American accent, I should add. We don't all come out of school yee-hawing, firing our six-shooters in the air and shouting about gold in them hills. We sound like the kind of Americans who have at least seen the sea. But American it is nonetheless. No official studies or inquests have been conducted on the International School Accent as far as I know, but I imagine it is just the natural result of smooshing together people from all over the world with a lot of different accents into one space. Which is – I guess – what America is. When you mix all the paints together you get brown, and when you mix all the accents together you get American. American: the brown of accents.

It is also what happens when you learn so much of your English from television, which is predominantly American. Even today I sometimes have to make an effort to sound English when I'm shopping for a new pair of suit pants at the thrift store for the prom so that I can impress the homecoming queen who must think I'm a dork after she saw me drop that can of soda (made of aluminum) in shop class, hot dang.

After a decade and a half in the UK, the American has mostly left my accent and I sound rather English these days, apart from a few exceptions. One friend is endlessly thrilled by how I pronounce 'record': *reh-kud*, like I'm about to cut a studio deal with the hottest new doo-wop star this side of the Mississippi. But what's interesting is that now, to add to this transatlantic mess, my Malaysian accent is starting to come back too. Maybe it's a natural return to an old self as I gain confidence in my own identity. Maybe it's to stand out more. Or maybe I just like it.

Mandarin in the Bin

My second and third languages of Malay and Mandarin have withered on the vine during my years in England, with no one to practise them with and no need for their use. My Malay has fortunately remained serviceable. It is a relatively easy language to learn, and a mercifully hard one to forget, which has made it a handy *lingua franca* among the many traders, officials, and labourers that have busied themselves around the Malayan peninsular and Indonesian archipelago over the centuries. Although it's not as sharp as it once was, a passable Malay lies dormant in my blood like chicken pox. It takes just a few days back in Sabah to reacquaint myself with its vocabulary and rhythms; its dips and crescendos, and soon enough I am impressing everyone again, their eyebrows lifting in delighted surprise to hear this White(ish) apparently American man speaking their humble and homely dialect.

Mandarin, on the other hand, is such a difficult language it is like it *wants* to be forgotten. Some languages feel like they wish to be understood, others feel like an extremely long password. Chinese and its many dialects are of the latter. Without constant practice and study, Chinese is quickly forgotten. It is as if the language was designed specifically to punish those who would dare to leave China, and curse them with muteness if they ever returned from their treacherous gallivanting abroad. Chinese is punishing to its speakers – with aurally identical words separated in meaning by subtle differences of tone – and sadistic to its readers, with an army of thousands of unique symbols to memorise where most modern languages use a phonetic alphabet. If Malay is like learning to ride a bike, then Chinese is like having to memorise the names of everyone who has ever ridden a bike. You might remember a few for a couple of weeks, but leave it a year or two and it's as if you never learnt them at all. At best you have a faded patchwork of incomplete memories. James . . . something? I think he had a Brompton.

I spent traumatic years at Chinese school in Malaysia learning as many words (or 'characters', as Chinese's words-cum-drawings are called*) that my teachers could cram into my little head. Homework would consist of writing the same character over and over again into a blank grid, in the hope that each pattern of lines and curves and squares would sear itself into our tender brains like a hot branding iron into raw beef. But it is a never-ending pursuit. As soon as you've memorised one, you've got another more complicated one to commit to your mental library. Chinese is like the Marvel Cinematic Universe

* Although a 'cum-drawing' sounds more like something from Japan.

post *Ant-Man and the Wasp*. It has too many characters and I just don't have the time.

You've got to admire the confidence of the ancient Chinese, who assumed they'd locked in all the words they would ever need and had no requirement for a more adaptable writing system, like say, the Roman alphabet. The reappropriation of existing words that Chinese is now forced to do when something new comes about can be pretty entertaining. 'Computer' is *diànnǎo*, or 'electric brain', which has a cool science-fiction feel to it. It certainly adds some much-needed intrigue to the otherwise unflattering 'Phil was looking at porn on the electric brain again'. Mobile phones are called 'hand machines', which sounds like something I might be caught using along with the electric brain. On the poetic end of the spectrum are movies, which are called 'electric shadows'; and on the wondrous: aeroplanes, which are called 'flying machines'. Every flight in China must make you feel like Phileas Fogg off on another one of his hair-brained adventures in his wacky airborne contraption. Chinese has also faced a similar problem whenever a new animal is discovered. It is the fault of Chinese's own lack of foresight that it has to call kangaroos 'bag rats', dolphins 'sea pigs', and skunks 'stinky weasels'.

My school made us take calligraphy lessons too, in which we all had to learn to write Chinese in the classical way, with a *máobǐ* (literally a 'hair pen') – the traditional Chinese writing brush that is essentially a small piece of bamboo with what looks like a ponytail on one end (just in case you were wondering if a stick can look like it's going through a mid-life crisis). Looking back, I'm not sure what practical purpose it held for us to learn traditional Chinese calligraphy, a writing method that can reach speeds of up to five words an hour. Perhaps to prepare us for a career in the Imperial Court should the Ming Dynasty ever return, or as extremely slow house painters.

The Chinese teaching/torture worked for a time, and I was reasonably proficient in Mandarin for periods of my childhood. But in the years that I have lived in England, my Mandarin has ebbed away from the shores of my mind like a receding tide, each year exposing a new strip of ignorant sand, as I forget another word, another rule of grammar, another expression. After some time I found that if I sat down to write a character from memory, I would get halfway, maybe four strokes in, before my mental image of it became blurry, and I drew a line in the wrong direction, or a tail looped the wrong way round.

It is a gently traumatic experience to forget a language. A partial dementia; the gradual death of an old self; heavy doors to a world you once knew slowly shutting you out. Chinese lessons were always an option once I had moved to England, of course, but I had another life to live now, other people I needed to learn to communicate with, and glorious, universal English to master. I felt I didn't have the time. And even if I did, why would I spend it on Chinese? I'm not moving to China and the Chinese aren't moving here (and if they are, they'll most likely be from Cantonese-speaking Hong Kong, and you can go suck on a hair pen if you think I'm going to learn a dialect with *nine* tones as opposed to Mandarin's mere four). So I let it slip away, as I replaced it with the knowledge that my new British life would require of me: that England are bad at penalties; that the UK is terrible at Eurovision; that the eighties were both excellent and terrible; that 'pants' means *under*pants (which is why people give me a strange look when I say I only have two pairs); that pornography is freely available on every newsstand in the country but you aren't allowed to swear on the radio; that everyone hates the Conservative Party but can't stop voting for them; that people's teeth here are fine, actually; that cars are meant to be ugly; that houses are meant to be small; that everyone longs for the summer but has no idea what to do with it when it comes; that the night can start at four o'clock, and the day can last till nine; that snow is both a miracle and a nuisance; that trains are on time often enough, but it is never to be taken for granted; that it is acceptable to get drunk with your family; that fingering is commonplace but asking someone out on a date is 'a bit intense'; that to fix a problem is human, but to complain about it – divine; that you are free to do as you like; that you need to get planning permission; that a man's home is his castle but he mustn't boast about it; that privacy is sacred; that silence is golden; that we're all in this together; that I need to mind my own business.

When I was asked to present a TV show that would take me on my first ever trip to China, I jumped at the opportunity, both to see the place and to rehash the old Mandarin and put it to the ultimate test in its natural home: China. The Motherland. The Big C. Asia Classic™. Chinatown Plus. Birthplace of lactose intolerance, and the Land of the Lightweights. *China.*

I got to work. I found an old textbook, my dictionary, and I practised. I set myself homework and watched *Mulan* (1998) again and again, which is in English so didn't really help. I did what any good Chinese kid would. I studied. As Benjamin Franklin once said: 'Fail to prepare, and your Chinese won't be very good. Now watch this kite.'

When I arrived in Shenzhen, I hit the ground running. I instantly greeted our local guide, Angela, with a confident *nǐ hǎo*. She looked impressed. 'Wow! You speak Chinese!' I let myself enjoy the compliment, ignoring both for her pride and mine that *nǐ hǎo* is known even by most British racists, mainly for the purpose of shouting it across the street at Vietnamese people.

I soon found that my Mandarin was about the level of a toddler's. And looking Chinese enough in the face to be occasionally presumed a local, I must have given off the impression of being an enormous child, or some simple giant of lore. I saved myself from the worst embarrassments for the most part. At one dinner I checked with Angela if my word for 'Miss' was correct for getting the waitress's attention. She was shocked by what I'd said. 'No, no, no, no, no! You must never say that!' I had come extremely close to shouting 'Oi! You old prostitute!' across the restaurant.

The greatest test of my skills came when I was forced to infiltrate a housing estate in order to look at their recycling bins (it was a truly thrilling show)* . We'd had word that this housing estate had installed smart bins that could identify residents who'd put the wrong type of waste into the incorrect bin. Now this we had to see. We had not obtained any express permission to film on the premises, but production was determined to get to these dang bins. It was decided that the director and I would try our luck anyway and just walk through the front gate. I was nervous enough about playing fast and loose

* The programme was about new technologies emerging in the US, Japan and China that sought to solve the world's many immediate crises – food shortage, global warming, the energy crisis, and the like. I was chosen to front the China expedition because, well . . . you know. My famous enthusiasm for ceramics.

with Chinese authority (not exactly *famous* for its sense of humour) as it was, so the further revelation that Angela would not be able to join us – making *me* the translator should we come up against any resistance – was just the icing on the mooncake. Fearing indefinite internment in a cobalt mine and making a last-minute attempt to learn the Chinese for 'That's my pickaxe, get your own!', I entered the estate, the director and his small camera following closely behind. We were spotted straight away, of course. A security guard, who for some reason noticed a White man with a camera and the tallest Chinese person he'd ever seen, began tailing us with a curious stroll, hands in pockets. I noticed him, but kept my eyes forward, trying to act like I'd lived there all along and they'd simply forgotten about me and my European friend who was always filming the staircases and the drains. After what felt like a lifetime, we found the infamous bins, but before we could get any good footage the guard had caught up with us and asked what on earth we were doing. My director, not understanding a word of what he'd said, turned to me. Here it was: my greatest test. It had all led up to this.

'We want to see your bins,' I said, in my best Mandarin.

'Our bins?'

'Yes. We came from England to see your bins. We heard your bins.' I'd wanted to say that we'd heard *about* their bins but 'We heard your bins' was the best I could do.

'You *heard* our bins?' said the guard, even more confused.

There's no other way to say it. I sounded fucking insane. Soon, more people surrounded us. Old, *old* people who it turned out were the residents' association and had come down to see what all the fuss was about. So, I had to repeat my little bin speech to them as well.

'I want to see your bins. I heard them.'

'He wants to see our bins,' one lady said to the others.

'Our bins?' said another. No one had a clue what was going on, and I couldn't help.

Here I was, having prepared myself for a *Mission Impossible*-style infiltration of a secret facility, struggling to explain to a group of confused pensioners, with the Mandarin of a child, why I had come all the way from England to look at their bins. By that point, I didn't know why, either.

Eventually, the kindly security guard decided that he'd had enough and (very politely) asked us to leave. I gave my Chinese one last go to try to get him to say on camera that what we were doing was forbidden, in an attempt to charge the footage with some semblance of drama: a little jeopardy. I wanted to say, 'You won't let us film here? *You won't let us film*? My God, man. What has this world come to, that you and I, brothers in humanity, will not allow one to film in the home of the other?' But I found my vocabulary coming up short once again, and all I could manage under the pressure was:

'You do not like the? You do not like the?'

You do not like the. That's what I said. What exactly it was that I was accusing him of not liking never became clear to anyone. And he, having given up trying to understand us, calmly guided us back out towards the gate to be on our way.

Of course, that was the only bit of the confrontation that made the final edit of the show: me saying to a baffled Chinese security guard, 'You do not like the? YOU DO NOT LIKE THE??' The very public result of months of revision and practice.

★ ★ ★

During my UK stand-up tour the following spring, a Malaysian woman came up to me after a show in Liverpool. She lives in England now, and had seen me on the China programme.

'Your Chinese isn't very good.'

It was nice to see that her quaint Malaysian directness (aka rudeness) hadn't worn off. Not to worry, though, I thought, a couple more years of British life should file that prickly candour down to the cold passive aggression that we Brits proudly call *manners*.

In that moment, I was overcome with the feeling that I would never get a grip on my Mandarin. No matter how hard I tried. And you know what? I did not like the. I did not like the, at all.

Manglish

A common phrase a Malaysian might say to you is: 'Come, *liàng zǎi* , we go *makan*.' Which translates to 'Come on, handsome (sarcastically), let's go eat'. *Come, we go* – English. *Liàng zǎi* – Chinese for 'handsome boy'. *Makan* – Malay for 'eat'. The language of this sentence altogether? Manglish.

If English is the unofficial official language of the world, Manglish is the unofficial official language of Malaysia. A contraction of 'Malaysian English', and also by divine coincidence, 'Mangled English'. It is primarily English, but with little to no adherence to the rules of English grammar. In many cases, Chinese and Malay sentences are translated verbatim, without changing the order of the words to account for the new syntax. Words and phrases are distilled down to the bare minimum required for comprehension, and past tenses, which don't really exist in Chinese and Malay, are ignored entirely.

For example, 'Now go where?' means *Where are we going?* and 'He come here and then? Explode' means *He came here, and then spontaneously combusted.* Some phrases have become so common, they are understood entirely on their own without context – mostly to be used in moments of great exasperation, the definitive Malaysian emotion. 'How can?' – *But how can that be?* 'Where got?' – *That seems unlikely.* 'Confirm cannot' – *What you are talking about is simply not possible, dumbass.*

It might seem impenetrable at first, but you'd be amazed at how quickly it can be picked up, even by you: a speaker and reader of the good old Queen's Anglo. It is accessible by design. And because it isn't entirely any single language, it doesn't belong to anyone in particular. So there is no sense of ownership over it, and anyone can give it a go without fear of offending anybody. 'This is for everyone,' said Tim Berners-Lee, creator of the World Wide Web, when he gifted his invention to the world. So too say the Malaysians about Manglish, an open-source language for anyone on our planet to enjoy completely free of charge. And historians will look back on these two great gifts to humanity for centuries to come, arguing until the end of time about which was the more generous.

The jewel in Manglish's crown is without a doubt the word *lah*. *Lah* is a magical word with no equivalent in English. It is a suffix for everything; a piece of conversational punctuation that no written symbol can represent. It is as malleable as it is effective. It can be used to reassure: *Don't worry, lah. Your lovely wife will be here soon.* Or it can be used to compel: *Come on, lah! We need to leave! Your awful wife will be here soon!* It can be used to hurry (*Quickly, lah!*) or to calm (*Relax, lah*); it can be used to harangue (*Don't be stupid, lah!*) or to sheepishly deny one's own culpability (*Eh, it wasn't me, lah. Haha. There was shit on the floor when I got here, lah . . . haha*).

A succinct definition of *lah* is difficult. The best I've come across is that *lah* turns a sentence into a command, but at the same time, softens that command. No command ending in *lah* is all that urgent, really. In a word, I suppose that's what *lah* is: a softening. It will make casual whatever has preceded it. It is incredibly effective. It always works. There is almost nothing *lah* can't soften. *Turn off the life support, lah. He had a good life, lah.* Or, *We should probably call an ambulance lah. That vial I just dropped was full of a flesh-eating bacteria, lah.*

No other culture I know is so committed to chilling the heck out that it has created a word completely dedicated to it. In regular English, if you wanted to finish a sentence with an appeal for calm, you'd have to say 'So just calm down, OK?', which, if anything, makes whoever you are speaking to even more annoyed.

These few pages may prove the most official Manglish lesson currently committed to paper. Manglish is not taught in school. It has no formal recognition as a language. But it is what is spoken among Malaysian friends and in Malaysian families, in the shopping malls, on adverts and slogans, on breakfast radio. Its vocabulary is mostly English, but borrows many words from Malay, Chinese, and Tamil, so its ownership is shared. Manglish is a warm, welcoming language. Like Malaysian food, Manglish is the natural product of a junction of cultures; a collision of worlds.

I have always loved Manglish. It is light and easy and almost always steeped in good humour. It has a charming awareness of itself. An awareness that it is not technically 'correct'; a cheeky acknowledgement that it breaks the rules. It is a language so casual that rules of grammar don't even apply – a kind of gentle linguistic revenge against English's colonial monopoly. Every sentence of Manglish is spoken with a tongue firmly in a cheek. It is jokey and friendly. And every time I hear its soft, limping staccato, I am warmed. My shoulders relax, my arms hang. I smile and slump over like a cat with the back of his neck pinched.

As a child, I spoke proper English at home with my family, but Manglish at school with my friends. And even after all these years, deep down I am still fluent. Whenever I return to Malaysia, my Manglish comes back. After only a day or two, I shape-shift like Benjamin Button into the boy I once was.

Even when in the UK, my sisters and I keep it up, asking each other 'Pass the salt, can?' or 'Eh! Why like that?' It makes us feel at home and it makes us laugh. Because Manglish is funny. It lies at the heart of the Malaysian sense of humour, which is largely about the rejection of formality. Even when people speak Manglish in anger, they are funny. Even if they don't want to be. They can't help it. I had an IT teacher at my Malaysian secondary school who once got so angry with my class for talking that he began telling us off by screaming at the top of his voice: 'You don't make me piss, ah! You don't make me piss!' I still laugh about that now. Good times. I still have no idea how to rename an Excel file, but it was worth it.

Knowing a pidgin language like Manglish or Jamaican Patois or Southern African Fanakalo has benefits beyond its country of use. It imbues a young person with an appreciation of the adaptability of language, and the shared features of our planet's seemingly disparate tongues. It is especially useful for anyone who is primarily an English speaker in the task of speaking English abroad (or at home for that matter) with people whose English is very limited. Understanding how English gets adapted helps you identify the crucial elements of a sentence, and which simple words you can use to get across the most important pieces of information that you need to. I've always been decent at this – a skill I had presumed was universal but which I now realise may be the fortunate result of having learnt Manglish. I went on tour through East Asia with an Australian guy called Jim, who, despite being extremely well-travelled, had absolutely no skill at speaking English to non-English speakers. To make himself understood, he would, at most, say the same words again slower. But strangely, he would slow down on short, simple words, and then say long, complicated ones just as quickly as if he were speaking to someone fluent in English. So, if we were checking into a hotel, he would say 'Caaannn yooooouu plllleaaassse expedite-with-immediate-haste-the-process-of-sanitising myyyyyy roooooom'. Naturally the person behind the desk would be flummoxed but required by their job to smile and nod. But because they hadn't actually understood what Jim had said, they would then just do nothing, which would make Jim all the more worked up. I should have explained to him that a more fruitful attempt would have been something like, 'My room clean, can?' which gets across all the important ideas and stands a much better chance of being understood.

Of course, ideally, you'd learn a translation of the phrase in the local language. But why waste that luxury that we English speakers have? That unique privilege fought so hard for by the empire builders, Hollywood directors, and the Internet's meme creators before us: English's chokehold on the world.

Lah-terature

Multilingualism is a wonderful thing. A large part of the reason Malaysia has enjoyed relative social harmony, despite its many different ethnic and religious groups, is a mutual involvement by those groups with each other's languages. The downside, however, is that no one speaks their own language all that well. In this sense, Malaysians are jacks of all trades and masters of none. When your attention is spread across three or more languages at all times, it's hard to commit much energy to being expert in any particular one. My own English is pretty good, but only because I had a British mother and a home in which we all spoke it to each other. But, conversely, the cost was that my Chinese never reached the level of most Chinese-speaking Malaysians and my Malay was similarly affected. Even my English didn't really get good, as in 'book-worthy' (though, I suppose, you'll be the judge of that), until I moved to the UK and could concentrate on it completely. And even then, my Chinese took a nosedive in exchange.

It is no coincidence that England (a country of monoglots) has a rich and extensive literary tradition, while Malaysia (a land of linguists) does not. Malaysians have their focus divided. Everyone knows a bit of Malay, a bit of English, and a bit of Chinese, and even when attempting to speak entirely in one language, will routinely adopt a word from another when their vocabulary in the first fails them. For example, my father, uncles, and aunts, when speaking Chinese to each other will regularly throw in an English word to substitute the Chinese equivalent that they either never learnt or have forgotten. It is fun to listen to them talking to each other in Chinese only for words like 'confused' or 'basking shark' to pop up out of the blue, and it's a gas to try and figure out what their conversation is about from those clues alone. A typical, and often highly animated, story told by my father to one of his siblings at a family dinner will sound something like this: '[*Chinese Chinese Chinese Chinese*] . . . accountant [*Chinese Chinese Chinese*] . . . daredevil [*Chinese Chinese Chinese Chinese*] . . . skydive [*Chinese Chinese Chinese*] . . . uninsured! [*Chinese Chinese Chinese*] . . . mechanical fault [*Chinese Chinese Chinese*] . . . tailspin [*Chinese Chinese Chinese*] . . . fireball [*Chinese. Chinese Chinese*] . . . ambulance [*Chinese Chinese*] . . . too late [*Chinese Chinese Chinese*] . . . dismembered [*Chinese Chinese Chinese*] . . . spinal fragments in a bush [*Chinese Chinese Chinese*] . . . nothing they could do [*Chinese Chinese Chinese*] . . . funeral [*Chinese Chinese Chinese Chinese Chinese*] . . . widow did not seem that sad to me [*Chinese Chinese Chinese Chinese*] . . . good buffet! [*Chinese Chinese Chinese*] . . . hired [*Chinese*] . . . new accountant now, *lah*'.*

But hey, Malaysia is a young country. A literary tradition may emerge yet. In 2012, Tan Twan Eng became the first Malaysian to be shortlisted for the Man Booker Prize for his English-language novel *The Garden of Evening Mists*, which is also what I call my pubic area. It's an extraordinary accomplishment for someone who grew up with numerous languages to master one well enough to be recognised by an international literary award. Hopefully Twan Eng is the first of many to come. Maybe I (with this humble offering) am following in his foot-steps. Though I don't think a prize exists yet for doorstops.

* By the way, I hope you knew that the repeated word 'Chinese' here was a stand-in for actual Chinese, and that you didn't think that that's actually how Chinese people speak.

The true test of the Malaysian literary spirit will be the first novel to be written entirely in Manglish. Now that would be something. Perhaps in time, Malaysians will have our very own unique claim to the world's literary firmament. Our own Dickens ('The times were best. The times were also worst, *lah.*'); our own Shakespeare ('Friends, Romans, countrymen, borrow me your ears, can?'); our own Austen ('Mr. Darcy – no manners. Made Elizabeth piss!').

FOOD

Welcome to the Black Country

Jason and I just stared. We couldn't believe our eyes. Plain cooked chicken. Completely plain. Cold, white, unseasoned pieces of chicken just lying there on a large platter. Limp and tasteless. Waiting to be eaten. Truly, we were in Wolverhampton now.

Our friend George had very kindly invited us to his father's fiftieth birthday blowout – a raucous Black Country* affair in the clubhouse of a local public golf course†. Jason, George and

* The Black Country is an area of the West Midlands in England named after either the thick seam of coal that runs through the region, or what happens to your memory after five pints of the local ale. In 2016, William Henwood, a candidate for the far-right party UKIP told the British-Jamaican comedian Lenny Henry to 'go and live in a black country' in response to an appeal Lenny Henry had made for more black and ethnic minority representation in the creative industries. Henwood, it seemed, was unaware that Lenny Henry is in fact from Dudley, a town firmly in *the* Black Country, and so Lenny was already way ahead of him.

† The birthday boy was one David Potts, George's father, and my occasional online (and in-person) nemesis. I'm not sure how our weird little rivalry began. Only that I enjoy roasting him – a mild-mannered Wolverhampton librarian who has never done anything to me – for no real reason. I like to tweet him random little jibes and photos of him in his garden when he didn't

I are in a comedy trio called Daphne – the most racially diverse one in the country by our count. George holds a unique selling point as 'the White one' of the group and he had been eager to show us a good time in the Black Country fashion he had grown up with. We got drunk on Banks's bitter ale and danced to pop and punk from the eighties, successfully keeping out of mind the knowledge that our parents almost certainly had sex to all of those songs. In the smoking area, George's cousin, a Royal Marine, took it upon himself to show me precisely where on my body he would stab for a quick kill in the heat of battle. 'Here! Here! Here! Here!' he shouted, cigarette in hand, as he punched a deadly constellation, without warning, fist tilted as if holding a knife, into my chest and belly. It was, in short, a brilliant night.

However, the buffet, and the buffet alone, stands out in Jason's and my collective memory as a sobering, horrific trauma. An image is etched into both our minds of us looking down at that trestle table in stunned silence, ears ringing in shellshock, at an unflavoured platter of pale chicken (I almost think we held hands).

'What do we have this with?' we begged to passers-by. A sauce? A dip? A gravy? A *jus*? Some *salt*? Surely there was some accompaniment to this undressed bird. Perhaps it was a build-a-burger situation, and guests were invited to flavour their chicken from scratch, to cater to each partygoer's individual

know I was watching to get under his skin. I hope that as he places this – my very own book – onto one of his precious library shelves, between the masterpieces of David Foster Wallace and Evelyn Waugh (anyone can learn the Dewey Decimal System, David, it isn't hard), he takes a moment to realise that I have finally, and quite decisively, won. I am in your place of work now, David. Forever and ever. You will never escape me.

preferences. How naïve we were. There was no sauce. There was no dip. There was no hope. The chicken had been served as it was meant to be eaten; to be 'enjoyed'. Plain. Neat. To Jason and me it simply did not compute. Jason had grown up with the bombastic flavours of Caribbean cuisine – his aunt running a Jamaican restaurant in his native Bristol – and I had grown up with the spice, salt, and earthy char of Malaysian cooking. Two cultures that don't so much eat to live as live to eat. We had both been brought up to believe that the chicken meat itself was merely the *foundation* of the dish; the canvas on which one built a mosaic of tastes and textures. Not the final result. Until this fateful day we had not even known that what we were now seeing – plain unseasoned chicken considered ready to eat – was even possible.

'Yeeeeeeeeppp,' waddled over a grinning George, nursing another Banks's and wearing a sick pride on his lips, 'Welcome to the Black Country.'

Welcome to the Bland Country

It is no controversy to say that British food has a bad reputation. A cuisine described by George Orwell as 'simple, rather heavy, perhaps slightly barbarous'. It is infamous the world over for being, as the French say, 'disgusting'. Even Americans think British food is gross, and that's coming from a country with dishes called 'candied yams' and 'sloppy joe'. In recent decades, food and food culture in the UK has gotten much, much better, of course. That we could have the East Asian, Italian, Mexican, and cheeky piri-piri high-street chains that Brits now enjoy would have been unthinkable in even the nineties. But despite the beginnings of a shift towards food adventurousness, there still exists a vast and powerful eating culture in this country that is defined by a distrust of flavour and a fear of the unfamiliar. What's especially strange is that this attitude of what is essentially cowardice is often accompanied by a bizarre patriotic pride. In my Bath years, I recall a man walking into a Chinese takeaway, looking up at the menu and ordering only a portion of chips, clarifying that he wanted 'None of this foreign shit,' as he swept his hand across the stir-fried, the sweet and sour, the kung po. Why he had chosen an obviously Chinese takeaway when all he wanted was chips baffles me to this day. Was he drawn in by the luscious red signage, or do those waving golden cats on the counter of every East Asian shop in the world hold stronger powers of allure than I had given them credit for? Perhaps he had fully intended on trying something Chinese but backed out when the numbers on the menu scared him off. 'Foreign food *and* maths? Too rich for my blood. I'd better just order the one thing that I can get literally anywhere else'*.

British picky eating doesn't just apply to foreign food. There is plenty this country produces itself that is not to its inhabitants' tastes. In no other island nation is the phrase 'I don't eat fish' so common. *Fish.* You know – the food source the country is surrounded by? I have met so many Brits who are flat-out

* Early on in my stand-up career I got on stage at a gig in Shoreditch only to be heckled before I'd said a word. Looking as I do, a grotesque man in the front row slurred menacingly at me, 'Number 69, please', something I imagine he says to East Asian people a lot and thinks is brilliant – the suggestion being that all Chinese people work in a Chinese takeaway and know the menu off by heart. The joke was on him however, as far from offending me, 'Number 69' simply made me a little horny, and hungry for Shredded Duck Fried Rice (Large).

disgusted by the idea. There are plenty who occasionally partake, of course, and I know that fish and chips is a national dish. But really that's just an excuse to eat batter. And the fish used – primarily cod and haddock – are plain-tasting white fish, deep fried beyond all recognition. What's more, whatever fishy taste is left is then dominated with lemon, vinegar, and – sometimes – curry sauce. That's right, some British hate the taste of fish so much they're briefly willing to suspend their distrust of foreign food to enlist its help.

The thing is, cod is not even that abundant in British waters, which are more heavily populated with flavourful, nutritious, oilier, 'fishier' fish like mackerel and pilchard. But the vast majority of these have to be sold to Europe, where they're in greater demand. Only 5 per cent of what British fishing fleets catch is cod. They catch much more herring, but because that's too fishy for Brits, 93 per cent of it is exported to countries like Norway and the Netherlands. Meanwhile, in Britain, we have to import cod (the fish we actually eat) from Iceland and have been known to wage the odd *naval war* with them just to try to get more of those beautiful bland bastards (cod, not Icelandic people, who are not bland at all. They're just a bit eerie).

It's not as bad as it used to be. I mean, to my mother's generation, onions were exotic. My generation of Brits are comparatively lucky to enjoy the choice we have, what with our green *or* red pesto and our lemon *or* blackcurrant Lemsip. Progress has moved surely in the right direction, but slowly. British shops now stock a greater variety of flavours than ever – soy, Jamaican pepper sauces, harissa, salsas, reduced sugar barbecue sauce – an exciting development. But in 2017, it was mayonnaise that was crowned the nation's number one most popular condiment. *Mayonnaise*. Edible moisturiser, essentially. Presumably ketchup had too much fruit in it. 'I'll have the sour egg goo, thanks!' the nation cried.

Mayonnaise is not alone in its pasty blandness. At Christmas we have *bread sauce*. Bread sauce, for God's sake! A sauce made of *bread*! Famously neutral-tasting *bread*. What other country on earth could have tasted *bread* and thought, *Oh wow! Why this is a flavour jamboree! Turn it into a relish this instant.* I often think that if the taste 'plain' came in a bottle it would sell out in every British supermarket immediately. There would be early morning queues outside every corner shop, like the launch day of a new iPhone. Dads around the country would pour it over their sausages, because *someone* had accidentally bought the *herby* ones again.

Now you might think, *Come Phil. That's not fair. Some English sauces are very flavourful.* Oh, you mean overpowering? The British palate seems to teeter between the two extremes of 'tasteless' and 'too much of a single taste'. Marmite, for example, is just an excuse to put salt on toast. And the excruciating strength of English mustard will always baffle me. *Ooh no I don't like chillies thanks, they're too spicy. Now would you please pass me that yellow explosion paste? My beef tastes too much like it's supposed to.**

In all fairness, British bland-food culture is not the fault of the British *people*. There are factors here beyond our control. Most significant of all is the unavoidable effect of geography. Britain's

* A quick side note: if you are a proud British picky eater and are getting upset or insulted by what I'm saying here, remember that self-deprecating British sense of humour, and your commitment to the British tradition of laughing at yourself. Checkmate.

physical placing in the world puts it at a culinary handicap. Great food cultures almost always sit at the crossroads of civilisations, absorbing culinary influences from many peoples at once and combining their best elements to create something truly exceptional. Italy sits at the crossroads of North-Western Europe and the Mediterranean. Mexico sits between the United States and South America. And India, China, Korea, and Japan have traded with each other along the Silk Road for centuries. All the while, mixing, experimenting, and refining their dishes to perfection. Britain, however, sits at the edge of the world, looking in at everyone else, tutting. It is the dead-end of Europe, a culinary cul-de-sac. An island left adrift to figure out food on its own. In the large family mansion of the world, Britain sulks alone in the attic, thrown occasional buckets of fish heads. Which it finds too fishy, by the way.

Don't Even Talk to Me Before I've Had My Kopi

Food has a predominantly functional value in the UK. Ever since the Industrial Revolution, the British worker has been overburdened. Technological advances, from the steam engine to the computer, have only demanded more productivity in half the time. The British worker's sandwiches and pasties and pasta salads and wraps are chosen more for their ease than their taste. Lunch hours are eaten into more than the lunch. The food itself just nutritional enough to keep you going. To keep you building ships, to keep you mining coal, to keep you answering phone calls, to keep you replying to emails, to keep you digitally consulting, whatever that is.

Malaysia is a different story altogether. Food is the national pride and pastime. Ask anyone who has been on holiday to

Malaysia what the best thing about Malaysia is and they will say 'the food'. Ask any Malaysian what the best thing about Malaysia is and they will say 'overcharging tourists for the food.' And then they will say 'the food.'

In Malaysia, food is life. It is everything. It is the point and purpose of each day. Every meal, no matter how busy you are, is hot, filling, and delicious. There are no compromises made with the pleasure of eating, no sandwiches over keyboards, no sad salads, no cut corners for the sake of improved productivity. If you asked a Malaysian to work through lunch they'd quit. Which is probably why there'll never be a Malaysian empire. That and because they'd never be on time to any of the battles.* Plus, the spices are already there so what would be the point?

Malaysians are obsessed with food. I mean, they eat it *every day*. Malaysians live to eat. Every meal is an opportunity for joy, not just an inconvenient process to be rushed before getting back to photocopying. Eating out in Malaysia is cheap and casual and what you get for your money is the best food in the world.

For the uninitiated, Malaysian food is defined by mixture. The national dish that sums up Malaysia's delightful tangle of peoples is *laksa*. Chinese noodles in a broth of Indian curry spices, brought to life with the pungent twist of Malay sambal.† Eating out is no big deal, as the cost is comparable to cooking at home. And there is plenty to choose from: Indian curry

* This joke requires you to know that Malaysians are, as a rule, late to everything. Malaysian time is eight hours ahead of Greenwich Meantime not because it is in a different time zone, but because that's how much extra time you have to give a Malaysian you're meeting for lunch.

† Sambal is a ubiquitous paste in Indonesian and Malaysian cooking made of (essentially) fermented shrimp. It is as delicious as it sounds.

houses where rice is heaped on cool banana leaves; Malay canteens where smiling ladies in headdresses serve pan-fried fish and beef *rendang* – a curry of coconut milk, aromatic spices and slow-cooked beef; and there are even places that will serve you (if you really need a break from all that foreign shit) chips.

At the heart of the Malaysian eating experience, however, is the coffee shop.

The Malaysian 'coffee shop' is something of a misnomer in that coffee is not really the point of the place. In the same way that 'meeting up for a coffee' in the West is not actually about the coffee either, it's about an ill-advised catch-up with your ex. The Malaysian *kopitiam* encapsulates the country's mixed heritage even within its name – *kopi,* the Malay transliteration of the English 'coffee', and *tiam*, the Hainanese (Hokkien/Hakka) Chinese word for 'shop'. These unassuming restaurant-cum-cafés* are ubiquitous throughout the country. Open-air shop lots, too hot for walls. Like giant pigeonholes full of people and chatter. Just walk in and take a seat.

My memories of Malaysian eating are of wobbly tables and plastic chairs; of ancient ceiling fans with blackened blades, exhausted by decades of labour, spinning precariously overhead – comforting and threatening at once, like a dancing grandmother holding a cleaver. Diners (though the word feels too formal) spill over from tiled floors onto the concrete pavement outside. It is year-round al fresco weather. Girls in knock-off Disney T-shirts appear out of nowhere and take your order, before spinning on their heels and screaming it at the relevant corners of the room: chicken rice to the chicken rice lady, *laksa*

* Although a 'cum-café' sounds more like something you'd find in Amsterdam.

to the *laksa* man, and drinks to the women in the back, busying themselves among their tea strainers, ice and Kasturi limes. It has been almost half of my lifetime since I moved to the UK, but still nothing excites my stomach and pinches the back of my gums with anticipation like the thought of soy-stained noodles tossed in a wok by a man in cargo shorts and an old Manchester United jersey, hunched over the roaring gas flames of a loosely connected Shell canister. An Asian Hephaestus at his forge.

Different *kopitiams* have different specialties and become famous through word of mouth for the best so-and-so in the city. One place will have the best minced pork noodles, while another the finest *bak kut teh* (a herbal broth of pork bones, mushrooms, and offal). Those who insist on the best value for their £3 meal (which is everyone) will drive across town to the number one joint, and finding it already packed, will wait on the street outside for a table to become free. Meanwhile, the restaurant next door, selling the exact same thing but to a fractionally lower standard, will lie empty and jealous. If the star cook retires, or leaves, or dies, with them go the crowds, the *kopitiam*'s imaginary Michelin star lost. One *kopitiam*, a family favourite after Saturday night *Kempo*, had a dumpling stand womanned by a pair of cool middle-aged lady twins. They made the tastiest, juiciest pork dumplings I've ever had. When they retired, a dumpling-shaped hole was torn into my heart and we stopped going. I never got the chance to call those twins Tweedledum-pling and Tweedledee-licious to their faces (mainly because I've only just thought up those names now) but I wish I had.

A trip to Malaysia will make you see food in a new way. One that eschews presentation for the pure ecstasy of taste and texture. Appearance is an afterthought. Food clatters onto your table on cheap plastic orange plates and service is purely transactional.

Perfect. Any clean freaks considering a culinary trip to Malaysia needn't worry, the hygiene in coffee shops is not an issue. By which I mean, they're filthy, but you'll quickly stop caring. The quality of your dinner will make you forget you ever did. Growing up, it was not uncommon for me to greedily shovel a spoon of food into my face while maintaining calm, unbroken eye contact with a cockroach riding a rat across the floor like the heroes of some tiny Western. I'd simply smile and wave. You know the food is good when you don't mind sharing the space with beasts of pestilence (like at your family Christmas dinner, am I right?)

The Chicken

This is not to say that Malaysian eating has gone untouched by Western influence. In the seventies and eighties the fast-food chains arrived – adding a brand-new feature to the dining landscape. However, contrary to their low status as cheap conveniences in the West, in Malaysia, fast-food restaurants were (and still are) considered upmarket. Because KFC and McDonald's were from distant, glamorous America, and their menus were actually more *expensive* than the food available in local coffee shops and canteens, fast-food outlets became the *fancier* option in Malaysia. The façade of every branch is grand and polished, and inside the floors and tables are clean and wobble-free. Families dress up in their Sunday best for lunch at Pizza Hut like they're attending the Church of Dough. And air conditioning units take the place of the *kopitiams'* rattling fans, lest Ronald McDonald's clown make-up start running in the heat. His is the proud McDonald clan, after all. And he, an ambassador of the noble Highlands in this far-flung corner of the globe, must keep up appearances.

The loyalty to Malaysian food is so strong, however, that even these multinational fast-food giants must buckle to it. Their menus are Malaysian-ified to honour local tastes, offering meal options that serve rice with the Colonel's original recipe chicken and sambal with your Whopper. Like the Caesars before him, The Burger King knows what any successful imperialist does: that the emperor ignores the customs of his conquered peoples to his peril. Always better to accommodate the local traditions than to convert outright.

KFC holds the throne in the fast-food wars of Malaysia. Arriving there first in 1973, it firmly embedded itself into the national psyche, becoming the nation's go-to foreign treat. In my family it was the reserve of special celebrations – anniversaries, exam results, another sports day successfully avoided with a well-timed cold. Colonel Sanders became our nation's smiling White overlord, looking down at us from his ubiquitous billboards like Saddam Hussein with a bow tie. KFC almost felt like part of the community; the infrastructure of public life. If you'd told me that they ran the electrical grid I would have believed you. I still hold a deep-seated obsession for fried chicken to this day, which is partly why I was so traumatised by my Wolverhampton buffet experience. How could I understand chicken with no seasoning when I had been raised on chicken with, if anything, *too much*?*

★ ★ ★

* In Japan, KFC is a Christmas tradition. Instead of toiling over turkey, the Japanese opt for its smaller, tastier cousin. The special KFC Christmas dinner package has to be ordered weeks in advance. On the big day itself, lines of people pour out of every KFC in the country as they wait for their turn to celebrate the birth of Our Lord, who took on our original sin so that we could enjoy Original Recipe.

Looking back, KFC's hold on my childhood was at times outright bizarre. A peculiar memory comes to mind. My sisters and I went to the same Chinese kindergarten – Tzu Yu (pronounced 'tser yoo'). Our Aunty Lily was one of the teachers there. The school was an open-air affair. To cope with the heat, schools in Malaysia are built a bit like army barracks or prisoner-of-war camps, with all the areas outside of the classrooms out in the open. Multiple storeys are stacked on top of each other, with classroom doors opening right onto long balconies that link them up. Assemblies take place in covered courtyards, or sometimes just fields. Tzu Yu had just two such storeys of classrooms built in a large diamond shape that began and ended at the school entrance.

On my sister Aimée's sixth birthday – she was a year younger than me (still is) – Aunty Lily came up to my first-floor classroom (I liked to think of it as the penthouse) to collect everyone to witness the very special celebration happening downstairs. I, along with the other children, walked out onto the balcony and looked down at the school entrance. Below, my sister and her class were gathered excitedly in the school foyer while an enormous chicken danced and wiggled and hugged everybody. Apparently, my aunt had arranged for a KFC visit to the school for my sister's birthday. This was a service that KFC Malaysia offered, I guess. School visits. Like your school might have done with a recovering drug addict who had come to tell you to never do drugs. Except this was a giant chicken who wanted you to keep doing chicken. The humongous chicken (who I have since learnt was in fact a man in a chicken *costume*, which is appropriation if you ask me) was really holding court, delighting his young crowd with the universal repertoire of mascots: a shuffled playlist of blowing kisses, covering his face in mock shyness, and grabbing his belly and shaking with silent laughter at some unspecified joke. The whole time his enormous bird eyes remained fixed wide open, staring, like in a trance, far into the distance, as if always on the lookout for new schools to visit, new children to win favour with. Then someone turned on The Chicken Dance on a CD player and he began marching around the school to it, with my sister and her classmates in tow, like the Pied Piper of Poultry. All the other children in the school watched with astonished glee, heads out of windows, leaning over the banisters of the upper floor, screaming and clapping with all the sound and fury of some Amazonian ritual sacrifice, cheering the procession on like the whole thing was some fucked up royal visit from The Chicken King. It was pandemonium. Everyone loved this chicken. All around the school the parade went: the chicken, swinging his enormous, useless wings; my tiny sister, beaming from ear to ear; and then her classmates following behind her, flapping their bent arms in loving mimicry of their feathered leader, all in whichever direction the gargantuan fowl deigned to go. They would have followed that chicken anywhere, man. At one point, my sister, as the birthday girl, was sort of promoted to second-in-command and was handed a large bucket of KFC that she was encouraged to distribute among the kids as they passed, all of whom had their hands outstretched in famished gratitude as this nightmarish train graced their vicinity. I cannot adequately express just how happy every single person in that school was to have that chicken there that day – the kids, the teachers, even the chicken himself, gleaming proud in his white feathers, crowned with his regal comb of red.

When he eventually left, we didn't even bother trying to get back to schoolwork. We all knew that wasn't going to happen. Not today. Instead we just collapsed into our seats, full-bellied and exhausted, faces covered in a happy sheen of sweat, as we spoke of the large chicken and shared tales of his benevolence.

A few years later, when Aimée and I had left the school, our sister Anna, who is four years younger than me (still is), also had her birthday at Tzu Yu. Again, Aunty Lily called in the chicken. But it was different this time. The years had taken their toll on the old god. He had visited too many schools, hugged too many children, and his magic had run out. In an old photograph of Anna's big day, she is peering up with sad, confused, disgusted eyes at the same chicken I saw that spectacular afternoon. Except now, he is dirty; grey. His feathers weathered by a thousand birthdays, the pads on his feet worn ragged by the cruel twists of the Chicken Dance, his wings arthritic from applauding the lives of others. His warped eyes no longer watch the horizon with hope. They now stare lifelessly into the abyss. He has seen too much. Blown too many empty kisses. Faked too many chuckles. His shoulders hang heavy with the shame of a chicken who has smilingly handed out deep-fried pieces of his own kind – his friends, his family – all for the fickle approval of children who have long forgotten him.

But I remember you, chicken. I will always remember.

Ball Boy

Now you might be thinking, between the coffee shops and the chicken visits it would be hard to live in such a society without getting fantastically fat. Well in my case, you'd be right! Although I was a skinny little Wang until the age of eight, I quickly learnt the joy of overeating, while also (disastrously) failing to acquire any interest in sport (except for *Kempo*, which was really just a weekly justification to eat even more on Saturdays). I was soon having multiple dinners a night, like some corrupt feudal lord, engorging myself with food from lands near and far. Noodles and dumplings to start, hot dogs and lamb chops to finish. I inflated dramatically over the course of three years. Slow for a puffer fish, but quick for a boy. By the time I was eleven years old – a prepubescent Wang – I was at my peak pudge. My top tub. My nipples receded into my new breasts; pink islands sunken by rising tides of flesh. I had become perfectly spherical. As wide as I was tall. Like a ball. Perhaps planning to save myself the effort of walking places by instead starting at the top of a hill and allowing gravity to do the rest. There is a photo of me at that age on stage in a school production of *Mary Poppins*. I have a lot of make-up on: red lips, pale face, rouge cheeks. Enormous, wobbling, rouge cheeks. I look like a geisha who is also a darts champion.

Compounding the shame was Malaysia's relatively low rate of obesity. People in Asia are pretty thin on the whole, despite all the marvellous food on offer. I don't know how they get away with it. Perhaps I had a European gene that stocked my fat stores for a winter that never came. Or maybe everyone else was simply able to exercise some restraint, instead of eating with all the control of a stray dog. So not only did I stick out of a line-up for looking Whiter than everyone else, but now with my new gut, I literally stuck out of a line-up. There was no body positivity back then either. So if you were big, you just had to deal with the taunts that came with it. Even from your own family. Asian families are close but they tell it like it is. A Chinese aunt will tell you you've gotten fat before she's even looked up from her mah-jong table. When I told my father that my dream was to become a professional WWE wrestler (I was really into professional wrestling), he just laughed in my face (I was his *child*, remember) and said, 'A *sumo* wrestler maybe!'

I lost a lot of the fat throughout my teens, as I grew both in height and in self-awareness. But the appetite has stayed with me, as has part of the belly. It hangs from me now like a reminder of where I came from; of who I used to be. Like a tattoo, except harder to get rid of and less of an interesting talking point. No one ever asks what the stretch marks around my belly button '*mean*' or if I got my bingo wings in Thailand (although pad thais did play their part).

It didn't help that it was a strange point of masculine pride in Malaysia to be able to eat a lot. Like you were some great warrior. A literal devourer of worlds. I was the source of much admiration and honour thrown at my father from his friends. 'Wow! Your son can eat!' the other dads would say, crowding around me as I gorged unaware of them, congratulating my father on siring such an insatiable boy. 'Yes, he is a brave fighter. The Northern armies will drop their swords and flee in terror when they see his powerful chins,' my father would proudly say, nodding as I heaved another full duck into my mouth. So, for a while I thought I was doing a *good* thing. Eating all that food for Daddy. Mum was no help either. 'He's a growing boy!' she would proclaim with delight, using her doctor status to lend my girth nutritional virtue. If only she'd noticed the direction that I was growing *in* was purely lateral.

Sober Noodles

But what chance did a growing boy have in such a culture of eating? Malaysians eat the way Brits drink. It's no wonder British cuisine has never taken off – it must be hard to create and develop recipes when you can't remember dinner the next morning. The *kopitiam* culture of Malaysia takes the space that drinking culture holds in British life. Late at night, friends arrange to meet not at the pub, but the *kopitiam* or the *mamak* – the Indian/Malay Muslim equivalents that offer spicier dishes without the forbidden pork of their Chinese counterparts. Both are open all night and are buzzing social hubs. Jokes are told, arguments are had, and gossip is shared over plates, not pints. Pubs exist, but they are invariably seedy – the reserve of local delinquents and ne'er-do-wells.

Alcohol is legal in Malaysia, but it is still a Muslim country. As a result, alcohol carries more of a taboo than it does in Europe. Pair this with the baseline relative disinterest Southeast Asia has for booze, and you're left with a culture that unwinds with sambal rather than sambuca. Indian Malaysians are known to like a drink (and are joked about for it) and native peoples often distil their surplus rice into a diabolically strong wine. But these are exceptions in a generally sober nation.

The central role of alcohol in everyday British life was a shock when I moved to the UK. At sixteen, I found myself suddenly under constant social pressure to get served booze. The fact that it was, you know, *against the law* was considered a mere inconvenience to be sidestepped. Getting served underage is the national sport when you're sixteen and seventeen. And anyone who says we don't make anything in this country anymore is obviously not aware of our thriving fake ID industry, which employs thousands of people, all of indeterminable age.

I only ever attempted underage drinking in Malaysia once. Around the age of ten, my friend Renky and I were invited over to a kid called Calvin's house to play computer games. We didn't like Calvin but we did like computer games, so we went. Halfway through, Calvin asked us if we'd like a beer. Renky and I were unsure, but Calvin insisted it was 'fine' because he was (and probably still is) a fucking idiot. He popped out of the computer room and came back a minute later with a small can of lager.* We cracked that baby open and took turns taking sips and pretending it wasn't the most bitter, disgusting thing we'd ever tasted. Soon the door burst open and standing there was a furious bald man who, it turned out, was Calvin's loser uncle who had noticed one of his beers had gone missing. Behind him was Calvin's mother, hanging her head with the kind of shame reserved in the West for parents of serial killers. The uncle started shouting at us for daring to drink beer so young, something that was specifically for – in his words – 'uncles to relax', which remains to this day the creepiest description of beer I've ever heard. As Calvin's uncle screamed at us, computer screen glowing in the corner, beer warming rapidly in the equatorial heat, and Calvin's mother close to tears over her reprobate son and his alcoholic chums, I thought, *To hell with this 'beer'. It isn't even nice! Chocolate milk is nice. And chocolate milk doesn't get you shouted at by a pound shop Mr Miyagi,*

* Beer only really comes in small cans in Malaysia. The same way rice only comes in pathetic little packets in the UK. Priorities, huh?

interrupting a perfectly good afternoon session of Half-Life. After such a traumatic experience, and with basically no peer pressure to drink otherwise, I didn't think about alcohol again for the rest of my years in Malaysia.

I have now, of course, become a complete booze hound. Or as the British call it, 'integrated well'. On my occasional adult returns to Sabah, I have had a terrible time finding drinking buddies. The few friends I have left there don't enjoy getting hammered (if you can imagine such a thing), and my family could not be less interested in any of it. One Christmas dinner back in Kota Kinabalu, I thought I'd get a little festive cheer going and asked Dad if we had any beer in the house. 'I think we have some downstairs,' he said, like it was leftover paint. I headed down to the basement and found a small cardboard crate of little Heinekens. Bingo. I quickly carried them up, excited to finally get this Yuletide going. The cans opened with an apathetic hiss, and the beer was flat and strange-tasting, like dried leaves steeped in urine. The expiry date revealed the beer was off by a long while. It had been down there for two years. No one had wanted a single beer in that house for *two years*. We had, however, run out of chrysanthemum tea for the third time that day.

For King and Curry

Food is the reason Malaysia became a country in the first place. A jumble of quarrelling principalities brought together by the invading British, who wanted in on those spices. It really says something about the food back home that you have to launch a naval campaign across the world to find something edible. It is no coincidence that the two East India Companies came from the worst food nations in Europe – Britain and the Netherlands. Dutch food is so bad it's no wonder they have to be high all the time. One of their national dishes is genuinely sprinkles. Like you put on a cake. It's called *hagelslag,* which sounds rude but it's just sprinkles. They put sprinkles on toast and have it for breakfast, like the last meal of a simpleton in a Steinbeck novel. Aside from pickled herring (most likely bought from the UK), the traditional Dutch meal is *rijsttafel** (pronounced 'Rai-star-fel') which is just a large selection of Indonesian food, brought home by Dutch colonists in the 1600s after the largest munchies-inspired takeaway hunt in history. How mad is that? To simply transplant your largest colony's cuisine over to a completely alien climate and treat it as your own. That would be like if there was a widespread tradition in Britain of stuffing yourself with butter chicken and naans every weekend— oh.

Now you might be thinking, *But the Spanish also had a large Empire and* their *food is alright.* Is it? Tell me the last time you were satisfied by tapas. Exactly. There isn't much that I can say with complete certainty, but I can say this: the Aztecs would still be around today if it weren't for small plates of cold omelette and tiny clay dishes with three prawns in them.

Still, the culinary riches of Britain's Empire took time to flow back into the country's everyday diet. Tea and sugar, of course, were profoundly popular when they were brought back from China to the East, and the Caribbean to the West. Caffeine and sugar are addictive, after all. But without a narcotic

* *Rijsttafel* translates literally to 'rice table', which sounds like a nightmare to assemble.

incentive, the British palate can be stubborn. When the celebrity chef Jamie Oliver campaigned to ban fast foods in school canteens in the mid-noughties, parents were outraged, even resorting to passing their children burgers through the playground fence.* Nutritional science didn't matter. Brits won't be told what to do, even when it's good for them. This national passion for self-sabotage even infected British progressives, who turned on Oliver and accused him of classism, denying people on lower incomes their God-given right to die of scurvy. In the years since his campaign, and with the replacement of junk food in school canteens by healthier, fresher options, students' exam results, attendance, and general level of health have all improved. An astonishing accomplishment for Jamie Oliver, who is nonetheless still ridiculed to this day, simply because he is, to be fair, quite annoying.

Class rears its ugly head in every debate in the UK. And food is no different. The quality of state school meals before Oliver's intervention, and the widespread resistance to their improvement, was proof of our national unconscious belief that healthy and tasty food is the preserve of the wealthy. But, of course, it is not expensive to make food delicious or good for you. The dishes of the world's favourite food nations were created by their poorest people. Starving French serfs picked up snails and turned them into a delicacy†. And Italians put bread, cheese and tomato together and created a global obsession.

* If this had happened in Malaysia, at least the parents would have hired a giant burger man from McDonalds, who'd bring enough burgers for the whole school and teach everyone a Burger Dance.

† Fun fact: if you place an empty snail shell close to your ear, you can hear the faint sound of a French waiter mumbling something rude about you.

Sunrise, Sunset

I would like to end this chapter by offering an olive branch to the British Isles – as long as they don't find it too 'olive-y' – because there are two important exceptions to Britain's rap sheet as the bad food capital of the world. Two categories of food in which the British truly excel. The first is: breakfasts.

The full English breakfast is a work of humble genius. Eggs. Bacon. Sausages. Mushrooms. Baked Beans. Eat any one of those things on their own and you'd look like a psychopath. But put them together and you have a filling, thrilling smorgasbord of all the tastes you need: salt from the bacon, sweet from the beans, sour from the ketchup or brown sauce, and egg from the eggs. I have never had a bad day after a full English breakfast. It isn't always a *productive* day. But it is never a *bad* day.

Asian breakfasts are . . . fine. Though it is hard to say, as the contents of breakfast rarely deviate all that much from the other meals of the day. Dishes are more or less interchangeable between breakfast, lunch and dinner.

As for Europe, don't even get me started. It wasn't until I first travelled to France that I truly came to appreciate the full English. Nothing ignites the patriotic fervour of a Brit like the first meal of the day in continental Europe, where breakfast goes to die. Pastry and cheese? Cold ham? Dusty oats? Sprinkles on toast? European breakfasts are like the panicked improvisations of a Martian guessing at what humans are supposed to eat. British breakfasts are made *for* hungover people, but European breakfasts look like they've been made *by* them. 'Just . . . I dunno . . . just throw that wholewheat cereal into this pot of . . . what is this . . . fennel yoghurt?'

The other exception is puddings. Man oh man do the British know how to pud. Custard, cake, sticky toffee, custard, trifle, tarts, custard, pie, custard pie, custard, custard, custard. All brilliant. Enriching, hearty, warming, comforting, delicious. Dessert is where simplicity matters, and when it comes to food, no one does simplicity like the British. The French novelist Marcel Proust had his famous madeleines dipped in tea, the taste of which always sent his mind back to a childhood memory of eating them with his aunt. I have many madeleines; many tastes that take me back to many different memories. But every sweet one is British. A sticky toffee pudding at university, the childhood Christmas trifles that Mum would somehow hold together in the Malaysian heat (which became a favourite of all the Wangs), and the greatest dessert of all time: a banoffee pie, made by my English uncle, Mark, with toffee made out of condensed milk boiled in its own can*.

Before the UK, the only desserts I was willing to commit any time to was stuff from the supermarket: ice cream, cheap sponge cakes, and cookies. Because Asia – and I say this with all the love in my heart – can't make a dessert for shit. Thousands of years of the oldest and greatest civilisations on Earth, and not a single good sweet to show for it. Have you ever looked beyond the main courses at a Chinese restaurant? Of course

* For those unfortunate enough not to know what a banoffee pie is, it's a pie with a biscuit base, toffee filling, sliced bananas, and whipped cream. It's the greatest dessert in the world and the first time I had it on a childhood visit to England I was both overjoyed to discover it and hot with fury that I hadn't been eating it every day of my life. The salty-sweet density of the toffee marries perfectly with the cool airy cream. And the banana basically makes it a salad so it's good for you too.

not. Because it rapidly descends into terrifying nonsense. Coconut jelly? Tapioca balls? Buns filled with red bean paste? *Beans*? For *dessert*? *Beans*?? Where were they at breakfast when we needed them?! The only dessert we ever got at our large Chinese family gatherings as kids was a slightly sweet clear soup with doughy balls in it. Yeah. Me neither. I still don't understand what it was supposed to be or who it has ever appealed to. As kids we looked at it as a punishment for finishing our dinners. I guess in Asia the starters and mains are so good, only the most demented gluttons ever had any room left for pudding and were left to devise it themselves.

It is interesting to me that the two types of food Britain nails – breakfast and pudding – are the very first and the very last things you eat in the day. Why did the British just give up on everything in between? Leaving that tasteless, stodgy, depressing no-man's-land of sandwiches, potatoes and batter? Perhaps we'll never know.

But we mustn't lose faith. British food is getting better all the time. As our islands are gifted with new citizens from the world over, bearing their sesame and tzatziki and dashi and gochujang and jerk, a new spice trade is picking up where the last one left off. A spice trade of free people and free ideas. Food is like nuclear power: our future's best hope is in fusion. I dream of a day of tempura fish and chips, beef rendang wellington, and Peperami jambalaya. After all, great food lies at the crossroads of cultures. And you can build a crossroad anywhere.

There is one truly great, uniquely Malaysian breakfast now that I think about it. My father's favourite. Hainanese coffee, runny half-cooked eggs cracked into a bowl, and toast covered in *kaya* – a delicious sweet coconut spread. Essentially, soft-boiled eggs and soldiers. Ordered by the colonial British from their Hainanese cooks, who took the 'soft' in 'soft-boiled' to its extreme and created something new. Rounded out with the sweet Southeast Asian *kaya*, it is a marvel. The unexpected consequence of White men who plundered their way across the globe to find some goddamn seasoning for their chicken.

RACE

A Fuss on a Bus

The night buses of London are a spectacle. Every evening, the pomp and ceremony of the capital dissolve away as the sun sets and in their place emerges London's dreamy night life. It's a gritty, intoxicating performance, and Transport for London's travel network provides its most fascinating stages. You never know what impromptu drama you might be lucky enough to catch treading the speckled floors of the Underground, the Overground, or the city's iconic buses.*

* In the last few years I have begun to occasionally get recognised on public transport. Once on my way home, I secreted myself into a seat on the upper deck of a night bus and began chowing down on some chicken nuggets I'd bought from a leading Scottish-named, clown-approved fast-food outlet. Getting off at my stop, I felt a notification buzz in my pocket. Taking my phone out as the bus pulled away, I read the brand-new Twitter comment: '@ PhilNWang you eat those nugs'. At last, *I* was someone's night bus show: That Guy Who Has Been on TV Five Times Stuffing His Face with Reconstituted Chicken Parts Alone on the N98. I don't know who my voyeur was; I don't know where they were sat. All I know is that they watched me eat every one of those nuggets with greasy greed. It hasn't stopped me eating fast food on public transport. I now just make sure to do it in as fabulous a way as possible. Just in case some little pervert is watching.

It was on one such night bus that I stumbled into the middle of a rather peculiar duologue. I had missed the beginning of it, so couldn't be sure what it was about, but I could tell that it was a heated exchange. For lack of a more delicate description, a Black man and a White man were arguing. The White man was considerably more animated than the Black man, wearing the anxious, angry energy of someone who knows he's cornered in a debate.

'Where am I from? Where am *I* from?' said the White man in a cockney accent, 'I'm from *Africa*, mate!' Now, this was an odd thing for him to say for obvious reasons. I'm not saying there aren't any White Africans – there are. But I can't recall anyone in *District 9* sounding like the Artful Dodger. Naturally, my suspicions were aroused.

Expecting a physical fight to break out, and exercising my proud British right to Not Get Involved, I scurried up onto the upper deck to sit down. My chicken nuggets were getting cold. So that brief burst was all I caught of the argument: a White, southern English man indignantly shouting at a Black man of unestablished nationality (he did not speak during my time on the lower deck): 'I'm from *Africa*, mate!'

Now it would be very easy for me to take that one snippet of conversation I observed and use it and it alone to extrapolate backwards and then forwards in time to rebuild the full interaction and judge both parties. Extremely easy. So let's do it.

This is how I see that argument starting: the Artful Dodger (let's call him that as the image is in our minds now) approached the other man (let's call him Oliver Twist, why not) and asked him where he was from. Oliver Twist was British, but withheld the information from the Artful Dodger, feeling affronted at being asked about his country of origin simply because he happened to be a Black Brit. Instead, he returned the question and turned the tables: 'Why are you asking me where I'm from? Because I'm Black? Where are *you* from?'

At this point, aspiring young comedian and eventual author Phil Wang (some would say the real hero of the piece) got on the bus. He paid a reduced fare, having savvily (and sexily) registered his travel card with his Young Person's Railcard, saving a third on all public transport fares in London – including, you guessed it, buses.

The Artful Dodger, accused of having said something maybe a bit racist, became defensive and angry. So in order to claim a little academic nous and show everyone on the bus who may have been watching (including Phil Wang) that he was quite open minded, actually, he replied with the apparent checkmate: 'Where am *I* from? I'm from *Africa*, mate' – a reference to our understanding that Homo sapiens originated in Africa and all our genealogies – regardless of our race now – began in Africa.

Phil, upon seeing this unrest, escaped heroically (and sexily) to the upper deck, despite knowing that the bus would start moving again at any moment, and he might have to engage a good bit of core strength to stay upright on the stairs against the destabilising lurch forward. Good thing he had recently started Pilates.

From that point onwards, extrapolation and guesswork must return to continue the story of the argument. Again, completely unfair and very easy. But who's going to stop me? You? Didn't think so. Here goes:

OLIVER TWIST: Well, yes, obviously we're all originally from Africa. But if you're going that far back in time, why bother asking me where I'm from at all?

THE ARTFUL DODGER: You're right. To be honest, the Africa comment was a diversion. I had felt suspicious about your origins, and hostile to your presence here. Decades of multiculturalism and globalisation have left me feeling bereft of a cultural identity of my own. In that vacuum, I have found nationalism to define myself by instead. However, nationalism is an identity that can only be expressed through the exclusion of others – those I feel do not fit into my idea of Britishness. And so, in denying your claim to this country, I was merely trying to assert my own.

OLIVER TWIST: I understand. Perhaps I was too quick to judge and should have tried to see things from your perspective before assuming the worst of you.

THE ARTFUL DODGER: Well at least we have come to an understanding now. This has been an enriching experience for us both.

OLIVER TWIST: Agreed. Also, was that Phil Wang who got on the bus just now?

THE ARTFUL DODGER: Yes! I thought that was him. He's looking goo—

OLIVER TWIST: He's looking good. Oh, sorry.

THE ARTFUL DODGER: Ha, yes, I was about to say the same.

OLIVER TWIST: Great minds, huh?

THE ARTFUL DODGER: Hahaha. Yes, quite.

OLIVER TWIST: Not only do I think his stand-up is excellent, but I reckon he's got one hell of a book in him as well, whenever he gets around to writing it.

THE ARTFUL DODGER: Well we are just agreeing all over the place now, aren't we? Hahaha.

OLIVER TWIST: Hahaha.

THE ARTFUL DODGER: He smelt a bit like chicken nuggets though.

THE ARTFUL DODGER *and* **OLIVER TWIST** *both laugh and hug each other long into the English night.*

Now, there is no way for me to prove that it all unfolded that way, but you can't prove that it didn't, and I dare you to try. Regardless, I think you'll agree that what the story *tells us* about our attitudes to race is very true indeed. And if Hilary Mantel and the Bible can play fast and loose with the great conversations of history in order to make a point/sell books then I can too.

I think about those two guys a lot, and all the possible branches that led to 'I'm from Africa, mate,' and all the branches that might have followed. In some versions, the Artful Dodger is completely in the wrong – a seething bigot whose ignorant words have finally been challenged and whose conviction has been found wanting. In others, an oversensitive Oliver Twist has rebuked the Artful Dodger for simply trying to make conversation, forcing him into an exasperated outburst at the bad-faith presumptions associated with his own appearance and voice.

I think about them a lot, because I think about race a lot. For me, their confrontation was a vivid (if embellished) depiction of the problem we have with race in the UK: we refuse to talk about it openly until it is too late. The more the conversation is avoided in public, the more poisoned it becomes in private. Eventually, when we are made to confront it, we release all our accumulated feelings – our hurt, our paranoia, our distrust, our anger – in one toxic blast, and we start shouting at strangers on the bus.

Proper Hair

I think about race a lot because I have no choice. The child of a White woman and an Asian man, the subject of race has always been a part of my life and always will be. I don't mind it. It's not a chore. I find discussions about race enlightening, important, and on occasion (to my good fortune) funny.

Others are not always so open to the subject. 'I don't see race' is a popular get-out clause – a claim apparently meant to imply that the speaker is *so* inclusive, egalitarian, humanist, and advanced, they don't even recognise something that has shaped societies the world over and directed the course of human history. The sillier version of this platitude, 'I don't see *colour*', is even more insane. I happily put my hand up and say that I see colour. All the time, in fact. It's kind of the point of colour.

Denying the existence of race is to admit to living in a fantasy. You don't see race? Well, that must be nice. It still exists, I'm afraid. Claiming that you don't see race does not mean that you have solved racism, in the same way that saying you 'don't see trains' won't make it any safer for you to walk onto the tracks at Manchester Piccadilly station.

The word *privilege* has lost a lot of its power through recent overuse, so let's use the words *good bit of luck* instead. It is a *good bit of luck* to not see race. Because you can only get away with not seeing race if it does not affect you. This is why the people in majority-White countries who say they don't see colour are usually themselves White. They are able to ignore the effects of being racially different because they are not exposed to them. And it's far easier to put your hands up and say 'not my problem' than to confront the issue, as anyone who has had diarrhoea in a public restroom can attest.

There's a scene in *The Aviator** in which the young businessman Howard Hughes is having a tense and obnoxious lunch with the wealthy Hepburn family. When the subject of money comes up, the matriarch, Mrs Hepburn, quickly nips the topic in the bud, 'We don't care about money here, Mr Hughes'.

'Well that's 'cos you have it,' snaps an irritated Howard, shocking the table into silence.

Clearly affronted, Mrs Hepburn gives him a second chance at polite conversation, 'Would you repeat that?'

Howard doubles down: 'You don't care about money because you've always had it.'

This is how I feel about people who say they don't see colour, or that race doesn't matter to them and that people should stop talking about it. You don't see race because you don't care about it. And you don't care about it because you don't need to. You don't need to concern yourself with

* A good film, worth seeing if only to watch Leonardo DiCaprio neatly arranging milk bottles full of his own urine while completely naked. Boy did he want that Oscar.

thinking about how your race fits in among the majority, because you are in the majority. You don't need to worry about how to find your sense of racial belonging. You've always had it. You've always been White.

I just saw you roll your eyes. I can see you, you know. I understand – it has become tedious to read Whiteness talked about in this way by an out-of-touch metropolitan creative-industries luvvie like myself. But the arts aren't innocent here either. I've read numerous reviews of my stand-up that have complained of 'too much stuff about his race'. As if the racial elements of my life are cheap, unimportant and unpleasant things to discuss. Almost every non-White performer and writer has had to put up with the same whining plea: 'Do you have to talk so much about race?' The subtext being, 'Don't you know we're past all that now? Move on.' It is an ignorant person who proudly declares a disinterest in the different life experiences of others. It took me too long to realise that.

What always astonishes me is the conviction people have that merely not talking about race is a righteous act. Or that racism is like Bloody Mary or Voldemort and will only appear if you say its name out loud.

I remember once, after a show in central London, a married couple from the audience accosted myself and the comedians Pierre Novellie and Nish Kumar, who had also been on. Pierre being from South Africa, Nish being British Indian, and me being whatever the hell I am, each of our three sets had included material about race – all of which had gone down well with the majority of the audience, I hasten to add.

The couple were White, middle class and from Essex, and had been decent enough during the show. Although the wife was quite excited – and even a bit relieved – to hear my jokes about having a White mother.

'I thought so from your hair!' she had said from her seat.

It was a strange heckle, so I asked, 'My hair?'

'Yeah! It's, like . . . proper hair.' She explained, in front of a room full of people.

I was taken aback by this astonishing assertion that my Chinese Malaysian father didn't have 'proper hair' and my mother's genes were forced to really put the legwork in to save me from the same fate. Who in their right mind could doubt the East Asian ability to grow a great head of hair, anyway? Hadn't she seen Bruce Lee or the girl in *The Grudge*?

The outburst was easy enough to deal with on stage. It had made the rest of the audience noticeably uncomfortable, but it was nothing a bit of the classic Wang Charm™ couldn't put right. A bit of heightened exasperation, a bit of light ribbing about what 'proper hair' could possibly mean ('Like King 'enry used to 'ave!' I said, in an exaggerated southern English accent), big laugh, tension broken, and we were back on track.

It wasn't until after the show that the couple really revealed themselves. It was the husband leading the charge this time, putting his arm around us each – part congratulation, part threat.

'Well done, lads. Good show. But enough of the race stuff, eh?'

Pierre, Nish and I tried to get to the bottom of this guy's problem. It was certainly true that there had been more race-based humour that evening than at most comedy gigs – if he didn't like jokes about race and racism, then he had been incredibly unlucky with the line-up. However, what was wrong with a little thematic consistency over the course of the show? That's what good theatre is about, isn't it? The entirety of *Romeo and Juliet* is about two horny teens and people love it. No one comes out of it thinking, *Ugh, too much yearning!*

The man continued to berate us, making vague appeals (mainly to poor Pierre, the only White person among the three of us) about how race didn't need so much attention these days, and hearing our jokes, thoughts, and observations about it was all a bit much for a fun night out.

I pointed out to him that all the jokes were made in good spirit, and aimed *at* racism. We were making fun of racists, and everyone else found the jokes funny. It then occurred to me to ask him what should have been an outrageous question.

'Did you . . . feel *targeted* by those jokes?'

'Yes! I did!'

I was stunned. All the more so by his apparent comfort with what he had just confessed to. He had felt *targeted* by jokes about *racist people*. And instead of thinking, *Oh these jokes have made me feel that maybe I hold some racist attitudes that I need to address*, he thought, *Oi! Those anti-racist jokes are about me! How crass!* Extraordinary.

I don't wish to demonise that couple. They were decent enough folk – otherwise attentive, appreciative audience members, with at least the baseline generosity of spirit to come over afterwards and say well done, which made the wife's comment about 'proper hair' and the husband's indirect admission to being racist all the more sinister. Racism is not always an obvious monster, screaming epithets at you in the street or daubing swastikas on your house in excrement. It can exist dormant in someone's psyche without them even being aware of it. I do not know where that married couple are now (Essex, I presume) but I honestly wish them well. One thing I do know for sure, though: the husband would absolutely hate the subject of this chapter.

I use these examples to say that hostility towards racial minorities is not confined to the archetypal skin-headed toothless thug, but arts critics, and middle-class theatregoers too. It is a pervasive bigotry because it can sometimes appear on the surface to be palatable or even well-meaning. Saying 'I don't see race' is at best a naïve attempt to simply wish a racism-free world into existence without doing anything that is difficult or disruptive to your life, and at worst it is a get-out-of-jail-free card to let you say and do racist things.

So please, see race. See colour. It's OK. You're allowed to notice that I look Chinese. What matters is what you do with that information. Want to ask me which noodle dish I recommend on the menu? Go for it. That's why I'm here in the restaurant, offering advice from table to table to as many people as I can before the management kicks me out again. But want to dropkick me in the chest because you think Chinese people all got together and created COVID-19 in a big wok? Maybe hold off on that impulse. Living well in a racially diverse world is not about sticking your head in the sand and pretending that race does not exist. It's about acknowledging race, whilst exercising care and judgement.

Pedant of Colour

I used the term 'non-White' earlier to refer to people who are racially, well, not White. 'People of colour' was also an option – one that is currently more popular. But I prefer 'non-White'. A quick note on that, if you'll allow it.*

* Well, you have to allow it. It's my book. I mean, I guess you could skip ahead past this bit, but then you'd miss a pretty incredible story about the time I met Gal Gadot. Your call.

Neither is ideal. Of course, I understand the case against 'non-White': it is inherently demeaning to define people by what they aren't instead of what they are. It implies that the norm is to be White and everyone else, everyone who 'lacks' Whiteness, is a second thought. But to its credit, it is the more precise of the two. There are White people, and 'non-White' refers to everyone else. 'People of colour' is a little kinder, in the sense that you are defining people by what they *are*. It's literally a positive description. These people are not merely *not White*. They are *of colour*. However, it is vague. What is 'colour' in this case, exactly? Black skin? Brown skin? How many shades off A4 does a person need to be to qualify for inclusion? Does a tan count? Would it be possible, say, for my mother to leave for a holiday in Mykonos a White person, forget her sunscreen, and return a woman of colour? That colour being tomato? I've known some very pale-skinned Chinese people in my time. Are they people of colour? Is 'people of colour' instead a socio-economic term for disadvantaged ethnic minorities? If so, Indian and Chinese Brits would lose their membership, being the highest-earning ethnic groups (including 'White British') in the country.*

'Person of colour' is specific enough to exclude White people, but still too vague to actively and clearly include whoever it is supposed to represent in any meaningful way. 'People of colour' tries to claim a collective group identity for an enormous and disparate collection of different ethnicities in a way that 'non-White' does not. Which is better because not all the people who are not White are united by some great shared cause of being 'of

* This is according to a study by the Office for National Statistics based on data between 2012–18 (my first six years of pursuing comedy professionally). I can't imagine I was part of that particular survey sample.

colour'. Being part Chinese and part Native Bornean, I qualify as a person of colour. But to then suggest that that means I have the same desires and needs, or face the same challenges due to my race, as, say, a Bangladeshi woman or an old Inuit man is obviously absurd. So what is the point of making the distinction at all, if not only to define me against White people, which is what 'non-White' already does quite well?

'Colour' is also an odd choice of word to use considering its less-than-heroic participation in racist language of the past. You're playing with fire to encourage its use. When in a BBC radio interview in 2019, Amber Rudd referred to the MP Diane Abbott as a 'coloured woman', I almost felt sorry for her. Of course, 'coloured' is an archaic and hurtful word with a great deal of painful history attached to it. But when the word 'colour' has been encouraged to remain in the updated terminology, that kind of mistake is *going to happen*. Many jumped on Rudd's gaffe as a Freudian slip that revealed the Work and Pensions Secretary for the old-school fifties racist she really was. And with her legacy as the Home Secretary who presided over the shameful Windrush scandal of 2017 and 2018, in which hundreds of Jamaican Brits were wrongly detained and deported for little discernible reason other than the colour of their skin, who can blame them? But her slip of the tongue was obviously an honest blunder. And not a very difficult one to make when 'woman of colour' – what she was supposed to say – is semantically the same. I get the same uneasy crinkle in my bones when I hear 'person of colour' as I do when I hear 'coloured person'. The exoticism, dehumanisation, and condescension of both are equivalent to me. I am not convinced that merely swapping the words around produces a different result. Two plus three equals five. Swap them around and three plus two does not equal a better society. It still equals five.

'Person of colour' is such a trivial modification of the unacceptable term – 'coloured person' – that it almost seems like a trap intentionally designed to catch people out. And to have such a dramatic difference in correctness between two seemingly identical terms merely provides evidence to truly racist people that anti-racist people really are unserious language-obsessives who care more about words than action. Besides, wasn't it the 'colour' part that was the problem anyway? The suggestion that non-White people have something strange added to them? A deviation from the normal human state?

The fundamental problem is that there are a lot of different types of people in the world who are not White, and every attempt at a single term to refer to them all is going to be imperfect. How do you group together so many different folks? You can't. The best term must therefore distinguish the people in question as being not White without implying that that itself is some unifying identity. So I will be using the term 'non-White' throughout this book. It is not perfect, but it is the least bad choice. I just wanted you to know that I had thought about it*.

Back to the Otherland

I hope it doesn't seem like I'm obsessed with race. But if it does, it's because I am. I've always found it fascinating. And after open conversations about it among people from different racial backgrounds, I often end up feeling more – not less – human. It was strange when I arrived in the UK to notice how instinctively uncomfortable people got whenever the subject

* I lied about the Gal Gadot story. I just didn't want you to skip ahead. Hey, you've got to respect me for that.

was brought up. I suppose I got thrown in the deep end as a child in Malaysia, where race is just an undeniable and unavoidable reality of everyday life. Malaysia is a highly racially diverse country. The largest ethnic group – the Malays – make up only half of the population, with the other half split among the Chinese, the Indians, and the non-Malay indigenous peoples (including the Kadazan-Dusuns of my own Grandmother Sanoh). In comparison, White Brits make up between 80 and 90 per cent of the UK's population. That's a pretty large chunk of people. Unsurprisingly, the less racially varied a country is, the easier it is to brush race under the carpet and pretend everything is fine. There aren't enough people to complain about the bump in the rug. Malaysia, however, has been a racial and cultural melting pot since its inception and race has been at the forefront of the Malaysian consciousness ever since. There is no taboo around race. Someone's race is as pedestrian and inoffensive to ask about as their height or favourite fruit.

Although tensions inevitably rise from time to time, overall, Malaysia's different ethnic populations live side by side in extraordinary harmony, especially considering the many religions that have to coexist – Islam, Christianity, Hinduism, Buddhism, Animism – combos that have led to pretty devastating fisticuffs elsewhere in the world time and time again. It is a testament to the Malaysian commitment to celebrating the country's many different races and cultures that there isn't a civil war every weekend.

Malaysian culture itself is defined by its diversity, and the pleasure everyone takes in sharing each other's festivals, music, art and – especially – food. The 'open house' is a uniquely Malaysian tradition. During each of the many religious and cultural festivals – Chinese New Year, Hari Raya (the Malay celebration of Eid),

Deepavali (aka Diwali), Christmas, Ka'amatan (the Kadazan-Dusun harvest festival) – people host an open party in their houses for all to attend, whoever they are and whatever they believe, with long tables heaving with food – *nasi lemak* in Malay homes, *roti* and curries in Indian homes and noodles in Chinese homes. Nothing teaches a young kid the value of cultural harmony like years of what is essentially food bribery. Malaysians are all raised tasting the glory of diversity.

However, even in that rich racial jumble, I never really fitted in. In the same way that I am seen as Chinese in the UK, in Malaysia, I'm a big old honky. It's perfectly understandable. Compared to most Brits, I am quite Chinese, and compared to most Malaysians, I'm pretty White. And we are always identified by what makes us different from the majority. Before we get to know anyone, we first characterise them by their most obvious distinctive feature. Think about when you're trying to point someone out in a crowd. The lady in the red shirt. The guy with the short neck. The child with the evil eyes. It is not reductive to use these markers because you know nothing else about those people at that point.

But this first act of othering can have lasting effects. 'Othering' is a term that has found popularity in recent years amongst people from marginalised backgrounds. It refers to the feeling of alienation a person experiences when they are treated as different, foreign, and unfamiliar, even in their own home country. I have never really known any other feeling. Being of two races means that you are neither, as often as it means that you are both.

Being mixed-race is a poisoned chalice like that. What allows you to enjoy two cultures, two histories, two identities at once, also leaves you alone in the middle, alienated from both sides for your insufficient purity. One needs only to look at the pivotal word used to describe people of mixed ethnicity: *half*. Half-caste, half White, half Asian. Half of a whole, half of something complete. I use the word myself! The word 'both' would be nicer, wouldn't it? I am not half British and half Malaysian, but *both* British and Malaysian. But even I subscribe to a language of lesser; of a split; of an accident. Half. Mixed. Or in my father's own story, not quite noon. As a result, far from being able to slot in easily on both sides of the planet, I've merely been gifted the opportunity to experience racism of both flavours. My cup runneth over!

Even in racially diverse Malaysia, I stood out for being White. I was called *orang putih* – Malay for 'White person'. Occasionally even *mat salleh*[*] – a more confrontational almost-slur with anti-White undertones[†].

Ironically, Malaysia was where I was first asked the question I would have to get used to for the rest of my life. 'Where are you from?' It came from everywhere. Grown-ups, other kids, shopkeepers, teachers, friends' parents, passport control (that one's fair enough I guess). People who knew my father would greet him cheerfully, then look at me, and with wide eyes say, '*This* is your son?', wondering for a moment if my Asian father

* There are numerous theories for the origins of *mat salleh*. Among the more ludicrous is that the first White people Malaysians ever saw were drunk seamen coming into port, or 'mad sailors', which eventually became *mat salleh*. Firstly, why would they have used English? And secondly, calling all British people drunk sailors is a gross and false generalisation – not all of them are sailors.

† The British aren't the only Europeans to bear the brunt of Malaysian taunts. The Malay term for the proboscis monkey – known for its long, bulbous, penis-like nose – is *orang Belanda*, or 'Dutch person'. This slam is further validated by the fact that proboscis monkeys are the only wild primates to legalise prostitution and recreational marijuana.

had adopted a White orphan from the West. Also known as a 'reverse-Madonna'.

Whenever I'd start speaking Malay to someone, they'd cock their heads, astounded that I spoke the language. 'Where are you from?' they would ask me. 'Here,' I would reply, before adding, 'but my mother is from England,' to save them from too much embarrassment, and give them the explanation they were looking for.

All those confused faces started adding up. *Well,* I thought, *I guess I'm White. I'll just have to wait until I move to the UK where I'm sure I will finally be accepted as one of the gang.* Not so simple, young Wang. When we moved to the UK, we moved to Bath, where I can safely say I have never felt more Asian in my entire life. The UK is very White in general, but Bath is *especially* White. Bath is a spa town for people who find Cheltenham too ethnic.*

At last, I felt like an Asian person. Seven thousand miles away from where I'd actually wanted to. I thought England was where I would finally feel normal. But all that happened was that my difference was flipped, and I felt equally foreign but in the opposite direction. I realised then that no matter where I went, where I moved to, where I lived, I would always stick out; I would always look different; I would never fit in. But hey, at least I've been easy to find in every school photo I've ever been in.

An Education

At sixteen I began my life in Britain and – more specifically – my academic life in the UK, starting A levels at a private school

* For any readers outside the UK, Cheltenham Spa is also a very White town. Hence this joke.

in Bath. I won't use the school's real name, so let's call it . . . I don't know . . . St Rugby's Academy for Problematic Boys and Girls Who All Wanted to Sing 'Summertime' at Assembly.

St Rugby's had a sixth-form block, where the A-level students could relax between lessons. The social hub of the building was the common room, which had a toaster and a kettle, and was also where the girls would practise holding hot drinks with both hands in that snuggling way only young women with a certain degree of financial security are able to do.

The sixth-form block also contained a rabbit warren of private studies. Your study was your home base at St Rugby's. It was where you'd keep your things, finish homework last minute, cry, and in my case, cough directly into a girl's mouth while trying to kiss her. We were dating at the time, and leaning in for a romantic smooch, a tickle in my throat caught me by surprise, and I barked a lungful of cough right into her unsuspecting cake hole. She broke up with me about a week later. Don't know why.

Each study was shared by three students. The kids who had already been at St Rugby's for a few years could choose their study mates so that they could be with their friends, as long as they were the same sex – to avoid any (at least heterosexual) hanky-panky (although you could always visit someone else's study if there was a mouth that needed a good coughing into).

As one of the new cohort of students, I didn't have the option of choosing my study mates, seeing as I didn't know anyone. So the school took it upon themselves to pick them for me. As part of my welcome letter, I was given the names of the students I would be sharing a study with: Ken Inoue and Keith Leung. Both from Hong Kong. Well, what a coincidence. What were the chances? Wang, Inoue and Leung (none of whom knew each other) placed together. I wonder what the running theme was there.

There was no need for the school to do this. There were other new kids who weren't Asian that they could have mixed the three of us up with. They could have got some real international, interracial mingling going. But no. 'There you go,' St Rugby's seemed to be saying to me, 'a couple of your lot. You'll feel right at home.' It was a blow to be starting a fresh life in a new home and find that I had been pigeonholed (quite literally) into 'Asian' from the get-go. I had also just come from a really wonderful international boarding school in Brunei (a tiny country right next to Sabah) with students and teachers from all over the world. Nigerians, New Zealanders, Nepalis, Peruvians, Australians, Malaysians, Bruneians – all mixing together. We were all friends with each other. It was quite a shock to then move somewhere so racially homogenous and quasi-segregated. It was like I had been living in *Star Wars* and was suddenly transported to *Downton Abbey*. I was lucky that Ken and Keith were good guys. Well, Ken was an extremely cool *both* Japanese and Hong Kong Chinese dude* who had incredibly nimble football skills and the cheekbones of Kate Moss. I may have been a bit obsessed with him, actually. Keith made fun of my goalkeeping skills once, and for that he will suffer eternal infamy in these pages.

It broke my heart that it was just assumed the Chinese kids would want to stick to themselves. And it added to my disappointment that they actually did for the rest of their time there.

* See? *Both* Japanese and Chinese. Not half and half. I'm learning. You're learning. *We're* learning. *Together*. This is a very important book.

But what chance did they have when the school itself didn't expect them to do any differently from the day they arrived?

Another one of the Hong Kong kids in my year, Kenny (yes, they all had names starting with K, which really didn't help the situation), was an eccentric, funny and sweet guy who made valiant efforts to be part of the broader school community. In our leavers' yearbook, in his answer to the question 'How do you want to be remembered?', Kenny summed up the success of his efforts: 'Not just another Chinese student'.

A year later, one of the leaving White male students adorned his yearbook profile with the parting motto, 'Genetics is everything'* – with no apparent intervention from the school. Sorry, Kenny. Hope you had better luck at university.

At least I was used to being an outsider. In a strange way, being treated as foreign in Bath made me feel like I was back in Malaysia. There were many things I had to get used to when I moved to Britain – the weather, the food, a new Sugababe every week. But fortunately, that familiar old question was there to remind me of old times. 'Where are you from?' everyone asked. Although, this time, it was a little more valid. This time they had a point.

The othering wasn't always so subtle. Once on my way to a lesson, I was accosted by a boy from the year above who had blue eyes and blonde hair that would have given Hitler goosebumps (to go with his steps). He caught my eye and motioned my gaze downwards, where I found him holding his penis, which was sticking out of the zip of his trousers. 'Now *I'm* Phil

* A scientific explanation he will eventually have to use when his kids ask him, 'Dad, why are we such dreadful wankers?'

Wang,' he said proudly, referring to his penis as a 'wang'. It wasn't a perfect joke, I have to say. It didn't make much sense because having a penis does not make you me, because I am not the only person in the world with one. And thank goodness for that. What a freak I would be. I'd be put in a cage and toured around in some cruel travelling circus. 'Worm Bottom' they'd call me. Or 'The Boy with a Sausage for a Leg'. They'd laugh at me through the iron bars and make me do tricks with it for nuts. But I got the older boy's point. That was how I learnt that 'wang' is slang for 'penis' in the English-speaking West. And how thoughtful of him to have brought along a visual aid, a real-life sample, for that particular lesson. That's just the kind of multimedia quality education you get at a private school.

The racism experienced by Chinese people often takes this form of ridicule, either for our appearance, the sound of our names, the sound of our voices, or the sound of our language. It rarely gets challenged – certainly less so than racism aimed at other groups. It is now broadly understood that the slurs represented by *the N-word* and *the P-word* are unutterable, but 'Chink' is still kind of OK to a lot of people. I've even heard people say 'the Chinky' to casually refer to the local Chinese takeaway. While the N- and P-words make most people reel with shock and disgust, 'Chinky' mainly makes them hungry. If further proof is needed that there is a hierarchy in place here, I haven't even felt the need to abbreviate 'Chink' like I have the N-word and the P-word! I knew I wouldn't get in trouble because *nobody cares*. But then again, I guess 'the C-word' is already taken.

Racism against East Asians is often brushed off as a bit of fun, light-hearted, or silly. 'They have little willies, tee hee

hee', 'they all look the same don't they! Ha ha ha'. 'Come on,' the unspoken consensus goes, 'no harm in that. They seem happy enough keeping to themselves. And what's wrong with saying they all look the same? It's not like we're beating them up over it.'

My university days found me in markedly more enlightened company, surrounded as I was by some of the smartest people in the world from many different backgrounds and walks of life. But even there, one evening, walking through Cambridge* with another half Chinese Malaysian friend (making us together one full Chinese Malaysian person), a drunk young man decided to impress the girl he was with by clocking us as we walked past and shouting 'Ching chong ching!' – a classic of the genre. At best, I'd underestimated the man, and he actually knew Mandarin fluently. *Qing* meaning 'green', and *Chongqing* being a megacity on the edge of Sichuan province. 'Qing Chongqing!' may have been an environmentalist call-to-arms to roll back the industrialisation of the municipality and protect the natural beauty of the nearby Yangtze river. At worst, this drunk was displaying a little *in vino veritas* and his *veritas* was that he was very racist.

When something like that happens, it takes you by surprise. You spend precious seconds second-guessing what you've just heard. 'Surely not. Surely he didn't just say "ching chong ching" at us in public like that. Not in Cambridge, of all places. There are no racists *here*, are there? Certainly not the kind of bottom-shelf bigots that say "ching chong ching". They'd do

* Clang. That's right. I didn't smash my exams and not go to any parties during A levels (my choice) *not* to mention it every chance I get.

it by quoting Voltaire, or using the Bernoulli Equation to prove mathematically that pak choi is gross, or something. Not just "ching chong ching". Actually, "ching chong ching" could also be Mandarin for "Please. Worms. Please". Like he's begging for worms. Ha. You eat worms, do you? You racist asshole. *You're* the worm, mate. Hahaha. Yeah, that's good. I'm going to tell him that.' And you look up and realise you're half-way across town, and your friend is asking you why you haven't said anything for the last twenty minutes.

In my less proud moments, I have fantasised about turning around that night and using the martial arts I learnt as a kid to kick that guy's ass. Although that would almost certainly have played into his stereotypes. And I don't think shouting 'I learnt this at my family's dojo!' would have broadened his impression of East Asian people.

The Virus of Racism

Now, if you're worried that epithets against Chinese people have gone stale, don't worry. The COVID-19 pandemic breathed new life into a dying art. When the new coronavirus was first discovered in Wuhan at the end of 2019, it quickly became synonymous with China and Chinese people. TV news was a rolling feed of fearful Chinese faces, half-obscured by now-familiar masks. Soon the virus spread to neighbouring countries and then further afield to Europe – Italy, Spain, and then France. The news cameras followed, but still, to my amazement, the Chinese faces remained. Wherever the report was coming from, whether it was Milan or Madrid or Paris, the producers had somehow been able to find a Chinese person somewhere in the European crowds to focus in on. It was like the news was playing an international game of Where's Wongy? following our itchy-footed contagious Asian antihero across the globe as he spread his deadly disease (and I'm *not* talking about his tenacious travel bug!). There he is on the BBC, poking his head out of the Coliseum! There he is on Sky News, strolling up the Eiffel Tower! And there he is on CNN, feeding ducks in Central Park as a SWAT team closes in behind him.

I'll never forget a story on the BBC News website about the first London Underground employee to test positive for the virus, for which they used an image of a Chinese woman sat in a train looking at her phone, *who wasn't even a London Underground employee.* On some occasions, news crews were apparently not able to find a Chinese person, so had to make do with a Filipino or Korean.

Eventually, the news broadened its outlook and gave equal opportunity to non-Asian COVID-19 representation, but by then the damage was done. A couple of weeks before the UK finally began its disastrously late first lockdown, I was startled by a man outside my home as I was about to finish the last few steps to my front door. Or rather, I startled him. While walking past me, he turned his head to look at me, apparently noticed the nature of my face and said 'Oop! Corona!' before quickening his pace to get ahead of me, intermittently looking over his shoulder to make sure he was keeping his distance.

Again, it took a few moments for me to register what had happened, and that I had been the subject of some stroll-by racism. As this was still early on in our understanding of the coronavirus, my upset was compounded by the thought that maybe this was how you caught it. Someone just had to quietly say 'corona' close enough to your face and that was it, you got it. And then you would say it quietly to someone else and they'd get it, and then they'd do the same to someone else after that, on and on, each transmission mutating the contagion ever so slightly. The new Chinese whispers.

A few days later, the then US President Donald Trump* began calling the disease 'the Chinese virus', and brutal physical attacks on East Asians – far worse than a hurried 'Oop! Corona!' – became a pandemic of their own all over the Western world. The victims often weren't even Chinese. Many were actually Japanese or Korean or Southeast Asian. But it didn't matter. It didn't stop them getting beaten up. We do all look the same, after all.

But Where Am I Really From?

Fifteen years on from my move to the UK, I feel British. Although I have still technically spent more of my life in Malaysia, the formative initiation rites of adulthood have all taken place in Britain: losing my virginity, voting, university, moving out of home, rediscovering my virginity, learning to drive, pretending to be 'into whiskey', calling the police on someone, buying a desk fan, giving up on *Infinite Jest*, replacing a boiler. Now, when people in the UK ask me where I am from, I say I'm British. 'But my father is from Malaysia,' I then

* In case you are reading this book a thousand years in the future, having found it lying in the dusty rubble that was once the human race, this is obviously a joke. Of course Donald Trump was never elected President of the United States. Please instead remember our species for the great things we *did* achieve: mapping the human genome and coffee culture. Also, I hope that whatever civilisation you are from has been able to figure out what we never could: how to satisfactorily fold a fitted sheet.

add, to save them from too much embarrassment, and give them the explanation they were looking for.

Perhaps it's a moot point anyway. Go back far enough in any of our families' histories and you're bound to find that someone was from somewhere you weren't expecting. And if you're willing to let me go back as far as I like, well then, I guess I'm from Africa, mate.

COMEDY

Mind Your Language

Pik-Sen Lim is seventy-seven now. But the legacy of the TV show that made her a star still weighs heavy. A recent BBC documentary on the poor representation of the Chinese community in Britain featured a clip of her, young and sprightly in vintage Technicolor, goose-stepping around a cafeteria dressed in full Chinese Red Army garb, before exclaiming to a perplexed White man in an exaggerated Chinese accent, 'This is uniform of People's Army of Ribelation as plesclibed by Chairman Mao . . . You not rike it?'

The documentary was part of a series focusing on the histories and experiences of various immigrant communities in the UK, and in the episode about Chinese Brits, 'They showed *my* clip as how *not* to be depicted,' Pik-Sen despairs. 'It was absolutely awful.'

The show was *Mind Your Language*, a British sitcom from the late seventies set in an English-as-a-Foreign-Language night class in London. The class is made up of a smorgasbord of foreign characters: a man from Spain, a lady from India, an Italian guy, and a Japanese businessman to name a few. They are all taught by the beleaguered Mr Brown, the new teacher at the adult-education centre, who must juggle their ropey English, inter-cultural grudges, and the lustful distractions of the class's French, and then (to really secure the programme's male audience) Swedish, femme fatales (this was the seventies after all). All the while, Brown has to dodge the curmudgeonly principal, Ms Courtney, who is for some reason always on the lookout for an excuse to fire Mr Brown, despite being the one who hired him in the first place. Pik-Sen (who goes by Pixi in person) plays Chung Su-Lee, the Chinese student in the class. Premiering in 1977, the show became a smash hit in the UK, running for four series and bringing in around eighteen-million viewers. It was Pixi's big break as an actor.

'It got all of us known instantly,' Pixi tells me, when we meet on Zoom, her eyes still bright with the memory of it. Although her goose-stepping days are behind her now, her face holds that same sprightliness; that engaged and youthful energy that some seem blessed to keep forever. However, speaking with her now, through that glow, it is easy to see that her relationship with *Mind Your Language* is a complicated one. 'It took me years to shake off the stigma of that show.'

Unlike Pixi, *Mind Your Language* has not aged well. A British comedy from the seventies about a group of hapless foreigners is about as sophisticated in its humour as you might expect it to be. The Sikh, Ranjeet, bobs his head along to his own sing-song voice, smiling wide, hands joined as if in constant prayer, offering Mr Brown 'a thousand apologies' every time he makes a grammatical mistake (which is often, naturally!). Japanese electronics executive, Taro, responds to every question with a hearty 'Ah-so!' and insists on getting out of his seat and bowing whenever he is called upon for anything.* German Anna – blonde hair in orderly plaits to complement her severe facial expressions – is typically stern and humourless, proclaiming outright at one point 'I do not know any jokes,' just in case the message hadn't gotten through to the viewers. Meanwhile, Italian Giovanni and Greek Max pit their Mediterranean machismo against one another, for the attention of sultry French au pair, Danielle. Yes, don't you worry, the show is also excruciatingly sexist, with the female French and Swedish characters serving no real purpose beyond eye candy, and who the live studio audience are almost encouraged to loudly wolf whistle at every time they say anything remotely sexual (which is often, of course!).

And then there is Pixi's character: Chung Su-Lee, an intense Mao-quoting young communist, who – get this – can't pronounce her R's and L's. In fact, far from settling for the occasional 'Herro!', the show insists on her swapping *all* her R's with *all* her L's and vice versa, which no real Chinese person actually does. The result is quite lidicurous. Sorry, ridiculous. Su-Lee sets her character's stall out the moment she appears in the first episode, joining the lesson late: 'Mr. Blown? Prease folgive my rateness. I aporogise but I rost my way.'

'It was extremely difficult to learn to talk that way,' Pixi laughs now, in perfect English and an accent as crisp as the Queen's.

Mind Your Language is undoubtably of its time and would not get made today without the immediate resignation of everyone

* It took Pixi to explain to me why everyone laughed so much at Taro saying 'Ah-so'. 'It sounded like "arsehole". That's what that was meant to be! The audience would roar with laughter.' Truly, I missed the golden age of comedy. I had never even noticed that it sounded like 'arsehole'. And I don't know whether to be proud or ashamed of that.

involved (and in Taro's case, hara-kiri). The show is a common feature of many scowling modern retrospectives on the UK's ignorant and problematic television of the past. 'A Brief History of Britain's Racist Sitcoms' runs the title of one such article on *Vice*:

> *Mind Your Language* is impressive down to just how many stereotypes the format manages to cram into each episode . . . managing to balance the distinct flavours of lazy xenophobia and smut-heavy misogyny so delicately.

I get a similar reaction whenever I bring the show up to British friends who happen to know it. They roll their eyes with embarrassment and shake their heads at the very notion that such a programme could ever have been on national TV.

This was at first a source of some surprise for me, because I like *Mind Your Language*. I actually kind of love it. And I am not alone. It was (and still is) profoundly popular outside of the UK, being broadcast in Pakistan, Sri Lanka, Kenya, Nigeria and more. It was huge in India, and I remember from my childhood how well loved it was in Malaysia too. It never stood out to me at the time as some backwards vestige of a politically incorrect past, but was merely another part of the tapestry of the great British comedy tradition – a tradition so great it was able to reach me even in far-flung Borneo.

Pixi and I first met as castmates in a short film about a family-run dim sum restaurant in London's Chinatown a couple of years ago. I felt like I recognised her at the time, but couldn't quite put my finger on where from. When she told me that she had been in *Mind Your Language*, my memory of the show came flooding back in an instant, and I was the most starstruck I've ever been. And I've met Tom Jones!*

Pixi is, in fact, Malaysian herself, from the beautiful city of George Town in Penang. 'Fate' has an egotistical edge – a superstitious kind of belief that puts your own life at the centre of the universe – but meeting her in a fake dim sum restaurant in London (my new home), realising she was in *Mind Your Language* – one of the first sitcoms I was ever aware of in Malaysia (my first home) – and then discovering that she was Malaysian too felt like fate to me. Pixi fell in love with acting (or 'the business', as she calls it) going to see American movies at the cinema – a reward from her cinephile father whenever she did well at school. Her mother was a lover of Chinese opera and theatre, and would similarly treat her when she'd earned it. Like me, Pixi had a large family: 'The house was full of twenty people . . . everybody could come and share the house.' Sounds familiar. And, like me, she had many cousins her own age, with whom she would put on small shows for fun. 'I produced. I directed,' Pixi adds with a mischievous pride.

It should have been no surprise to anyone, then, when Pixi told her parents that she wanted to pursue acting in the UK. 'There was a whole lot of horrified reactions!' she tells me over our video call, eyes wide, hands to the sky, selling the scene. Coming from a family of high achievers (one ending up the Malaysian Ambassador to Belgium†), a calling more robust and

* Well, saw him across a room. By 'met' I mean we met eyes. And by 'met eyes' I mean my eyes met the back of his head. It was definitely him though. And you know what, despite what he is known to have said in the past, it *was* unusual.

† That said, it was *just* Belgium. I'm not saying becoming an ambassador isn't impressive. It is. But Belgium is, well, not impressive. It's . . . *Belgium*. Being an ambassador, but to *Belgium*, must be the most unimpressive impressive job I can

respectable was expected of her. Her parents were relatively unfazed, but her extended family were appalled. 'They were all horrified. "How could you let your daughter go there and be an actress?" and my father's rather resigned reaction was, "Oh, she's female,"' Pixi re-enacts with a dismissive wave of the hand, '"She's going to be somebody's wife someday. It'll be alright. Just let her go."'

And so, at just seventeen, Pixi made her way to England and studied acting at the London School of Dramatic Art. After graduating, she quickly got a part on the medical soap opera, *Emergency Ward 10*, and then a short-lived flat-share sitcom called *Sorry I'm Single*. After that, her IMDb reads like a laundry list of typical Chinese drop-in characters – 'Sister Ling', 'Mrs Chan'. One appearance has her character down simply as 'An Oriental Friend'. She was even in three episodes of *Doctor Who* in 1971. But it wasn't until *Mind Your Language* that she became an internationally recognised face.

Although the bit of script she had to audition with was a little lowbrow for her tastes, she was delighted to get the part. It was only later, when the show was well and truly underway, that she realised the kinds of lines Chung Su-Lee had never moved on from what she saw in that audition material.

'My character and the Japanese guy's character were the only two-dimensional characters. I did not know that every single episode would not progress from there. Every single episode, the same old thing "Chairman Mao, he say . . . "' She's right. Chung Su-Lee has no meaningful character arc over her three series. Possibly because (and this is the writer

---

think of. Not so much the tallest dwarf of jobs, more the shortest giant. Sorry to any Belgians reading this, but . . . you know . . . come on. It's not France, is it? Which is actually the national motto of Belgium: 'It's not France . . . is it?'

Vince Powell's mistake) her English is already excellent upon arrival in episode one. In order to get enough R's and L's into her lines for her to mispronounce, they had to give Su-Lee some pretty advanced words and, ironically, a pretty sophisticated vocabulary for someone who was supposedly in need of an evening class for beginners. In one episode, upset about some homework the class are set – to write a story about going to a market – Su Lee starts ranting: 'Malketprace is full of capitaristic tladers serring inferior merchandise to ignolant working crasses at infrated plices!' I mean, aside from some pronunciation issues, that's a pretty good bit of English. So the character was painted into a corner from the very start. All Pixi had left to do was to repeatedly proclaim her loyalty to Chairman Mao and wave his little red book in the air and mix up her R's and L's again and again and again. It all gets a bit lepetitive.*

There is no doubt that *Mind Your Language* is crass. The writing is hardly sophisticated, you can successfully guess the punchline to a joke at least 1,500 times an episode, and its depictions of non-White people, if re-enacted today, would get you very intimate with your work's HR department. But is it *racist*?

'No, *lah!*' exclaims my Uncle David. *Mind Your Language* is his favourite show. It is currently being repeated on Malaysian TV and he couldn't be happier. I gave him a call to get his thoughts, unintentionally interrupting his drink of fresh coconut on the beach. I am not making this up. I do wonder

* Pixi has kept that little red book, by the way. And why not? Today's young communists would pay top dollar for such a trinket – something to spend their trust funds on.

why I moved to England sometimes. Just remember, Phil: the *museums*.

'There is nothing racist there,' Uncle David continues, lounging in the breezy shade of dancing palm trees, the waves of the South China Sea lapping at his sandals. 'It's just a joke.'

To hear him say 'It's just a joke' was rather striking. That's the excuse you'd normally expect from the *teller* of a racist gag, not the supposed target. Uncle David doesn't even *feel* targeted by Pixi's character. Not even Chung Su-Lee's exaggerated speech – 'Most of the Chinese spoke like that at that time!' Well, I don't know about that, but then again, Uncle David has a lived experience of the seventies that I don't. And we're supposed to respect the lived experience of non-White people, aren't we? When something like *Mind Your Language* is dismissed as racist bullying by well-meaning people in the West, it strikes me that the apparent 'victims' are rarely consulted for their opinion on the matter. And unfortunately for those who wish to expunge it from Britain's national memory, *Mind Your Language* is incredibly popular amongst many of the people it is apparently ridiculing.

Sindhu Vee is a comedian originally from India who now lives and works in the UK. I asked her whether she remembers *Mind Your Language* being big in India. 'Massive. I remember the adults loving it. It was something they understood perfectly. Everything about it – the values, the mores, the English. As a child, I thought it was funny. I got all the jokes.'

And you know what? Amongst the silly accents and clumsy plots, there *are* some pretty good jokes.

'You damn fool,' Pakistani Ali chastises Sikh Ranjeet after yet another grammatical mistake, 'you are not understanding the Queen's English!'

'I *know* the Queen is English!' Ranjeet spits back.

Now, I don't care what you think, I like that a lot. But the linguistic misunderstandings weren't all there was to it. Sindhu recalls her parents having a broader enjoyment of the show.

'They weren't laughing at the non-English speaking characters. They were laughing at the whole thing. They were laughing at how silly the English were. They were laughing at the stereotypes, the fact that the Italian guy always made eyes at the women. These were very innocent stereotypes.'

Not all the stereotypes were innocent, I argue. What about the fact that Ranjeet and Ali wanted each other dead? A running joke that relies on the sweeping stereotype that Sikhs and Pakistanis didn't get along?

'Well, they *didn't* get along!' says Sindhu. Fair point.

There are brilliant individual performances in *Mind Your Language*, too. The unflappable commitment of the cast to their characters and even the occasional flash of nuance really buoy a script that regularly fails on its own. When Juan, the Spanish character, is asked to tell the class a joke, he gleefully runs to the front and tells a very long story completely in Spanish, with no one understanding it but him. Completely unfazed, he reduces himself to hysterics, and it's genuinely great fun to watch. In another episode, Taro performs a song called *A Warrior's Lament-o*. Dressed in a business suit, he proceeds to screech eerily in a wavering high pitch and briefly impersonates some notes on an invisible Japanese lute, before miming decapitating the watching principal Ms Courtney. His stone-faced 'execution' of the principal is so sudden, juxtaposing beautifully with the motion of his tie flopping limply in the wake of his swing, that it leaves me in gasping convulsions of laughter every time I watch it. Despite the dated cheesiness of the show in general, there is quality here if you care to look for it.

To Western eyes, the sight of all those different caricatures in Mr Brown's classroom might look contrived. A lumping together of various cartoonish stereotypes. But to Malaysians, who share their country with each other as Indians, Malays, Chinese, Natives, and even the odd Eurasian, it's a natural set-up. In a peculiar way, the central premise of *Mind Your Language* was a reflection of Malaysian society itself – a hodgepodge of different races, religions, and cultures trying to get along in pursuit of a common goal: learning English; building a country.

We Make Fun of Singapore

Pixi thinks the explanation for *Mind Your Language*'s appeal to us Malaysians is easily explained. 'We have a more direct sense of humour, don't we? My relations still laugh if somebody farts on-screen.' In our conversation, I laughed immediately at her just *saying* the word 'farts', so I guess she's right.

This idea of a Malaysian sense of humour is an intriguing one. *Is* there a Malaysian sense of humour? Does every country have one? And if so, why are some more well-known than others? Everyone knows about the British sense of humour. How can you not? Along with cold sandwiches, the Beatles and the phrase 'oh dear', Britain's sense of humour is widely considered its greatest cultural export.

But of course, the British are not unique in enjoying a good joke. The ubiquity of the Great British Sense of Humour is more about the ubiquity of Britain's influence in general than the quality of its jokes in particular. It wasn't that the Great

British Sense of Humour was inherently better than anyone else's, but that Britain had the technology and resources to produce radio and television comedy before almost anyone else, and history's largest empire to export it to. The Great British Sense of Humour is known the world over because Britain got all over the world.

But, for a nation that has produced both P. G. Wodehouse *and* Mr Blobby, what exactly the Great British Sense of Humour *is* is quite hard to pin down. A lot like Mr Blobby.*

Is the Great British Sense of Humour absurdity and slapstick? Like *Monty Python* and *Mr Bean*?†

Is it parody and satire? Like *French and Saunders* and *Spitting Image*?

Is it character-driven? Like *Blackadder* and *Alan Partridge*?

Or is it wordplay and sexual innuendo? Like *Mind Your Language* and . . . William Shakespeare? That's right. You heard me – *Mind Your Language* has all the comedic merit of Shakespeare's entire catalogue of comedies, if not more. And with the added bonus of not having to watch it in a theatre surrounded by people who are, quite frankly, lying to themselves. Shakespeare's comedies must be the greatest scam in all of literary history. Puns and dick jokes. That's all they are. Both of which are fine, of course, but not from the supposed God of

* For anyone outside the UK, Mr Blobby is a nightmarish, man-sized pink-and-yellow bulbous bowling pin with arms and legs. He can only say the word 'blobby' in an electronically distorted voice and navigates the world in unsettling erratic, tortured movements. He first appeared in the nineties BBC variety show *Noel's House Party* hosted by Noel Edmonds. He is demonic and vile. And Mr Blobby is pretty creepy in it too.

† Also incredibly popular in Malaysia. It's funny that of the two most popular British TV comedies in Malaysia growing up (*Mind Your Language* and *Mr Bean*), one was about the intricacies of the English language, and the other was about someone who couldn't speak English at all.

Rhetoric. Putting on a ruff and then thinking up knob gags by candlelight? It just doesn't fit.* Imagine writing jokes about erections with a *quill.* Pathetic. It's not right. You can be one or the other, Shakespeare. Pick a lane.

If I had to categorise British humour into a single comedic quality, innuendo is probably it. In one word, the Great British Sense of Humour is innuendo. And not just sexual, but all kinds of innuendo – the act of not saying what you mean; of only hinting at the truth with a sly wink and a nod. This is the distinction Pixi was drawing when she said the Malaysian sense of humour is more 'direct', i.e. it is not innuendo.

Innuendo is vital to the British spirit. Not just to its comedy, but to its *everything*. Every description of Britain's past and present identity is laced with innuendo. What is 'empire' if not innuendo for invasion? What is 'manners' if not innuendo for class? What is 'expat' if not innuendo for an immigrant but one who is from Britain? And what is 'the Great British Sense of Humour' if not innuendo for the British domination of world culture? The British are infamous the world over for not saying what we actually mean. It's part of the reason why we've gotten ourselves (and others) into so many disastrous calamities over the course of history. Or as we'd put it, 'little spots of bother'.

Dr Jason Leong is a Malaysian comedian – ethnically Chinese and part of the country's exciting new generation of stand-ups. He is also, as his name suggests, a qualified doctor. I spoke to him to get the perspective of someone currently working in comedy in Malaysia, and also to be able to say that I interviewed a doctor for this book. Having become a doctor only

* That's what she said.

to later take up a career in comedy, Jason's mother and father are officially the proudest, and subsequently, the most disappointed parents in Asia.

Comedy is still in its early stages of development in Malaysia. It is still a very young country, and comedy equals independence plus time. Jason feels that Malaysian comedy still has some way to go before it can get to the 'sophistication' of British humour. He doesn't think it's in our bones in the same way that it is in the English-speaking West, having become familiar with that culture of humour after working in a pub in Ireland for two years.

'When it comes to small talk, Irish people, Australian people, and UK people – there is this sense of, *To get to know each other, we're gonna tell jokes. We're gonna laugh at each other, we're gonna make fun of each other. If you can take the joke, I can take the joke – that means we can get along; that means we're cool,*' Jason says. 'Malaysians? We tend to be a bit more polite.'

Asian cultures are often structured around respect and courtesy, an environment in which 'banter' – i.e., playful mockery – doesn't always come off well. At least not straight off the bat with someone new. 'In fact, sometimes, if you meet someone and you fling jokes at each other, that may be quite rude,' says Jason. Though Malaysians of course share plenty of jokes and light ribbing with their friends, it takes a while to get to that point. Friendly jibes are rarely what relationships start with, as is more often the case among Brits.

That isn't to say that Malaysian humour is entirely innocent and wholesome. Anything but. When it can be eked out of good friends who trust each other over the rickety tables of late-night *kopitiams*, Malaysian humour can be hilariously wicked. It is sarcastic and mischievous. And while Malaysians might be cautious about making fun of each other, they are more than happy to make fun of Malaysia the country. Often in exasperation at whatever dreadful howler a politician has committed this time, or some great failure of national effort. Local politics is an ever-dependable source of jokes. Jason laughs at the idea that the British think their parliament is chaotic when Malaysian MPs will literally challenge each other to fist fights. Getting things wrong is a cornerstone of the Malaysian comic identity. There is an almost nihilistic pride to it. Malaysians relish the opportunity to laugh at themselves as a whole.

Britain often prides itself on being a self-deprecating country, 'We know how to laugh at ourselves' is almost a national motto, alongside 'Hiya!' and 'Yeah it was alright, actually'. But if you ask me, it's Malaysia that has a better claim to that honour. Though Britain claims to make fun of itself all the time, most traditional jokes are aimed at others – particularly the UK's neighbours, making it not uniquely humble, but simply like most other Western countries. The French make fun of the Belgians, Americans make fun of Canadians, the Danes make fun of Norwegians, and Britain follows suit. In the 'An Englishman, a Scotsman and an Irishman walk into a bar' tradition, it is never the Englishman or Scotsman that does something stupid, but the Irishman. The French are pompous and smelly, the Germans are authoritarian and boring, but the Englishman's flaws are all rather likeable. He is, if anything, *too* polite. He queues. He apologises a lot. He is a bit awkward, but in a loveable way. And despite his (essentially charming) shortcomings, the Englishman is ultimately honest, uncomplaining, and gets on with the job at hand. He keeps calm and carries on. So while the Brits are more ready to mock each other as individuals, they are actually quite protective of the British identity in general.

That doesn't sound like self-deprecation to me. In my view, Malaysians have a far more self-deprecating national mindset. Malaysia is the only place I know where the butt of every joke is itself: Malaysia and Malaysians, whether they are ethnically Chinese, Indian, or Malay. When I put this to Jason, he agrees. 'You are right, *lah!* There is no trope where one particular person gets it. It's always: as a whole, *we* suck.'

Jason has a joke that I love. It's a play on an old classic which goes:

> In Heaven, the police are British, the mechanics are German, the bankers are Swiss, the lovers are French, and the cooks are Italian. In Hell, the police are German, the mechanics are French, the bankers are Italian, the lovers are Swiss, and the cooks are British.

Jason's version goes:

> In Heaven, the police are British, the mechanics are German, the bankers are Swiss, the lovers are French, and the cooks are Italian. In Hell, the police are Malaysian, the mechanics are Malaysian, the bankers are Malaysian, the lovers are Malaysian, and the cooks are Singaporean.

'We make fun of Singapore,' Jason admits.

Chong Are You

As a child there was nothing more exciting for me than making people laugh. And making adults laugh – especially my parents

– was the Holy Grail. It meant I was beginning to understand adulthood; that I was smart enough to trick and entertain mature minds.

Mother would often laugh at my silliness and attempts at gags, but my Chinese Malaysian father was always a tougher nut to crack. I felt a special impetus to make him laugh, more out of curiosity than anything else. But whether it was a language barrier, or simply his belief that I wasn't very funny, I could never quite do it. Not consistently. I've only ever seen my father really laugh – like completely lose it – twice in my life. And only the first time was my own doing. When I was about ten years old, I told him this joke that I'd heard:

> A guy is at his new girlfriend's house for dinner to meet her family. When he arrives, he is introduced to the parents and the family dog, Rover. He is naturally nervous about making a good impression as they sit down for dinner. He soon finds that, due to a combination of nerves and spicy food, he is getting quite gassy. He needs to relieve the pressure but is too embarrassed to ask to go to the bathroom. However, he can't just fart in front of his new girlfriend's parents. So, spotting that the dog is lying down under the table, he hatches a plan: *I'll blame the toots on the pooch.* And so, he gives it a go, and releases a mini guff, a squeaky little one to test the waters. *Fffffft.* 'Rover . . .' the father says in a low accusatory grumble. *Great! I'm getting away with it*, the boyfriend thinks, *Old Rover is taking the heat.* A few moments later, his bowels gurgle and our inflated antihero realises that he is need of further relief. So, he does it again, this time allowing himself a slightly louder trump. *Prrrrt.* 'Rover . . .'

> his girlfriend's father says again, raising the urgency in his voice ever so slightly this time. *Superb*, the boyfriend thinks, *I'm really onto a winner here.* A few moments later, an even larger amount of gas has built up in him, and with all the confidence of a man with the perfect scape-dog, he lets out his largest fart yet. *PRRRRAAAAAAAP!* 'ROVER!' the father shouts, 'GET OUT OF THERE BEFORE HE SHITS ON YOU!'

I can still see my father now, absolutely beside himself, shaking uncontrollably with laughter, trying desperately to keep it in but failing, tears streaming down his face, his arms buckling as he tries to keep his hands steady on the wheel and keep us on the road (I shouldn't have told it in the car). I was in joyful awe. I'd never seen him laugh like that. Pixi was right. Malaysians *do* like a fart joke.

The second time my dad really fell apart laughing was at the end of 2019 when I returned to Malaysia for a cousin's wedding. And it wasn't even from anything *I* said or did. It was his own story.

He'd recently been to a friend's wedding and was recognised at the reception by someone whose name he couldn't quite remember. 'Benny!' the mystery man said cheerily, approaching Dad for a handshake and a catch-up. Still, the Rolodex in his mind was coming up blank. What's more, the guy knew *his* name, which made matters worse. Thinking on his feet, my father decided on something neutral, returning the greeting with all the warmth of an old chum. 'Ah! My friend! How are you?! How are you, my friend?'

'No,' the man replied, 'Chong.'

'What?' said my father, a little confused.

'*Chong* Ah Yu. Not How Ah Yu. My name is *Chong* Ah Yu.'

In the retelling, Dad could barely get to the punchline intact. He was rocking back and forth. The pitch of his voice had risen to a register usually reserved for birds. His face was red with mirth, like the Ghost of Christmas Present, as he described Chong Ah Yu getting his identity card out of his wallet to prove to Dad that he wasn't messing with him.

I realise now: the two times I've seen my Malaysian father laugh the hardest were about farts and the misunderstandings of English as a second language. Go figure.

Foreigners!

For my Uncle David, the appeal of *Mind Your Language* was its characters. 'I like the characters,' he says (told you). 'Especially the Spanish guy.' I suppose that's the real genius of the show: there's someone for everyone to laugh at, even if you take a few shots yourself. Everyone gets their turn in the firing line.

The writer and creator, Vince Powell, always insisted that the hapless Brits in the show were figures of ridicule as much as the foreign students were. Having found inspiration for the idea during his own time at night classes, you can imagine him finding humour in the situation as a whole – people who struggled to learn English led by people who weren't quite capable of teaching it.

The foreign characters often got their own back, pointing out what was strange about the British. In an attempt to improve their speaking skills, a few of the students buy the Cockney caretaker, Sid, a coffee and sit him down for a chat. He proceeds to tell them a story about getting drunk in full Cockney rhyming slang: 'So I staggered home, took off me dickie dirt and me daisy roots, and fell backwards on the apples and pears!'

'Blimey,' Sanjeet says to Giovanni and Max, 'we are better off talking with each other.'

What's more, the accusation that the show was actively xenophobic and racist would hold more water if the character who held those attitudes the most plainly wasn't the principal, Ms Courtney, who is undoubtedly the villain of the piece. It is her character that embodies the fear and suspicion held by many Brits during those decades of intensified post-war immigration and the social upheaval that followed.

When she first meets the class and has to struggle through a conversation with the Sikh Ranjeet, Indian Jamila, and Spanish Juan, Ms Courtney turns on her heel, exasperated, and huffs, 'Foreigners!' before leaving the room. In a later episode, covering for Mr Brown, she asks the students, 'Can anyone tell me what the population of England is?' German Anna raises her hand, 'Ja. English.' The class and audience share a laugh before Ms Courtney rebukes, mostly to herself, 'Not any longer . . .' There is a sense that the viewer is invited to laugh at her frustration, but not to sympathise with her underlying sentiment.

'All of the non-British characters, they all had redeeming qualities,' says Jason Leong, 'The one person that didn't have any redeeming quality was the headmistress . . . She was the one that was the nasty character.'* And Jason's a *doctor*, remember.

★ ★ ★

★ While I think the casting of Ms Courtney as the bad guy relieves the show of some of the accusations of racism made against it, it certainly doesn't do anything to address the inherent misogyny of the show, which is unarguable.

Mind Your Language first ran for three series from December 1977 to December 1979. Pixi played Chung Su-Lee in all 27 episodes. The show was then brought back for one final series years later in 1986, but Pixi wanted nothing to do with it. 'I had got myself a rather good job in a drama series by then, so I was glad to be out of it!'

That final series was a flop. It seemed that tastes had changed since 1979. And by the nineties, *Mind Your Language*'s creator, Vince Powell, found that he could no longer get any interest for any of his scripts at all. These were different times. 'No one wanted his style of comedy anymore,' Pixi says, remembering a time he confided in her, 'He couldn't submit anything that got accepted. It was quite sad, really.'

Regardless, the influence of those first three series of *Mind Your Language* is undeniable. It inspired remakes in countries all over the world. In each iteration, following the same premise, but playing on the local languages and ethnic make-ups of its new home. Versions were made in India, Kenya, Nigeria, Japan, Indonesia, and the Unites States among others.

However, it is the original British version that still has adoring fans everywhere. Even Pixi's eleven-year-old granddaughter loves it. 'And she's a smart cookie!' says Pixi, who can't believe the show's longevity.

It must be quite something for Pixi's granddaughter to see someone who looks like her on TV. Someone who looks especially like her, in fact. Her grandmother. And this is why the show is popular in so many countries. There are people of so many different races in it. Even watching *Mind Your Language* now, I am struck by how diverse the cast is. And to be completely frank, it outdoes most British shows made *today* in that regard. It's easy enough for well-meaning Western progressives to now dismiss the caricatures on display as crass, but to the many Indians and Malaysians who watched it then, it was revolutionary to see themselves on-screen in a world-famous sitcom.

'I remember my parents were always very proud,' Jason tells me, '"Oh, that girl who plays Su-Lee, she's from Malaysia! She's from Penang!" I think that was probably the earliest Western show where there was representation.'

I hope Pixi's granddaughter knows that she is the descendent of a great. Pixi is something of a hero of mine. A trailblazing Malaysian on British TV, decades before I was even born. Her TV and film credits run from 1964 all the way to 2020 and counting. Very few can claim such longevity. I can only hope that I do. She has beaten up Rowan Atkinson in *Johnny English* and acted alongside Angelina Jolie in *Maleficent*, and there are no signs of her stopping yet.

Pixi is humble about getting through that fateful audition in 1977, playing down her talent. 'I had the right look,' she insists. But she does herself a disservice. She's an excellent comic performer, despite being given very little to work with compared to the others in Mr Brown's classroom. She had to work hard to imprint something of herself onto those scripts.

'You really must work on those R sounds,' Ms Courtney says to Su-Lee in an early episode. 'Try saying "Around the rugged rocks the ragged rascal ran."'

'ALOUND THE LUGGED LOCK THE LAGGED LASCAL LAN,' Su-Lee replies, unaware of her mistake, to raucous laughter. Not exactly a joke to win the Mark Twain Prize, but there is the smallest of looks Su-Lee gives Mr Brown after she says it. It is innocent, confused, and frustrated with these perplexing Brits and their silly English. It's so subtle, and so funny. A little work of genius hidden between her lines.

When I watch that clip of Pixi as Chung Su-Lee in that BBC documentary on Chinese representation, I am not ashamed like she was. I am proud of the young Malaysian woman who defied the odds and flew to Britain on her own, against the protests of her family. Who, having grown up in Malaysia speaking mainly Chinese, became one of the first East Asian faces on British TV before she was even twenty-five. Who was the first Malaysian in an English-language TV comedy. And an enormously – internationally – popular comedy at that.

In a world in which we struggle to find common ground, a common goal, and a common language, *Mind Your Language* is almost radical. If we can't laugh about each other's differences, what hope do we have of finding what brings us together?

'It's the jokes that bring about harmony,' says Uncle David as he gets back in his car, having had enough of the beach. The sun is setting on Sabah as we wrap up our phone call. 'If people take offence, it's because they don't understand. Jokes are the best way to solve differences among different people.'

I say goodbye and hang up. Refreshed by this reminder that there really is a Malaysian sense of humour. One that isn't eager to offend, but that looks for the fun in our differences. It is a sense of humour that lives in me, I now realise. I just hope I do it justice, thloughout the lest of my own enteltainment caleel.

LOVE

No, He's Chinese

In December of 2012, I had a gig at Roehampton University in London. Sometimes universities put on comedy nights to both entertain their students with some much-needed light relief from their courses, and also to prepare them for the job market with a demonstration of what insecure employment looks like.

I'd only just graduated from university myself, and was terribly excited (and very lucky) to be performing professionally already. The venue was decent enough. A sports hall with raked seating set up. School assembly vibes, but at night and naughtier, like everyone had been held back for detention but detention was an irreverent evening of stand-up from some of the country's most exciting and affordable comedians.

I was the first act on after the compère.* Once he had fulfilled his God-appointed duty to get the crowd, as it's known in the

* The compère is the comedian who hosts the show. Sometimes also called the MC. 'Compère' is fancier-sounding, but 'MC' has cooler hip-hop connotations. It's each comedian's individual choice as to which is better suited to them. Personally, I prefer 'Phil Wang MC' if I am hosting a show, as, if said too quickly, 'Phil Wang Compère' sounds like I'm about to do something awful to Pierre.

business, 'warmed up', he announced the first act: our good friend, me. I can still see myself as he said my name, getting psyched up in the dark, hidden from the audience against the side of the bleachers. After all these years of doing stand-up, that excitement hasn't abated. Which is fortunate.

'Your first act of the evening is Phil Wang.'

A little commotion emanated from the seats near where I was standing, culminating in a conspiratorial giggle*. When the compère asked them, two young White women, what was going on, they explained that after he'd announced my name, one had asked the other: 'Is he fit?'†

'No!' the other had replied, 'He's *Chinese*.'

She finished the story with less confidence than she'd started with, feeling the room fall into a tense and embarrassed silence.

The compère was understandably dazed by this. Not only by what they'd said, but by the casual and unafraid nature with which they had recounted saying it. He made a light-hearted attempt at chastising them. It was a bit too early in the evening to have a real go at them and potentially kill the mood for the rest of the night. Plus, the girls already seemed

* The mention of my name at gigs would often have this effect when I was starting out, for reasons similar to the punchline in the previous footnote. People often told me they presumed Phil Wang was a joke stage name or something I'd made up for a comedy character. Wang is a real name, I'd assure them, but don't be embarrassed, it's only the most common last name in the world. That's just how many Chinese people there are. If you collected the world's population in a large field and threw a stone, odds are: you'd hit a Wang. *Again*, wordplay not intentional.

† To any readers not from the UK, 'fit' means good-looking/handsome/sexy/beautiful/attractive. It doesn't necessarily mean the person is physically fit, in the same way that being 'hot' doesn't require the person to have a fever or be going through the menopause.

embarrassed about it. And they were also very young. What I'm trying to say is, these calls are hard for a comedian to make in the moment, and I don't blame the compère for not getting angrier. They were university students. Still kids, really. I was older and wiser and – at twenty-two – basically their dad. As such, it was my responsibility as the more mature figure to calmly, kindly, and patiently show them the error of their ways.

Needless to say, I tore those twats a new one the second I got on stage. I slammed them about how they were both silly little racists and the crowd laughed and laughed. A cathartic laugh of relief and cosmic justice. I imagine life on campus was *pretty* difficult for those two gals for a few days after that show. 'There go those racist twins' people would have whispered as they crossed the quad. They weren't twins, but it would be added to the rumour. Oh yes, I imagine those ladies would have been roundly ostracised from the rest of the student community for their bigoted outburst, and to be frank, the very thought of it still fills me with a righteous peace. My comedic persona has always been two things: very laidback and deeply vengeful, and the student of any mid-tier university forgets that at their peril.

The unfortunate thing was that at twenty-two, I did look fucking awful. So the girls' Aryan theory was not exactly disproved that night. Every time I see a picture of myself from those days I am disgusted and angered by my dweeby little glasses (I thought the smaller they were, the closer I was to not having glasses at all) and my checked shirts and my bulging second chin and my hair that was simply too short and emphasised my enormous head. So I had actually reinforced those girls' stereotype. I was *not* fit. But it had nothing to do with my being Chinese. It was my own *personal fault* for thinking that cardigans over T-shirts was an aesthetic, and that drinking fruit smoothies was the same as actually eating fruit.

I wish I had looked good then, to have really hammered the point home in front of that crowd. To completely invalidate that girl's comment without me even having to say a word. It would have been so sweet if she'd said 'No! He's *Chinese*,' only for me to appear on stage looking like Simu Liu or Daniel Dae Kim. What a gotcha that would have been. Without even having to say a word, the audience would have instantly laughed at those girls and their appalling assumption, wolf whistling at me in supportive celebration as I swept my hair back and kissed my biceps for ten minutes straight.

As it was, I dumpily shuffled on in old jeans, doughy paunch teetering over my belt buckle, my blue-denim pockets faded white in the outlines of my phone and wallet, and the crowd thought, 'OK, one-nil to the twins . . . Let's see if this tubby nerd can turn this around. I hope he brought his graph paper with him so he can calculate an effective comeback.'

I was shocked and hurt and embarrassed by what those girls said that night, but I was not surprised. It is an unspoken understanding amongst East Asian men in the UK (and in the West generally), that we are not what most women think of when they imagine their ideal man. Whether you're willing to admit it or not, every racial group has their stereotypical perceived strengths. Sex appeal is not ours. It is just not the feeling we tend to conjure up. Academic prowess? Sure. A good massage? Absolutely. Relief when you see us in the kitchen of a Thai restaurant you previously weren't sure about because it's called *Shirt & Thai*? You bet. Sex appeal? No.

But why not? It doesn't make any sense. There are more than 1.4 billion Chinese people in the world – more than any other type of person – and seeing as people are made by sex, that makes Chinese men officially, *scientifically*, the sexiest men on earth. East Asian men are history's sex champions and we have the stats to prove it. But that seems to count for little out on the street. We are still patronised as being unsexy despite all numerical evidence to the contrary. And yes, maybe it's sentences like that that are part of the problem.

Also stacked against East Asian men is the West's general feminisation of East Asian physical characteristics. East Asian men are typically smaller than Western men (the White half of my genes made me the tallest member of my Malaysian family when I was just thirteen), and generally have less body hair. I cannot grow body hair to save my life. I am less man, more mannequin. Every woman I've ever dated has been significantly hairier than me. Which is not to say that they were particularly hairy. It's just that I am as smooth as a silk catfish. My arms are (and this is no exaggeration) completely hairless. Like I've permanently just had a wax. My chest is bald except for a dozen or so rogue hairs dotted around each nipple, that droop and hang forlornly in their solitude. And, even at thirty-one, my facial hair has the appearance of weeds in an abandoned car park.

In the West, being small and being hairless are considered feminine qualities. As a result, dating in the West is an uphill battle for East Asian men, who have to overcome these perceptions to assert a masculinity that is assumed of other men.

Some armchair sociology there. But you're going to give me the benefit of the doubt, aren't you? And why? Because of my assumed academic prowess.

A Sexy Peril

The distrust of East Asian men's sexuality in the West is old and widespread. For centuries America and Britain feared the 'Yellow Peril' – the mysterious menace of China: that ancient and unscrupulous behemoth to the east.

The fears were of a general cultural and economic takeover of the West by Chinese immigrants, and measures were taken to mitigate this threat. By 1882, anti-Chinese sentiment in the United States had gotten so bad that President Chester A. Arthur signed the Chinese Exclusion Act which effectively made Chinese immigration illegal – the first law ever to prohibit immigration to the country based on race (the Chinese are always responsible for new inventions, one way or another). It also excluded the Chinese people already living in the United States from obtaining citizenship. As a result, it became impossible for Chinese Americans to be fully naturalised or even to hold secure employment. Laundromats and railroad labour were about the limit of what they were allowed to do for money. Essentially, the gigs no one else wanted. And even then, laws were enacted in an attempt to drive them out of *those* jobs. Still today, the Chinese laundromat is an iconic feature of America's landscape. But it was racist legislation, not some natural passion for clean clothes, that is to thank for it.

When it wasn't anxiety about economic domination, it was fear of ethnic displacement. The Chinese giant was waiting to rise and enslave the Western world, starting with its women. The Yellow Peril was coming to steal your wives and rape your daughters. Propaganda cartoons in the nineteenth century depicted caricatures of Chinese men with long pigtails, arched, menacing eyebrows, and buck teeth, standing over the body of a helpless White woman, or tangling her up in that famous Chinese silk, squeezed out of his own horrible spider body, to preserve her for later consumption.

Inspired by the hysteria in North America in the early twentieth century, the English author Sax Rohmer invented the character Dr Fu Manchu: a Chinese criminal mastermind with those iconic long moustaches – because there's nothing more suspicious than a Chinese man who has somehow managed to grow decent facial hair. Fu Manchu was a smash hit, featuring in books, radio, TV, comic books, and movies for the best part of a century. In these portrayals, the dastardly Fu Manchu drugs and captures Good White English Women to keep hostage and even wed. In Fu Manchu, Sax Rohmer created a single representation of the Western world's distrust of Chinese men, which included a paranoia that they would stalk innocent women in the street and have their wicked way with them. Which is pretty hypocritical from an author whose own name sounds a lot like 'sex roamer'.*

As the twentieth century progressed, the figure of the sexually aggressive East Asian man fell away, and was replaced by a new stereotype: the *asexual* East Asian man. The sexless East Asian man. This stereotype survives to this day. It is rare to see an East Asian man on-screen, and for as long as I can remember, whenever they do appear, they only ever hold one of two character traits: impossibly wise or embarrassingly stupid. No

* Rohmer himself claims an incredible story about how he came up with the idea for what would become his most popular character. Consulting a Ouija board, he asked it to tell him how he could become rich. 'C-H-I-N-A-M-A-N' it answered. Wow. The spirit world might be powerful, but it is *not* politically correct!

middle ground, and nothing remotely sexy. It's either Mr Miyagi, babbling on about wax, or some incoherent screaming fruit stand merchant with an absurd accent furious at the two maverick cops who have just run over his 'watelmerons', or Ken Jeong's over-the-top, degrading Chinese character, Chow, in *The Hangover* films, whose 'best lines' must have been thrown at Chinese boys in schools in America and the UK countless times since 2009. At best, the East Asian man is good at karate, but he is never the love interest or the hunk. He can kick butt, but he sure can't kiss it.

In this new version of an old prejudice, the East Asian man is a diminutive figure. Not so much to be feared for his conniving ways, but dismissed for his silly-sounding language and short stature. There are a few things I hear regularly from people whenever I am asked for a photograph. The most common is, 'No, sorry. I meant: could you take a picture of *me and my friend*.' The second is, 'Wow! You're taller than I thought!' as they look up at me in amazement. It could be perfectly innocent, of course, this assumption that I would be shorter than I really am. After all, a stand-up comedian is usually the only person on stage, so if they've only seen me on TV there is no one else on-screen to compare my height with. But I've not heard anyone say this about any of my non-Asian comedian friends – that they are surprisingly tall. I don't think it's their fault, and they're probably not even aware of it, but I think people expect me to be shorter than I actually am because the picture of East Asian men they have in their minds is of a short guy. Incredibly, people are even surprised by my height right after watching me in a *live show*. Maybe they thought I was merely performing extremely close to them. Even more extraordinary is when people *I know* who I haven't seen in a while say to me, 'I always forget how tall you are'. *Their* mental image of the small Chinese man is so strong it can actually override their *own experiences* of standing next to me in the past. Not only can these people not imagine a tall Asian man, they can't *remember* one.

Most demeaning of all for East Asian men, of course, is the consensus on our penises. They're small, in case you haven't heard. Tiny like our eyes, short like our bodies, silly like our voices. Those audiences from early on in my career who assumed Phil Wang was a joke stage name, must have considered the 'Wang' (slang for penis, remember) ironic, like 'Little' John or the 'Democratic' Republic of North Korea. Again, this is part of the general characterisation of the East Asian body as diminutive and feminine. The stereotype of the tiny Chinese penis fits into this generalisation with ease. Which I guess would be the advantage of a small penis.

I know you're wondering, so I'm just going to tell you. My penis is fantastic. All right? When erect, it is sturdy, effective, and rather handsome. When flaccid, it packs away neatly into a very manageable nub – about the size of a fat garden slug – exactly flush with my testicles, so that the entire package resembles a single small gourd. I then don't have to think about it and can get on with my day. My penis is an ingenious piece of practical design, perfect for the busy travelling man. Don't believe the bad PR. My penis is like Mary Poppins – extremely good at packing things into apparently small spaces, and practically perfect in every way with or without its hat on.

The small East Asian penis might seem like a harmless bit of fun. But it is not unrelated to the original Yellow Peril, in which Chinese men were sex-crazed rapists of White women. Sexual impotence might seem like the opposite of this old caricature, but it's just the other side of the same coin. The coin that says East Asian men are sexually abnormal, physically peculiar, and in every conceivable scenario, NOT TO BE FUCKED.

In 2018, the movie *Crazy Rich Asians* was released to much critical acclaim and commercial success, despite having not invited me to even audition. Nothing. The first I heard about it was the same as everyone else, despite me being in entertainment, from the region the movie was about, and, frankly, an intoxicating screen presence. But whatever. The film isn't exactly *Casablanca*, and most of the characters make no sense (I'm fine about it, really!), but when it hit cinemas people were wowed by a big-budget mainstream Hollywood movie that had an entirely East Asian cast, including, revolutionarily, an East Asian male love interest, played by Henry Golding*. He has since played the romantic lead to a *White English woman* in the 2019 film *Last Christmas*. Progress indeed. The next step now will be for an East Asian man to be the romantic lead in a *good* film (I cannot express how absolutely fine I am with not being a part of that *stupid* movie!).

Injustice aside, *Crazy Rich Asians* was undoubtedly a positive development for East Asian people in film. It is important for me to clarify that when I say 'film', I mean Western cinema;

* Henry Golding isn't actually Chinese at all as the movie suggests (really, I'm so over it, I really am). His father is White English and his mother is Iban, a native people from Sarawak in, where else, Borneo! Where he was born! Isn't that incredible. I'm not even the most successful *both* English and Bornean man in entertainment! Absolutely brilliant. It is safe to say that despite our rather similar origins, Henry and I have taken very different paths in life. His taking him mainly to the gym, and mine to whichever fried chicken shop is closest.

Hollywood; mainstream, internationally screened fare. East Asian people have of course long been featured in say, South Korean cinema, whose *Parasite* became the first foreign-language film to win the Oscar for Best Picture at the 2020 Academy Awards, but you know what I mean. There are two tiers of popular culture: localised popular culture and global popular culture. And although you could argue that what I'm calling 'global' popular culture is in fact Western (especially *American*) culture, what I mean is the stuff that people all over the world are likely to see. This is the exposure that *Crazy Rich Asians* achieved for East Asian people. This is what people mean by 'representation'. Of course, East Asians have long had representation amongst *themselves*, but that's not what I'm talking about. When Japanese people went to see the movies of Kurosawa, they didn't think, *At last, a Japanese face in Japanese cinema!* What East Asians have yet to enjoy is *global* representation on that international tier of popular culture, held predominantly by White people in, again, predominantly America and the UK.

Internationally recognised East Asian faces are few and far between. And because there are so few of them, each becomes overexposed into an overfamiliar kind of stereotype, with their nuances bleached out. But upon closer inspection, these figures, too, show their true, and deep, importance.

In 2016 I went to the long-running Bruce Lee exhibition in Hong Kong. I'd never actually seen any of his films in their entirety, just the same short clips everyone uses to paste together a collage of what he did and what he was like: fast kicks, 'hooowwaaaaaYA!'-ing about the place, dispatching wave after wave of hapless crooks, all the while apparently allergic to a

T-shirt of any kind. But this exhibition provided a fuller portrait of the man. A mixed-race kid (this is where Bruce Lee's and my physical similarities end) from San Francisco who moved to Hong Kong to make films and almost singlehandedly create an entire movie genre. He got the whole world into martial arts. There are few who can claim to have done as much for the global Chinese image as Bruce Lee. An image of power, strength, agility, and cunning.

And yet, perusing the many photos and costumes and clothes and looping footage at that museum, I was struck by another less-appreciated element of his life and work, more revolutionary for the East Asian male image than any number of flying fists: the man was sexy. Bruce was hot! Not just in the obvious physical sense. He was in good shape, of course. I mean, the guy was more shredded than a birthday card from Jeffrey Epstein. But he was also sexy in the way he held himself; the way he moved; the way he spoke. His smouldering smiles and piercing eyes lifted his Hong Kong accent to a seductive, sultry plane.

'Empty your mind' he says in an iconic recording, 'Be formless; shapeless. Like water. Now, you put water in a cup, it *becomes* the cup. You put water into a bottle, it *becomes* the bottle. You put it in a teapot, it *becomes* the teapot. Now water can flow . . . or it can *crash*. Be water, my friend.' His charm electrifies.

The man dressed well, too. Looking as good in aviators and leather jackets as he did with nothing but a long pair of trousers pulled up to his nipples. He is most striking in his outfit for the film he never finished, *Game of Death*, in which he is resplendent in a yellow jumpsuit with elegant black stripes down each side that flow from his neck down to his shoes: two yellow Onitsuka Tigers, with black stripes.

In pictures and interviews he never appeared to shy away from anything. He never slouched or feigned undue humility. He approached everything with his head high and his chest open. Confidence is the essence of attractiveness. And our Bruce had it in teapots.

It was a eureka moment for me. Chinese men were sexy. East Asian men were sexy. And here was proof. After that day, after Bruce Lee, I finally understood the value of that thing we call representation. Of seeing someone who looks like you in an otherwise White Western global culture that doesn't look very much like you at all. It isn't superficial. It isn't box-ticking. It isn't about showing off what 'your people' can do. Actual meaningful representation is proof *to yourself* that you can be whatever you want to be; that the scope of your life is not limited by your race. That you are like water, and with enough skill, with enough determination, you can fill anything.

My first televised stand-up performance that could be considered anything like a breakthrough for my career was my debut appearance on the BBC's stand-up comedy series and British TV institution, *Live at the Apollo*. I am not unambiguously proud of many things I have done, but I am unambiguously proud of that performance. I stood in front of 3,000 people in that room, and many more watching at home. But I felt confident nonetheless. In some part thanks to the new yellow-and-black shoes I was wearing. The same shoes Bruce Lee wore on the set of his final film. And you know what? I looked good.*

★ ★ ★

* I also wore the rest of the *Game of Death* outfit on another British TV comedy institution, *Taskmaster*. A tight-fitting onesie that was, altogether, less flattering.

The Chinese Exclusion Act was only repealed by the American government in 1943, after the attack on Pearl Harbour. The US had found themselves in a brutal war with the Japanese and needed allies in Asia. They had suspected the wrong peril in the East after all, and could now use a little Yellow Help, to be honest.*

In many ways, things are, of course, much better today. Chinese Americans are now free to work in any laundromat they like. And not just that, they can do other jobs too, and even become American citizens if they want. In the UK, East Asian men are making steady progress up the social ladder, thanks to an increasingly worldly population, and a slow upturn in the number of East Asian male faces in film and television. Hey – you're welcome, brothers.

That said, although its shape has shifted, the idea of the Yellow Peril still survives to this day. It is dressed in new clothes now. 'Chinese Virus' is its hip new name.

The Love Below the Wind

My parents were pioneers.

When Mother arrived in Sabah in the north of Borneo for the first time, she was a young woman in a young country on

* At the Museum of Chinese in America (MOCA) in New York, there is an extraordinary pamphlet from the Second World War on how to differentiate between Japanese people (the bad guys) and Chinese people (alright now actually!). Using the kind of skull-measuring phrenology that was considered racist by *the Victorians*, it points to small differences in the angles of each race's slanted eyes, and the relative heights of their cheekbones, as a way to correctly identify if you are speaking to friend or foe. It is, of course, nonsense. This is how you actually tell the difference between Chinese and Japanese people: Chinese people hold their chopsticks between their thumb and their index finger, whereas Japanese people buy used underwear in vending machines and watch tentacle porn.

an ancient island. Sabah is still known as the 'Land Below the Wind', an old seafarer's name for the part of the world under the Pacific Ocean's typhoon belt, dangerous because of its regular earthquakes and volcanic eruptions. Sabah just escapes it. Hence a land famed for its tranquillity. A perennial port in a perennial storm.

However, safe as she was from the elements, Mother was still a young woman alone in a strange new place, and men are men no matter what side of the wind they're on. So when a local friend told her about a new self-defence class he was going to, she decided to join. When she turned up at the dojo (where I would be handed my hard(ly)-earned black belt years later), who should be her instructor but Benny 'Phil Wang's Dad' Wang. If It feels like I am giving *Shorinji Kempo* – my family's martial art – a lot of attention in this book, it is only because I owe it my life. Well, martial arts and the British Empire. Violence, essentially. But that is how my parents met. My father was my mother's kung fu teacher. I come from a long and proud line of Chinese stereotypes. My father is a kung fu teacher, *his* father was a communist, and *his* father was a dragon made entirely of noodles.

A martial arts class might seem like a strange place for a romance to blossom – hard to know if someone's touching your arm to flirt or because they're about to demonstrate a devastating wrist lock. But it happened. Father used his position as instructor to his advantage, singling Mum out for all his demonstrations, during which he would go just a bit too hard on her, and hurt her just a little bit, so that he would then have an excuse to visit her on the weekend with Chinese medicines, to help heal the injuries that *he'd* inflicted. And sure, nowadays, in our oversensitive culture of victimhood, that might be called 'abuse'. But in the eighties, that was just sweet, sweet chirpsing, my jive cats (I don't know any eighties slang).

Eventually, the sexual tension at kung fu class got too awkward, and was making everyone else uncomfortable, so Mum stopped going to lessons. She started dating Dad officially, without the complications that close-quarters combat can bring to the courting process.

Their first official date was a trip to the movies – or 'talking pictures' as they would have been called back then. Dad insisted that Mum had to check out this crazy new Hong Kong action star – Jackie Chan. For the uninitiated, Jackie Chan is essentially Bruce Lee with mumps. He's a goofy, family-friendly kung fu clown, but a world-class fighter nonetheless, and an ingenious choreographer. His fighting sequences are somehow balletic, brutal, and funny all at once. The true triple threat, if you ask me. His breakout hit *Drunken Master* had just been released, which provided Dad with the perfect excuse to invite his favourite new student to Kota Kinabalu's premium (and only) cinema: it will be educational! And the drunken element of the movie was sure to make her feel like she was back home in the UK.*

* For most of my childhood, Kota Kinabalu had just one cinema. A square, dusty, brutalist old thing with three screens and an open-air concourse, where you could buy snacks and brave the stink of the public toilet if you needed to go badly enough. Its most extraordinary feature, however, was its billboard outside – a huge, raised canvas upon which would be the poster for the latest big release, painted entirely by hand. I never saw any painters up there, but whenever a new movie was in town, up went an enormous hand-painted version of its poster, seemingly overnight. Looking back, I only now appreciate the scale of this task. The results were impressive, but always ever so slightly and eerily off, giving Hollywood stars the appearance of runaway criminals whose artist's impressions had been put up in town in the hopes that someone had seen Julia Roberts recently, as she is wanted dead or alive for having a huge mouth.

The date went well, of course. Otherwise this book wouldn't be in your hands. They spent the next seven years dating (or 'going steady' as it was called back then) going back and forth between Borneo and the UK.

As couples went, they were unique. A White archaeologist from the Midlands and an Asian martial artist from the islands. Like a gender-swapped *Indiana Jones* reboot. Though probably less controversial. Happily, they found little resistance or disapproval in Sabah, where people were generally chilled out about things, what with being below the wind and all. People in the UK (the 'Land Directly Underneath the Rain') were also accepting, and my grandparents greeted Dad with open arms.

The only rudeness Mum recalls them ever being subjected to was in France (*naturellement*), where she felt the Parisians poured scorn on her *Chinois* boyfriend in the same way they poured their wine – scornfully. When, as children, my sisters and I went to visit our French relatives, one particularly odious uncle looked at us and commented that the Chinese 'bred like rabbits', despite having many more unaccounted-for children himself all over the world from his army years whom he'd never met. Better to breed like rabbits than salmon.

Back in Malaysia, we bunny-kids thankfully didn't always feel like *complete* freaks of nature. There were a couple of other Eurasian families in Kota Kinabalu during my childhood to make us feel a little less peculiar. It was a small city, so odds were that if another intercontinental family moved in, we'd know about it. We took some small comfort in seeing humans like us, who had some empathy for our experience. Those children also didn't fully fit into Malaysian society. Too Malaysian to be an expat, too White to be truly Malaysian.

This is the fundamental and inescapable cruelty of being mixed: you will never fully fit in anywhere. Nowhere are you a member of the majority. Nowhere are the particulars of your life commonly understood. Being mixed-race is a great way to feel foreign, no matter where you are. There isn't even a side of your own family in which you don't stick out. And this has a knock-on effect on every kind of relationship you try to build for the rest of your life. At the base of most successful relationships is a feeling of recognition; of similarity; of shared experience. 'We just have so much in common!' is the most promising indication of a new friend. This refers in part to shared interests and outlooks on life and moral principles, all of which can transcend race, of course. But a lot of what people usually have in common is also cultural; experiential. And the experience and cultural identity of being mixed-race is a unique one; a messy one, which few people are likely – through no fault of their own – to share.

Dating as a Eurasian is not just dating as a minority – as, say an ethnically Chinese Brit would experience – but as a minority *within* a minority. Not only am I ethnically foreign in the UK (because of my Asian-ness), I am ethnically *native* (because of my Whiteness) within that foreign minority. So as well as being a minority among White Brits for being half Asian, I am a minority among Asian Brits for being half White.

All of this is to say that the quintessential experience of being Eurasian; of being mixed, read on the face of every Eurasian person I've ever seen, whether in Malaysia or in Britain, is loneliness. Every Eurasian face *sings* with loneliness. The next time you are in a dim sum restaurant – the unofficial meeting place for Eurasian families in every city in the world – have a look at those latte-coloured faces. No matter their height, no matter their accent, no matter the quality of their clothes, no matter the straightness of their backs, no matter their accomplishments or their talents, and no matter their beauty (and we are, as a whole, quite beautiful), the corners of their mouths and the downwards pitch of their gazes betray a lifetime of not knowing where the hell they're from, or where the hell they're supposed to be, or why no one else looks like them outside of this dim sum restaurant.

By the way, I recommend the shrimp and chive dumplings.

But have faith, my half-brothers and sisters. The world is transforming. Ours is a global age and our numbers are multiplying with rapid speed. It turns out our parents do breed like rabbits and it's working.

Mixed-race people are the fastest-growing ethnic group in the UK, and the second fastest-growing in the US. It is an observable trend even within my own Malaysian family. My sisters and I were the only mixed White-and-Asian kids in our generation, but two of our cousins have married and had children with Europeans – a German and a Bosnian, which really adds linguistic texture to our Christmases. That's now three mixed-race households in our extended family, up from just one a generation ago. And once *I* have children, seeing as how, because of me, my kids will be mixed-race no matter who their mother is, it'll be four in total. Then all our kids will be mixed-race, and they will eventually have kids of their *own*. Now, I don't know if you understand exponential growth, but essentially: mixed-race people = x^{rabbits} =

90 per cent of the world population within the next two Bond recastings.

I realise now that my kind is not freakish, and love is not the preserve of those with easily understood backgrounds, or cousins that look like them. I realise now that I am merely the latest in a line of lovers-across-borders. Not just my parents, but their parents too. English and French on my mother's side, bridging the linguistic divide of two historic rivals. Chinese and Kadazan-Dusun on my dad's side, whose children were 'not quite noon' to others, but bang on time to them. What they set in motion cannot be stopped, and I can but follow in their sexy footsteps.

Yes, He's Chinese

I have been lucky in love, really. Perhaps my days on dating apps would have borne more fruit had I been a full White English boy. With my Superdry T-shirts and my incurable conversational misuse of the word 'massively'. Perhaps dating would have been more straightforward. Maybe the familiarity and safeness and assumed masculinity of a young White man would have attracted more female attention over the years than my own vague and alien quasi-Asian-ness. But then again, maybe not. The upside of my looking different is that those who have braved the racial divide to give me a shot have all been top gals with open minds and a disinterest in stereotypes. Being in an ethnic minority can be a pretty useful sieve in that way. I filter out the racists before I've even met them. Which must have saved me from countless nasty surprises over the years.

Sometimes, being Chinese-y can even be a boon. There are some racial stereotypes that can work in your favour. Especially when meeting a new girlfriend's parents. It is much easier to earn their trust. East Asian boys are good boys, and unlikely to take their daughter on meth-fuelled motorbike rides or entice her into the occult. Plus, free technical support with their computers every time she brings him round.

In my doubtful moods, I wonder where I would be without stand-up. Without that clear proof to others, men and women alike, of my confidence; my way with words; my good humour. Without that, would I just be assumed to be 'another' shy and dorky Chinese guy?

I suppose it made no difference to those girls at Roehampton. Some people are beyond help. But if they saw me now, would they be forced to retract their words? Accept their assumptions were wrong? Looking in the mirror as I write this, it's anyone's guess. Maybe first thing in the morning. After my shower but before breakfast.

But if you ask me, and put aside the bias, I look pretty good at thirty-one. A lot better than I used to, that's for sure. I have a straighter back and better-chosen clothes. My large spectacle frames accept and accentuate my face where my old narrow glasses were an act of retreat. My good angles outnumber my bad, and I smile wide and stand tall in photos.

Confidence is the essence of attractiveness. And I have confidence now. From comedy, from heartbreak, from success and failure, from the things I've made, from time on the road, from the life-affirming electric connection of jokes shared with strangers. I have the Bruce Lee confidence of a man who knows his strength, and takes his virility as a given. I have the confidence of a man who has heard it all about East Asian men, but who knows from the inside of his bones to the outward gleam of his terracotta skin, that he is without doubt, unequivocally and absolutely, *fit*.

HISTORY

Paper Rain

The end of the Second World War spelt the end for the Empire of an exhausted Britain. Lady Britannia was showing her age and was – to put it lightly – 'completely fucked' having fought two Earth-changing, record-breaking, deadliest-in-history mass conflicts in a row. And, after years of casting Hitler and the Nazis quite emphatically as The Bad Guys (I would totally agree, by the way!), holding dominion over the non-White peoples of the world had become a good deal less palatable to everyone all of a sudden. Britain was broke, and the independence movements in its colonies had gathered an unstoppable momentum, encouraged in no small part by their own indispensable contributions to the defeat of the Axis powers. India – the MVP of the Empire – gained freedom in 1947, and by 1957 the dominoes of liberty had tumbled all the way to the Federation of Malaya, just across the water from Borneo. The world was changing, the age of empires was coming to a close. And on 31 August 1963, British North Borneo was British no more . . . neo.

My father remembers paper rain; planes buzzing low and loud overhead, leaflets floating softly down onto the streets of his hometown of Tuaran, just up the coast from Kota Kinabalu. *'Independence!'* each sheet cried in English, Chinese, Kadazan, and Malay. Excitement thickened the air, and although no one knew what independence would mean, exactly, the people partied. All they knew was that change was coming. And what is a party if not a mark of change? A birthday; a wedding; a new patio; a new era. Dad was fourteen years old, which is an impossible age for me to imagine him being. There are no photos of him from his youth, so I'm forced to picture him as he looks now but just smaller, same button-up shirt with a pen in the pocket, same khaki shorts, same open-toed sandals, same mobile phone holder on his belt. He's never smoked, but he does love ice cream. So instead of a cigarette, I have to imagine him rebelliously eating a cone of ice cream, leaning against a wall, bopping his head, his free hand holding a gramophone on his shoulder.

Celebrations were soon underway. The Chinese marked the occasion the only way they know how to celebrate anything – fuckloads of lanterns. The Chinese love a lantern, which is essentially a hollow paper sculpture with a candle lit inside it to make the whole thing glow.* Every Chinese festival calls for lanterns: Chinese New Year; Mooncake Festival. And Lantern Festival? Well that's just double lanterns, my friend. A jubilant night procession was held in

* In recent years flying lanterns have become very popular at weddings, including Western weddings. The bride and groom light candles in lanterns that are then meant to rise up like hot air balloons and sail away into the sky – a symbol of the newlyweds' journey of love. But they almost always crash to the ground instantly. If they do take off, they usually float away briefly into the horizon with the best of intentions, before catching fire like a tiny Hindenburg and *then* crashing to the ground. They are, therefore, an excellent representation of most marriages.

the town to celebrate Borneo's big news, and Dad made a crescent-moon lantern, with a face, a nose, and a mouth cut into the inner curve. Which is adorable for someone who I can only picture – regardless of age – as a fully-grown father of three.

Malaysia was officially formed on 16 September 1963. The peninsula of Malaya, the island of Singapore, and the Borneo territories of Sarawak and North Borneo came together, founding a new independent nation.* My father was born in 1949, which makes him older than the country he lives in. But in the ancient fella's defence, Malaysia is pretty young for a country. To emphasise the point, here are some other things that are older than Malaysia: power steering, Tom Hanks, fibre-optic technology, Oprah Winfrey, *West Side Story* (film *and* stage production), the original *Lady and the Tramp*, bubble wrap, breast implants (though hopefully not one specific pair), Slurpees, Tipp-Ex, the phrase 'Hey, cool it!', Fender guitars, Velcro, Super Glue, Mr Potato Head, Sony, 3-D movies, and – get this – Tom Cruise. *Tom Cruise* has existed for longer than *Malaysia* has. Isn't that something? However, I have found out in my research that Malaysia is exactly as old as the lava lamp. Figure out the significance of that on your own. I sure know I'm stumped.

* The Federation of Malaya had already had its sovereignty for six years by this point. It is now known as Peninsular Malaysia or West Malaysia. West Malaysians (particularly those in the capital Kuala Lumpur) enjoy a light snobbery over the people of East Malaysia (the Borneo Malaysians), accusing us of living in trees and lacking even the most basic modern technologies. But none of these mean words will stop the Peninsula looking like a big poo hanging out of Asia's ass.

British North Borneo now had a new, less British name, too: Sabah. Brand new name, same great taste™. A ceremony to mark its newfound independence was held in Tuaran's town field or *padang* – the Southeast Asian equivalent of a town square. Everyone was there. Chinese, Malay, Kadazan, and all the other native peoples of Sabah, young and old, adults and children – dragged kicking and screaming away from the lava lamps they'd just got. Politicians from the newly formed political parties gave speeches on the magnificence of this historic moment and the bright future that lay ahead for the people of Sabah. Faith leaders took turns blessing their infant country – a Muslim imam, a priest from my father's own school who led all the Christians in an 'Our Father'. A scattergun approach to blessing a country: get *all* the religions to bless us, *one* of them has got to be right. All bowed their heads in prayer. All asked their gods to smile on this new nation called Malaysia.

Tom Cruise had just turned one.

Oh, Willy be Goode

The last colonial governor of North Borneo was an Englishman from Twickenham named Sir William Allmond Codrington Goode, which sounds made-up. I guess all names are made-up, strictly speaking. But regardless, that's what the man was called. Sir William Allmond Codrington Goode. Sir William Allmond Codrington Goode is such a colonial-sounding name I suppose he had no choice but to pursue a career in the Empire. It is also such a *long* name that there's an 'almond' and a 'cod' in the middle of it to provide the reader with a snack before attempting the second half.

A year or two into sovereignty and Malaysia was beginning

to stand on its own four feet – Malaya, Sarawak, Sabah, and Singapore. It was time for William Allmond Codri— look, let's just call him William or the word count of this book is going to end up like *War and Peace*. It was time for William to head home.

Kota Kinabalu was then called Jesselton. On the day of William's departure the locals crowded around Jesselton Port, waiting for a final look at the governor. My father took a bus down from Tuaran specially for the occasion. The bus was made of wood, which is mad. If you ask me, there are enough things to worry about on public transport (crazy people; rowdy lads; an Agatha Christie-style murder mystery) without the added threat of splinters. A wooden motor vehicle is quite the thing. Taking your wooden car to the garage for repairs must have been weird. Whimsical, even. The mechanic would roll out from underneath and shake his head: 'Well, that's your problem right there,' he'd say, wiping tree sap from his hands, 'Termites. Yyyyyyyyup. We're gonna have to order in a new trunk. Oh and a barn owl's taken up residence in your gearbox.'

By the time Dad got to town – the termites nearly full; the bus by this point a single wooden plank balanced on a wheel – William Goode was boarding his ship back to Britain. The crowds waved him off, cheering him goodbye. Not a spiteful hiss at a defeated tyrant, but a bittersweet farewell to an old friend. He had been respected and liked, and although Sabah was eager to take hold of its own reins, many were sad to see him go. Malaya and Borneo never quite had the tumultuous imperial history of rebellion, suppression and violence that, say, India or the Caribbean had. Life under British rule was relatively peaceful and stable (before the war at least). So, Malaysians were (and are) mostly ambivalent towards the

Empire. My own father still misses the British-run buses. Which were always on time, even if they were made of wood. A free NHS-style healthcare system had also been put in place by the British, as well as a civil service and a legal system. So you could get a splinter on the bus ride into town, get it treated at the hospital, *and* sue the bus company, all in the same day.

Also saying farewell to Sabah was Singapore, who, not being able to see eye to eye with the Malaysian leadership, was forced to abandon the project of Malaysia in 1965 – just two years after they'd started. Singapore was now an independent island state, and being too big to get on a ship and sail away like William, it simply had to stay put and figure things out on its own. Without even a sufficient source of drinking water, its future looked rocky to say the least. In an extraordinary televised interview from the time, Lee Kuan Yew – Singapore's steely and eloquent first prime minster – breaks down in tears as he mourns his vision for Singapore as a part of a united Malaysia, 'A people bound by geography, economics, and ties of kinship.' His eyes shine wet with loss, his voice breaking. 'Will you mind if we stop for a while?' he asks the assembled press.

Tom Cruise was three years old.*

* You're probably aware that Singapore did alright in the end. Not content with simply solving its water problem, it committed itself to becoming the centre of world trade in the region. Today, Singapore is a bustling metropolis, a shining beacon of culture, business, and art, and envy of the capitalist world. In the sitcom *Friends*, young Chandler makes fun of young Monica for being fat and unattractive, rebuffing her romantic advances one Thanksgiving. In revenge, Monica undergoes a health kick and makeover, returning slim and beautiful the next year and shocking a now regretful Chandler; their positions in the sexual pecking order now decisively flipped. Malaysia is Chandler.

God's Soft Power

I don't think we appreciate just how much of the world sounds British. Because of the Empire, the world is covered in English (and Scottish – don't let them forget) names. There's a Birmingham in Alabama. There's an Aberdeen in Hong Kong. My father's name is Benny. My Malaysian uncles are David, Ricky, Gilbert, Alex, and Bobby. My aunt? Lily. They still have their original Chinese names, of course, but they don't use them.

That is what is known as 'soft power' – overseas influence gained or held without physical force, usually through diplomacy, trade, and exports of culture: music, literature, and (over the last century) film and television. Although the British Empire is gone, and America is now the leading Western influencer, the UK still has soft power in boatloads.* Not all of it intentional, but potent all the same. James Bond, for example, has been cited as the reason many defectors from hostile nations contact MI6 over the intelligence services of other countries like France or the United States. They want to go to the one with the Aston Martins, the laser pens, and the laissez-faire attitude towards workplace sexual harassment. Mr Bean portrays the British as bumbling, foolish, and ultimately harmless. All the better the surprise when an SAS unit parachutes into your compound and snaps your guard dogs in half. And *Mind Your Language* reinforced the idea that English was a language one was *meant* to learn, regardless of what you grew up speaking. It might be a silly old sitcom, but multiply it by the number of Asians who

* It used to have *hard* power in boatloads too, also known as battleships.

have absorbed it, and it's a significant piece of influence. Pixi may not think herself the equivalent of a nuclear submarine, but I sure do.

Before the days of film and TV, however, most of the winning of hearts and minds was done by the church. Albeit under pain of eternal damnation for any who weren't interested. Where British soldiers and merchants went, so did missionaries who had a book to flog and a Hell they just could not *wait* to tell you about. Borneo was no exception. A missionary named Father Groot (Groot!) arrived in my dad's hometown of Tuaran in 1917 and eventually built a Catholic school there. St John's School was the name, converting was the game. Dad and his army of siblings decided to attend. 'It was the trend!' he explains to me now. It's funny to hear Catholicism described as a *trend*, as if it were The Twist or fidget spinners. But I suppose it was. A hot new deity from the West that's got *everyone* confessin'! And with the offer of eternal salvation thrown in to sweeten the deal, who can blame them for taking up such a potentially high-reward craze? Wild swimming can't offer that.

Lessons at St John's were taught in English by English-speaking locals. And English was insisted upon even when class wasn't in session, with five-cent fines for anyone caught speaking their mother tongue. In the beginning was the Word, and the Word was with God, and that Word was in *English*.

There were many new and exciting sins now on offer to Dad, but the confession he dreaded the most was the one to his father. Dad and his siblings had converted without telling their old man and sooner or later he'd find out. Along with his brother, Alex, Dad mustered up the courage one day and went home to tell my grandfather.

Gong Gong wasn't especially happy. But most of all, he was just confused. He didn't understand the appeal. 'But we don't have any religion,' he said to his sons, 'We worship only our ancestors.' Fundamentally, though, he had no objection. Christianity was not especially at odds with any of his own beliefs. Jesus had nothing against barbers, and any belief system in which 'God' and 'Father' were interchangeable was fine by him. All that mattered was that his children, and his children's children, honoured their ancestors. And as we still light incense and burn paper money at his and Po Po's graves, next to that unfortunate fire station to this day, I suppose he was right not to worry.

Christianity continued its sweep across the island, overthrowing the native animism. Fortunately, much of the indigenous culture survived, able to live side by side with the New Testament. However, if there is a tragedy in the Christianisation of North Borneo, it's the loss of its names. I grew up among descendants of the people of the jungle called James, Edbert, and Hannah. There was even a Bathsheba at school. Which is as biblical as it gets, and admittedly, badass. But it is a shame to lose names like Anavau, Mojigoh, Jupinon, and Ongkili. In the course of writing this book, I found out that my own grandmother Po Po's name was Sanoh, which is lovely. I'd never asked before.

Nevertheless, Dad was in for a penny, in for a pound. And having come to the Lord and Saviour later than most, he had the unique privilege of getting to choose his own name. Which is far better than having it fished out of a hat at random, if you ask me. Dad now had before him the full collection of Catholic names to pick from, and to be fair to him, his first choice was anything but dull.

'Bonaventure,' he tells me on the phone, like that's in any way a sane choice for someone living after 1683. '*Bonaventure*?' I reply. He can't remember where he first heard it or where he got the idea, he just knew that he liked it. He wanted to be called *Bonaventure Wang*. Which, actually, now that I see it written down, rocks. The appeal fades a little, though, when he tells me that he liked the name mainly for its shortened form – Bona. Malaysians are addicted to abbreviations, and my father is no different. He wanted – and I'm as surprised as you are here – to be called *Bona*. *Bona* Wang. *Bona* . . . *Wang* . . . Are you seeing what I'm seeing? Bona Wang. That's just 'boner' in a Boston accent. His surname was already *Wang* and he wanted his first name to be BONER? Boner Wang. I can't believe how close I came to a lifetime of saying 'my dad, Bona', which sounds far too much like 'my dad's boner'. No thanks! My school years were difficult enough, thank you!

One of Dad's schoolteachers suggested that he go for something a little more ordinary; a little less . . . well, *Bona*. 'How about Benedict? Benjamin?' 'All right,' Dad agreed, '*Benny* it is'. And I would say 'thank Christ for that' if He and His Big Book of Crazy Names weren't the reason the whole mess started in the first place.

Now, usually Benny is the short, unofficial nickname for someone whose birth certificate says Benedict or Benjamin or – hell – maybe even Benaventure. Not in my father's case. My father who loves an abbreviation so much he was almost called Bona. Benny was what he put down on the form, so Benny is his full, official name in the eyes of local and international law. The same goes for his brothers and sister. Ricky, NOT Richard. Full name: RICKY WANG. Bobby, NOT Robert. Full name: BOBBY WANG. Same with Alex, and Lily. Now that I think about it, only my uncles David and Gilbert carry the complete original form of their names. Though I have to wonder if they were in fact originally short for Davidandgoliath and Gilbertandsullivan.

One year in England, Dad joined Mother and her folks for their first Christmas there together. My French grandmother thought it very sweet and open-minded of him to join them for midnight mass and go along with all the hymns and prayers. When Mum told her that not only was he Catholic, but the rest of his family were too, she was shocked, slightly confused, and then delighted. She had not thought that someone from deepest Borneo could have heard the Good News! She was thrilled that he had. All those pennies in the mission box had been used after all.

The Club

All over the world, in all of its former possessions, British power stayed long after its rifles left. My English grandfather, Gordon, found work for a few years as the manager of a tea estate in India in the fifties, after the country had become independent from British control. My mum was born in Britain during this time, straight after which she flew with her mother to Assam in the east of India to join the rest of the family (which must have been where she got the inspiration for my own jet-setting first month of life).

Mother still speaks of India with wonder. Even now those early childhood years of hers are sharp and bright and full of colour. She remembers leopards' eyes glowing in the dark; the vistas of Assam from the backs of elephants; the suspicious shuffling of the jungle at night. She can still feel the cool months on her skin, the dry heat that followed, rising with each day, and the monsoon rains that split the sky open and came down in sheets to quench the gasping soil. 'It's the monsoon!' someone would shout, and she'd whip off her clothes and join the others outside in the downpour.*

She lived with her parents, brother, and sister in a bungalow by the Brahmaputra river. A humble house by most modern standards, but pretty grand for the time. On the dime of Williamson Magor & Co., the tea company that my grandfather worked for, this small house enjoyed an army of Indian staff. Help was cheap. They had a cook, a guy who just swept the floors, and a groundskeeper who'd bonk snakes on the head in the garden and flick their limp bodies over the hedge. Out of sssssight, out of mind.

Although India was no longer part of the Empire, centuries of British rule still hung in the air. Williamson Magor & Co. itself was originally established to satisfy the thirst of the colonies with Assamese tea, and they still sent out British managers like my grandfather to oversee the local pickers. Mum remembers watching him testing the quality of a harvest, downing

* There is nothing quite like the smell that comes off hot earth in the rain. After the food, it is what I miss about Southeast Asia the most. Cold rain on concrete releases no aroma. English rain has its comforts too, of course. But only if you happen to be at home at the time. It feels great to shut that shit out, knowing what you're safe from. Scottish rain has its own misty romance, but is so persistent it usually outstays its welcome. The Edinburgh Fringe Festival, where I and many other comedians cut our teeth, is synonymous with a month of wet cobblestones and rivers of rainwater that appear out of nowhere and flow down the city's many inclines. Though they might simply be the tears of the countless university improv groups who've performed their show to an audience of three every day for two weeks straight.

cup after cup set out in a line in front of him like liquid soldiers gathered for inspection. Grandad must have looked like a tea-obsessed madman chugging all those cuppas in a row. Or a normal English person.

He had good relationships with those under his watch. He respected them and their knowledge, learnt their languages as best he could, and is laughing and smiling with them in many of the photographs Mother has shown me. But still there hung between him and the Indian workers under his supervision an invisible boundary, an impassable membrane that neither had done anything to create, and neither could do anything to take down. He and they were separated by a centuries-old chasm that no amount of smiles and handshakes and expressions of gratitude could ever fully bridge.

There was a country club nearby – remembered by Mother simply as 'The Club' – that my grandfather and grandmother would frequent to take in the evening air or sip away a lazy Sunday with gin and tonics. My mum and her siblings would occasionally join them – most memorably, once on Christmas Day, when Santa Claus arrived in a helicopter like a crazed American GI.* Similar members' clubs were built all across the Empire, and many survive to this day. I have visited a couple myself. In Singapore; in Hong Kong. They are beautiful places. But their impeccable colonial-era decor and luscious bars conceal an unpleasant truth about their original purpose. The tea estates of Assam had their own such place. Indians were not allowed to join The Club. But they were allowed to serve.

* 'I love the smell of cinnamon in the morning.'

The VSO

The next time Mother was in Asia she was in her twenties, fresh out of university, and a budding anthropologist. With the heat of India still coursing through her veins, she set her gaze East, and signed up with the Voluntary Service Overseas (VSO).*

The VSO started in 1958, when the Bishop of Portsmouth put out a call asking for people to teach English in – where else – *Borneo*. Thanks, Bishop of Portsmouth! Wouldn't be here without you. It still exists today, organising volunteer programmes to aid in the development of some of the world's poorest regions. At the time of writing they are adapting their work to address the COVID-19 pandemic across the developing world. But in 1978, COVID-19 was a mere twinkle in a bat's eye. Mother had heard through a network of equally itchy-footed friends that a museum in Sabah had a post to fill and were looking for a VSO volunteer. She requested the post, and the museum took her, thrilled to make the most of her great expertise and her low, low volunteer's salary.

The humid air hit her first. It engulfs you like a crashing wave that never recedes. Malaysian air is heavy, hot, thick, and

* It's a strange order to put the words in, if you ask me. Surely it should be: The Voluntary Overseas Service. Which makes for the much cooler 'VOS', which you can say as 'Voss' instead of the laborious and time-consuming 'Vee Ess Oh'. 'The Voluntary Service Overseas' also makes the 'Overseas' part sound like a sinister surprise reveal. Like they're exiling someone who isn't expecting it. 'Congratulations. You are now part of the Voluntary Service . . .'
'OK, cool.'
'OVERSEAS!'
'What?! Noooo!'
'Take her away boys!'

moist. As if God is breathing 'huhhhhhhhh' directly into your face non-stop, like an annoying kid. You are ever so slightly wet the entire time you are there. Which sounds sexy, though it's anything but. Especially if your genes are not acclimatised to that kind of weather. In fact, if you have a White partner, and you want to be absolutely sure that you love them for who they are and not how they look, take them on a trip to Malaysia. Watch their skin bloat with moisture and redden with heat. Watch small hairs on their face that you were previously unaware of emerge from their hiding places and twinkle with sweat. Watch the wet patches expand under their armpits like pools of blood at a murder scene. Watch their hair frizz and explode from the humidity. Watch them pant and fan themselves and throw your hand away in instant fury whenever you try to touch them because *it . . . is too . . . HOT*. If you still want to have sex with them after all that, congratulations. You're in love.

Mother got straight to work in her new post at this mysterious museum in Sabah, which it turned out was called . . . The Sabah Museum. Why not? There weren't any others. What followed was a rollicking tropical adventure: dark caves, untouched islands; sea turtles and mangrove snakes; remote tribes and their ancient customs; villagers with their own unique rites and rituals who alerted each other to Mum and her team's arrival by blowing on actual conch shells like in a movie. A fantasy land indeed.

There is a black-and-white photo of Mother from then. She is stood on the lip of a cave facing inwards, rainforest erupting in its verdant endlessness behind her. She has her hands on her khaki hips and is looking down at the ground as if scanning for a spot to dig. I don't think she knows the photo is being taken but she has wisely hidden her certain-to-be-frizzed-to-hell hair under a hat anyway. She looks ready to take on the world. Young and powerful. It is hard to imagine this is the same woman who gets terrified every time I drive a car.

I suppose the VSO embodied the softest of Britain's soft power. What's softer than helping people with their museums? But still, Mum's arrival in Sabah was a late consequence of the Empire's long legacy, through a volunteer service initially founded to spread the English language. But also, in the end, a fledgling state in Borneo got a good anthropologist for a great price. And, very importantly for me, my parents met. It's always interesting to trace back through the twists and turns of history that led to your birth. History that may have been less kind to others. May even have killed others. Should you be grateful for them? For example, I owe my life to (among other things) the Sabah Museum, the Voluntary Service Overseas, the Bishop of Portsmouth, and the British Empire.

Should You Be Ashamed

Growing up with a White English mother, attending English-speaking schools, and watching *Mr Bean* on local TV stations gave me the suspicion not that Britain *used* to dominate the world, but that it still did, albeit with its head occasionally in a turkey.

As I learnt about Britain and that I was part British, I became fascinated with the idea. As a child I could not get my dormant Britishness out of my mind – constantly reminded of it by Britain's subtle presence in everything. Not just by the television I watched and the language I spoke and the names my cousins had, but also by how different I felt from everyone because of my relative 'Britishness' in an otherwise very un-British setting.

As children, we desperately want to fit in, but we also desperately want to feel special. And I have to say, being different in this way – being British – made me feel special. It was either feeling special or feeling like a freak. So I leaned into the more favourable interpretation. I'd be lying if I said there weren't times when I really kind of liked it. I liked that it made me unique amongst my classmates and the people in town and even my own extended family. Added to this was the sense of a residual affection for England in Sabah. Restaurants served fish and chips, the local intelligentsia took pride in their good English grammar, and England was the favoured nation during every World Cup – introducing Malaysians to another proud British pastime: disappointment.

As I got a bit older, I began to play up my Britishness. Particularly from the age of ten onwards when you start to build your identity. I held myself in what I now realise to have been a particularly British way: a sort of apologetic arrogance, a bumbling and shy sense of absolute superiority. I would say things like 'Henceforth!' completely devoid of any context, not really knowing what it meant. Just that it sounded very English. I'd start quoting Shakespeare in conversation to the girls at school, 'But soft! What light from yonder window breaks?' before realising I had no idea how the rest went, 'So . . . you know . . . somebody fix that window.'

I guess I've always enjoyed the spotlight: to stand out in a room; in a school photo; in a group of friends. Or maybe I was simply born an ethnic outsider and developed a taste for attention out of necessity, because I was going to get it whether I wanted to or not.

My sisters and I weren't completely alone in our experience. There were a few others like us; other chestnut-haired, confused-looking children of eccentric expats. But none ended up my friends. I liked my unique mixed-race identity, and I wasn't going to let some other vague-faced upstart take any of my limelight.

I was proud to be British. I was proud to have partly come from a powerful, history-writing nation. So I was surprised when I came to the UK to find that people were actually a bit embarrassed about it all, and would rather not talk about the Empire, if you don't mind. Unless, of course, there's a good fight to be had about it. Then everyone has something to say. Conversations about the Empire in Britain can only ever be had as combat; only in the form of some controversy, big or small, about whether or not to sing 'Rule, Britannia!' at the Proms, or the appropriateness of a supermarket ready meal called 'Empire Pie', or the toppling of statues.

There is very little balanced debate about empire because there is very little balanced opinion on it. What evokes grandeur and benevolence for some, evokes murder and pillage for others. Britain is often guilty of whitewashing its imperial legacy, but there is a strong anti-empire culture here, too. And it is this attitude that I am most personally familiar with. Even when I had just moved from Malaysia at sixteen, I sensed a quiet shame about the Empire. I didn't understand it. Why wouldn't you be proud of all that influence and power? A world so vast, conquered by so few people. The schools, the hospitals, the wooden buses. A planet of English speakers. A Mr Bean *movie*.

Then I learnt of the atrocities of empire. Of the slave trade, of the massacres. Of the establishment of a racial pecking order in so many parts of the world that placed White people on top. Of 'The Club'. And the guilt started to make sense.

I suppose shame always follows a splurge. That's certainly how I feel after one. Britain's splurge only really ended in 1947 with the independence of India, and technically continued to dribble on until the handover of Hong Kong to China in 1997, when Tom Cruise was already a substantial thirty-five and had *Top Gun*, *Rain Man*, AND *Jerry Maguire* under his belt. This is all pretty recent history. Britain's post-coital shame is still fresh, and a large section of the population still shiver with regret whenever it is brought up, and roll over to face the wall. I'm making a sex analogy.

Then there's the other side of the country, who sing the glories of the lost Empire and rattle their Union Jack tea mugs like sabres. Their history is selective, too, and often overemphasises the benign, giving side of empire. In many of their heads the British Empire was little more than Oxfam with cannons.

But their numbers may be waning. The polling company YouGov conducted a survey in 2014 amongst British citizens, asking about their feelings on the Empire. More than half said that it was something to be proud of, while only a quarter said it was a cause for shame. That is quite the majority. However, 2014 was a long time ago at the twenty-first century's pace of events. British pride was at a high then. The 2012 Olympics had been an astounding success, surprising everyone, none more so than the British themselves. In addition, I had just finished university, obtaining a perfectly decent 2.1 in my Engineering degree, an achievement that lifted the hearts of the nation.

The picture is quite different now. YouGov conducted a similar survey in 2019, when Tom Cruise was a mature fifty-seven, and still looking, frankly, fantastic. This time, only a third of Britons said they were proud of the Empire. That's quite the drop over five years. What happened? More young people had come of survey-answering age, I suppose. British society had become more multicultural, more thoughtful. And the ongoing racial tumult in the United States, inflamed by Donald Trump's presidential victory in 2016, caused many Brits to examine our own uncomfortable history with non-White people at home and abroad. But I think it was also Britain's withdrawal from its global duties in those intervening years that made the idea that it should ever have had an empire feel illegitimate. It's abandonment of the European project, it's reluctance to receive refugees made homeless by the war in Syria. These were not the actions of a country that could hold the world together.

However, the attitude of British exceptionalism can go both ways. People who characterise Britain's past as particularly evil also think Britain to be more special than it is. Britain is not alone in its colonising past. There have been other empires too. Of all races and creeds. Many nations have sought global conquest over the course of history. Was Britain uniquely ravenous, or just the most successful?

Interestingly, out of all the recently imperial nations of Europe, the Dutch are currently the proudest of their empire. Half of them remain proud of the Dutch Empire in 2019. Though most of that sentiment is just gratitude for Indonesian food, which saved them from pickled herring and sprinkles on toast.

The Netherlands, France, Spain, Belgium, and Portugal all sailed the seas and made men and women kneel at the ends of their guns, with a brutality that equalled, at least, that of the British.

Regardless, all these empires would crash and break against the rocks of the twentieth century. The colonial era was coming to an end. But not without a final bloody hurrah.

The First World War was a gruesome orgy of old empires pitted against one another. The Second World War, however, was a challenge to the old empires by newer ones that wanted to replicate and replace them – Hitler's Third Reich and, on Malaysia's side of the of planet, the Empire of Japan. They would all fall apart in the end.

Turning Japanese

On a low hill in the middle of Kota Kinabalu is a small, white clocktower. Its ticking hands have been carrying out their dutiful spirals for over a century. It is the oldest structure in the city and very handsome indeed. Backed by trees that stood there long before it was built, and looking out onto the concrete that grew after, the Atkinson clock tower stands in distinguished and solitary relief. Its brilliant-white wood panels line its four sides fifty feet into the sky, and the black edges of the planks and clock face pop elegantly in contrast – colonial architecture at its simple best. Its roof and wind vane (in the shape of Malaysia's crescent moon and star) is metal and terra-cotta-coloured, with wavy Oriental edges – the tower's marriage of styles a meeting of East and West.

It stands to this day a reminder of the British who put it there: foreign but familiar, orderly and incongruous. An inter-cultural improvisation. Also, it is white.

* * *

When the mighty Japanese navy landed in 1942, the small British forces of North Borneo surrendered. It was under the rule of a new empire now. One that was a lot less interested in cute clocktowers.

The brutality of the Japanese still haunts those islands. Growing up, we were told of the notorious *Kenpeitai* military police that terrorised the land; the tortures and executions. Train engines slowly rolled over heads until they burst like cherry tomatoes; mass graves dug by the people who were about to be put in them. The stories gave my sister nightmares. Captured Allied forces and locals were conscripted into forced labour, starved in prisoner-of-war camps, and forced on the infamous death marches from Sandakan to Ranau. Of an estimated 4,660 prisoners of war in North Borneo, only 1,393 saw the end of the war.

The Japanese were particularly interested in putting the sword to any Chinese on the island, who they suspected might be loyal to China and eager for revenge after the war crimes committed there, in particular the six-week long Nanjing Massacre of 1937–38.* A Chinese Bornean, Albert Kwok, decided it was all a bit much, and organised what became known as the Kwok Rebellion, alongside local Sikhs and the native Suluks, Bajaus, and Kadazan-Dusuns. With only three pistols and a box of hand grenades between them, the rebels managed a decent amount of disruption, armed mostly with knives and spears. But the Japanese soon retaliated and Kwok and Co were forced to retreat and hide.

Now a search was on for rebellious Chinese men. *Any* rebellious Chinese men. And Gong Gong – my grandfather – fitted

* The Chinese and Japanese have never got along, which is why I find restaurants that sell wonton soup *and* sushi to be suspicious to say the least.

the bill. Leaving Po Po at home, he fled into the cover of the jungle and found refuge with local tribespeople. There, he had to subsist solely on chickens and coconut water, which I think is a diet now.

The Japanese then issued a final ultimatum to Albert Kwok and his militia: surrender or we kill your families. The rebels had no choice. They gave themselves up and were executed. The Japanese, satisfied that they had quashed the revolt, calmed their crackdown. With the pressure off, Gong Gong was able to return home, but the occupation continued, and the war raged on. A memorial is still held every year in honour of the men of the Kwok rebellion.

Liberation came at the end of 1945.

My uncle David remembers metal rain; bombers flying loud and low overhead, his father bent over, shielding him with his body. The Australians had arrived, and they were putting *shrimp** on the *barbie*†. The Land Below the Wind had never seen a downpour like this.

The same was happening in Jesselton, twenty miles down the coast. Australian planes were bombing the capital that would eventually be my hometown of Kota Kinabalu. It was levelled. Destroyed. The Allies were saving the town from the Japanese even if it meant there was no town left when they were done. Eventually, the guns and planes fell silent, the dust settled, and Jesselton was flat. All that stood now was a lonely white clocktower, ticking quietly on a small hill.

* Bombs.
† Island.

The Freedom Medal of Valour

For an enterprise so heavily associated with death, I ironically owe the British Empire my life. The Australians who saved Borneo, the VSO that brought my mother. I would be dead without it. Or never born, if you want to be less dramatic.

Britain likes to congratulate itself for winning the war, with the occasional nod to America for its help in turning the tide (and Russia often gets forgotten completely). But it was Indians, Canadians, New Zealanders, South Africans, Kenyans, and Australians too, who saved the world from a new age of tyranny. The brave and dispersed peoples of the British Empire.

In 2019, a third of Brits said the British Empire was something to be proud of, down from over a half in 2014. However, also down was the number who thought it was something to be ashamed of – now at less than a fifth. A new option had been given on this survey: the British Empire is neither something to be proud nor ashamed of; 37 per cent agreed with this, making it the majority opinion.

Maybe in time we will find our peace with it, when the years add enough distance, and a more measured, informed national conversation allows for a true reckoning. Perhaps a new national identity will emerge that includes every Briton. Or maybe, in a century or so, the British will feel the way Italians seem to about the imperial history of Rome – a kind of detached acceptance – and pith-helmeted drama-school graduates will take photos with tourists in Piccadilly Circus, holding plastic elephant guns and wearing fake curled moustaches, smiling at the camera but dead behind the eyes.

* * *

Tom Cruise continues to make films to this day. At fifty-nine, he has three children and a cabinet of awards for his decades of excellent work, both as an actor and as a producer. In 2004 he became the first person to win the Church of Scientology's Freedom Medal of Valour (a special variant of the Church's annual Freedom Medal) for 'humanitarian work of a larger global scale'.

ASSIMILATION

Mixed – Other

It isn't always easy for me to feel British. Particularly whenever I am made to fill out the 'Ethnicity' portion of a form, an activity which – this being Britain – is required at least four times a day. The options are usually some version of the following main categories:

- White
- Asian/Asian British
- Black/African/Caribbean/Black British
- Mixed

And:

- Chinese and other groups

Just in case you missed it, here is that final option again: 'Chinese . . . and other groups.' What? Excuse me? Chinese and *other groups*? The Chinese in Britain are so far down the list of concern on British forms that we don't even get our own group, instead only thrown the lean bone of leading the 'Other' category. I mean, at least we are the poster ethnicity for 'other groups', I suppose – that's something if you squint (and according to the stereotype, we do) – but why don't we get our own group? Why do we have to share it with *the rest of the world*? Why are the Chinese the only ones on the list who sound like they're the lead singer in a band from the sixties? 'Now here's a boppin' new number for your jukebox, it's 'Box Ticking Blues' by Chinese and The Other Groups'.

The Chinese are a pretty major proportion of the world population, last time I checked. Don't we at least get our own tick box? Did the person who was designing the form simply forget about Chinese people until he'd reached the end? 'Oh! Chinese people! Nearly forgot . . . there we go. Hmmm. Look, I'll add "and other groups" just in case I've forgotten anyone else; some other equally obscure ethnicity. Chinese? Tick that box. A member of the indigenous Sámi people of Lapland? Tick the same box. That feels right. Ahhh, it sure is sweet to be good at your job!'

What is most baffling is that the whole issue was entirely avoidable. There's already an 'Asian' category. Why aren't the Chinese just in that? Why are the Chinese separated from 'Asians'? Isn't China quite famously a part of Asia? In fact, I'd go so far as to say that China is *most* of Asia. Strictly speaking, the Asian category on the form should be called 'Chinese and other Asians'. What happened to China? Was China kicked out of Asia at some point and no one told me? Did I miss this? I feel like that would have been pretty big news!

Now, if I were ethnically pure Chinese, this wouldn't be too bad. Sure, I'd for some reason been deemed not Asian, but at least there's a clear box for me to tick in order to carry on with this form and join this gym. But that isn't my – Phil

Wang's – ethnicity. I am – as the premise of the entire book has hopefully made clear by this point – 'Mixed'. So 'Mixed' must be my category. Again, easy enough. But, ah ah ah not so fast. Because now I have to pick a tick box *within* the 'Mixed' category to say precisely what mix I am. It is at this point of the form that I feel unpleasantly picked over, like a dish of food being presented to a vegan. 'Yeah, I know it's mixed, but what's in it? Is the White heritage ethically sourced? Oh, and I can't eat "other groups". They make me bloat. Sorry to be annoying!!'

The choices of ethnic combinations within the 'Mixed' category are then usually: 'White and Black Caribbean', 'White and Black African', 'White and Asian', and 'Mixed – Other'. Now, again, at first glance the choice seems simple enough. My mother is White British (and French and Irish, but for God's sake let's not complicate this any further) and my father is Chinese Malaysian. I am therefore 'White and Asian'. *But* we already know from the main categories earlier on, that this form – for some untold reason – does not consider Chinese people to be Asian. So if I tick 'White and Asian', will the form think that I am half White and half *South* Asian (e.g. Indian or Pakistani or Bangladeshi)? Well, if past form (the perfect pun? Could it be?) is anything to go by, then yes. That means that if I tick 'White and Asian', I will be answering this questionnaire incorrectly, and I don't do that. I'm good at exams. It is not my style to write down wrong answers. Plus, a wicked cycle is at play: if I select 'Mixed White and Asian', and they assume that that means I am White and *South* Asian, then they will not be notified that there is a fundamental problem with their form and will continue to use it, assured that no considerations for Mixed

White and *East* Asian people need to be made. I could tick the rather surly 'Prefer not to answer', but I *would* like to answer! I'd love to answer! And so, every time, I – with slumped shoulders and hanging head, finger gliding listlessly across my laptop's trackpad – tick that my ethnicity, my heritage, the name of the unique and miraculous culmination of peoples, cultures, and genes that have survived millennia of war and hunger; disease and destruction, to get to this point – me filling out this form – is 'Mixed – Other'.

Now I have to say, there is nothing more othering than having to literally select the word 'Other' to describe yourself. Black and Brown Brits are often made to feel othered in this country too. But at least they don't exist in the nation's data stores as, quite literally, 'Other'. What's ironic is that I am usually presented with this dilemma in diversity survey forms, sent to me by TV production companies, or arts bodies, or awards judging panels, who all feel incentivised in the current socio-political climate to be seen to be taking some sort of action with regards to ethnic inclusivity and representation. Their intentions are broadly well-meaning, but for someone like myself, who for the most part feels OK with his place in society, it is their questionnaire that snaps me back to the reality of a country that hasn't even considered the possibility of my existence. 'Do you feel underrepresented in the arts? Please select one of the following options, none of which describe you.'

The marginalisation that East Asians face in the UK is unique. It is not quite the same as the racism experienced by Black and South Asian Brits, who have put up with generations of institutional discrimination, verbal and physical abuse, and general unfounded suspicion, but have also, over the last few years, quite rightly begun to be celebrated for their contributions to British music, film, politics, literature, fashion, food, and history. Long overdue, too. East Asian Brits, however, suffer the same indignities (recently exacerbated by COVID-19-provoked hate), but silently in the shadows, without even the consolation of having their hardships or their contributions to society recognised. What East Asian Brits face is a kind of invisibility; a lack of acknowledgement as contributing members of this country, and a general treatment of alienation. We are almost never considered part of the UK's rich tapestry of faces. So complete is the exclusion, it is not actually possible to even *know* how many East Asian Brits there are, or how many of them are something other than Chinese, because of how vague and uninterested the data-collecting questionnaires are. 'Chinese and *other groups*'.

It seems this has been the case for a long time. In my conversations with Pixi Lim about *Mind Your Language,* she spoke about the isolation she felt when she arrived in the UK in 1961 as a Chinese Malaysian. 'In those days, we Malaysians, Chinese, Japanese – we were just oddities. There was no racist pointing the finger or anything. We were just oddities.' And although curiosity about her race and culture was predominantly innocent – 'They were just curious. They wanted to know what I ate at home and how many brothers and sisters I had,' – she recalls an experience of being East Asian in the UK that is all too familiar still today: 'I was just incredibly lonely'.

Despite the long history between the two countries, the Chinese of Britain still struggle to be seen as British. Even saying the phrase 'British Chinese' feels odd. Like I've never heard anyone say it before. 'Chinese' and 'British' are considered, albeit subconsciously, by this nation as mutually exclusive identities to have. You can be one or the other, but not both. It's the reason I was placed in a study with other Chinese kids at school in Bath for no other reason than my surname. It is why Chinese Brits – and East and Southeast Asian Brits (also known as 'other groups') – aren't even counted amongst British Asians in the 'Ethnicity' section of diversity surveys. And it is why British Chinese people get asked all the time, even if they were born and raised in the UK, 'So where are you from?'

They Come Over Here

'Why don't they integrate?' So goes the classic charge against the immigrant in Britain. Integration. Assimilation. Learning the language. These are the expectations placed upon the good immigrant. And for the most part, they are fair ones. Any citizen of a nation should know the language and wield a workable knowledge of its history and values. Though I'd like to see the same standards applied to British people living abroad as immigrants. Or as they prefer to be called, expats. Here is a glaring double standard of the English language. People who have moved from elsewhere to live and work in the UK are 'immigrants'. But British people who move abroad to live and work are merely 'expats'. Expatriates – as the word's definition goes – are people who live outside of their native country. And that's what British people living abroad are. People merely living outside of their own country. Not *in someone else's country*, of course. Merely outside of their own. An expat of what country, you say? That detail seems to be left out? Well, Britain of course! What other country is there?

The language of citizenship is centred around Britain. You either live in Britain, or you want to, or you used to, and are now selling fish and chips and Carling on draught in Marbella, to other British people.

Britain can't seem to make its mind up about immigrants. The nation claims to be open to all, wanting to attract 'the best and brightest' from all over the world, but in the same breath deports British Caribbeans of the Windrush generation who helped rebuild the country after the Second World War. Aren't these the 'best' immigrants one can imagine? Immigrants who literally helped to repair the country and staff its services? If they aren't fit for citizenship, who is? Politicians in support of Britain's exit from the European Union speak of opening up the country to more people, in spite of the Brexit campaign's core promises of ending freedom of movement and 'taking back control' of the UK's borders. Either this country wants immigrants or it doesn't. And the UK has never been able to settle on an answer it is comfortable with.

But that's what happens when such a physically small country amasses history's largest empire. Britain's eyes were bigger than its stomach, and now that it finds itself having to repay the hospitality of a quarter of the globe, it has realised a little too late that it doesn't have the space. It's for that same reason that I don't accept invitations to dinner parties. Because eventually I'm going to have to invite the hosts over to dinner at my place in return and I only have three chairs.

Is Britain a racist country? Again, it suffers a similar schizophrenia. Unsurprisingly, the nation that both helped to establish the transatlantic slave trade and played a significant role in the abolitionist movement suffers from a split personality on the subject. I am – and always will be – proud to call myself British. But national pride's proximity to its darker form – national*ism* – will always temper my public exaltations. Although I am confident that Britain is on balance not a racist country, there are elements of the British identity that even I am too squeamish to celebrate.

In particular, the England flag. Now, I don't care much for any flag, and seeing one of any kind on a front lawn or in a window is usually an indication of at worst a fascist, and at best a dreadful bore – the kind that insists his particular corner of the country should be an independent nation for no apparent reason other than the quality of the local produce. But no flag instils in me the instinctive panic of a St George's Cross. I wish it wasn't so. Because I do love England. But after decades of misuse by racist thugs, the St George's Cross is a ruined brand. While there is nothing inherently wrong with the flag itself, unfortunately, like polo shirts and *Hamilton*, its most rabid fans have spoiled it for the rest of us. And as a Chinese person, that St George is famous for slaying a dragon – that most Chinese of beasts – only makes it worse. I imagine the Welsh are wary of the English for the same reason.

The sad fact is that pretty much every non-White person in England is made uncomfortable by the presence of an England flag. And thanks to our football hooligans, its link to racism and destruction is now known far beyond our shores. I just hope it hasn't gone too far. I think it's a cruel coincidence that the St George's Cross looks so much like the humanitarian Red Cross. I dread to wonder how many sufferers of drought and famine in South Sudan or Somalia have caught sight of a Red Cross medic approaching over the horizon, only to panic and think a van of Luton skinheads were on their way to finish the job.

Seeing as the England flag *is* now a ruined brand, I recommend that we do the only thing that can be done *about* a ruined brand: replace it and forget the old one ever existed. A new design is just what the doctor ordered. One that avoids the ugly insinuations of the St George's Cross, but still embodies the spirit and character of what it means to be English. Perhaps a young woman in heels, vomiting into a storm drain, resplendent against the backdrop of a starry, freezing Friday night. A man sitting at home, on hold to his Internet provider for the third time that afternoon having gotten through an hour ago but accidentally hanging up because he got too excited. Or a bird's-eye view of a roundabout packed with cars, at a complete standstill for no discernible reason at all. *And did those feeeeet, in ancient tiiiiime . . .*

Is Britain an open country? Again, yes and no. On the one hand, British society is notably liberal, and generally resistant to overtly racist politics. Occasionally, openly xenophobic parties make some progress, but not to the extent they have in say, France or the Netherlands, both of which have seen the unabashedly far right and anti-immigrant Marine Le Pen and Geert Wilders come perilously close to actual government. Now and then, parties like the British National Party (BNP) and the UK Independence Party (UKIP) gain some traction in the UK. But thankfully, neither has yet found a significant foothold in parliament. Britain claims proudly to be a free, open, tolerant place, in which racial discrimination is unacceptable, and for the most part I buy it. In my life here, I do not walk the streets worried about my safety as an East Asian person. It's what lies beneath the open liberal surface of British society that I am less sure about. The Britain that exists in whispers and glances; in codewords and unspoken paranoia.

I can think of no better illustration of this split-personality disorder than a night in Hereford some years ago. For those of you who don't know, Hereford is a town just on the English side of the border with Wales. With a major military garrison nearby and the native Hereford cow, it is known for two things: the army and beef – making it the most British town possible. It is also a very White town. There was a regular comedy night at the local arts centre (because soldiers and cattle need a laugh too) – a rather notorious night that I had previously failed at miserably. However, the central delusion that makes a comedian a comedian is not to accept a unanimous message that you're not wanted, but instead say, 'I'll get them next time'. And that I did. The next time I was there, a better, more confident comedian, I did great. The audience laughed and clapped and mooed with delight the entire time I was on stage. It was one of those nights when a comedian feels on top of the world, and as this gig had gone badly the last time, a distinct feeling of victory and progress was mine all mine.

Now, as a live comedian, and in particular as a live *single* comedian, there are nights when someone you find quite attractive is in the audience. These are lucky nights. There are also nights when you do really well on stage. These are also lucky nights. Then there are nights when you do really well on stage, *and* there's someone attractive in the audience who *sees* you do really well on stage. These are very lucky nights. This night in Hereford was such a night. In the crowd, amongst the heaving mass of beer, semi-automatic rifles, and shaking udders, was a beautiful woman sat with a few friends at a table near the stage, her hair in a bob cut and looking like a young Twiggy. As I performed my set and looked around the audience, I noticed that she was looking at me too. You might think this is no big deal as I *was* on stage with a big light on me and a microphone amplifying my voice. You would assume everyone was looking at me. But you'd be surprised how many people at a comedy show are quite happy to either look at their feet, talk to their friends, look at their phones, or just stare dumbly into the middle distance like they're having a war flashback (and in Hereford that was more likely than most places). Our lovely lady was, however, paying rapt attention and laughing at the jokes.

The show ended to raucous applause, the cows even giving me a standing ovation (though I guess they can't do anything else), and I stepped out triumphant from backstage with the other comedians. A group came over to say well done to us all, and who should it be but Twiggy's gang. It was then that I realised the spread of ages of the group was quite broad. Twiggy was around my age, but the others were in their forties and maybe even early fifties. Together they looked like the cover of an Open University prospectus. The person leading the charge was a fun aunt of a woman who said they'd all had a great time, and asked what we comedians were up to now. The other comics had to get in the car share back home, but I – it just so happened – had to stay the night in Hereford.

'Come for a drink!' the lady said.

'Oh, I don't know,' I said. Going out with the audience after a show can look a bit tragic, and also feel terribly awkward. My general rule is to say a polite *Thanks, but no thanks*. The lady then tilted her head in the direction of Twiggy, and said 'She is *chronically* single.'

'Let's get a bloody pint!' I boomed. The game was afoot. Or 'a-hoof,' as they say in Hereford.

I bid farewell to the other comics, who wondered why I was going for a night on the town with what looked like a conversational-Spanish evening class, and left the theatre with my new crew. Twiggy hung back to introduce herself and the other individuals of the group who turned out to be her colleagues. There was the fun aunt, a younger guy about Twiggy's age, and an older guy who must have been in his mid-to-late forties. They were all welcoming, cheerful, and very excited to have one of the comedians out with them, all looking at me with faces that seemed to say *You're the first one who has ever said yes*.

They took me into town and to a bar where they bought me drinks. We all chatted and shared our stories. I told them about the intricacies of the comedic arts, and they, proud Herefordians, enlightened me on the finer aspects of bullets and milk.

When we decided to move on to the second bar, Twiggy and I were the first out, and, while the others weren't looking, stole a kiss on the cobbled avenue outside. *Superb!* I thought. *Here I am: young and funny, delighting the far reaches of my adoptive nation like a travelling bard of yore, and making out with a sixties icon on the Welsh border. This – THIS – is what your twenties are all about*.

The others caught up and we continued through town to the second bar on their itinerary. This time the middle-aged man of the group fell back from the others to talk to me. Let's call him Cooper, after another icon of the sixties – the Mini Cooper. I asked Cooper about life in this picturesque part of the country and he spoke pleasantly of its slow, easy pace. Then we passed the town's taxi rank – cabs lined up sleepily on the pavement outside the town hall.

'I know a lot of cabbies,' Cooper said as we walked by. 'Well, I *used* to. They're all Pakis now.' Instantly, the chat stopped flowing. I had opened my mouth to continue the conversation before I'd actually processed what he'd said, and ended up simply hanging my jaw dumbly in the air, caught off guard. He then realised what he'd said, like he'd been woken from a daze. 'Oh, sorry . . . I didn't . . . I just . . . you know . . . it's . . .' He juddered and sputtered like a stalling, well, Mini, nothing he said able to get us moving again.

I was shocked, of course. This had come out of nowhere. One minute ago he was buying me lager and telling me how much he'd enjoyed my set and pointing out local landmarks, and now he'd just caught himself launching into the Best of Enoch Powell.

It goes without saying that my instant reaction to his use of the word 'Pakis' was revulsion. But my second reaction – and I'm not proud of this – was *flattery*. I was . . . kind of *flattered*. *Wow,* I thought, *he really likes me! He trusts me enough to use a racist slur. A slur I imagine he only ever uses around his closest friends. Many of whom used to be cabbies, apparently.* I can't remember a more bizarre moment of internal conflict in my life. I was both appalled by his use of that word, but also – and I have to say it again – flattered that he would use it in front of me. I felt . . . accepted, part of his group. And some Palaeolithic instinct of mine appreciated this acceptance so much that it temporarily overrode my moral code. *Maybe next time he won't even feel the need to apologise after!* said this dark corner of my mind, and I quickly stamped out the thought.

I wasn't sure what to say, so just replied with something to the effect of, 'It's . . . OK.' The kind of *It's OK* you say to someone who already seems to know that what they've done is wrong. Perhaps I should have been firmer. Angrier. He'd apologised, but was that just because he'd been caught? I should have stormed off. I should have told the others that they associated with a bigot and should ostracise him from their weird little comedy night out group for good. But I didn't. I said, 'It's OK.' The French have the term 'staircase words' – the righteous witticisms and devastating retorts you should have said in the moment but only come up with at the bottom of the stairs having already left the party/meeting/orgy*. My staircase words eluded me in that moment. And being outside as we were, and with Hereford's notable lack of multi-storey buildings, neither the words nor a staircase were likely to materialise any time soon.

It is always easy to know what one should have done in retrospect. I should have said, 'That is unacceptable,' I should have said 'I'm leaving,' I should have said, 'I always knew I preferred Aberdeen Angus! It's a tastier meat and has a more pleasant fat ratio'. But I didn't. I said 'That's OK.' You have to understand that in the moment you often don't say the thing you think you will when you imagine confronting such a situation. Those countless times when you drift off and daydream about encountering some faceless racist, or sexist, or homophobe, and setting them straight with the perfect demolition of their entire worldview. Something devastating and insightful and inspiring and even funny. The movie camera of your mind's eye spins around the imagined scene as onlookers and allies cheer you on. The villain hanging his head in shame, the world put to rights.

* Technically, the English translation of *esprit de l'escalier* is 'staircase wit' but I prefer the Yiddish version, 'staircase words', which is broader in definition and puts no pressure on the individual to have actually come up with a witty reply even after they've had plenty of time to think of one.

But the reality is always different. The bigot is never faceless. In my experience, they almost always have a face. And you have to understand that when you've established a rapport with someone – albeit over the course of one evening – it is all the harder to think badly of them in a single instant. Even when clear evidence is presented to you. And you have to understand that once someone has shown you a little hospitality, you feel a small debt to them, and are willing to give them the benefit of the doubt when they say something appalling. And you have to understand – you absolutely *must* understand – that Twiggy was really, *really* pretty. Not that I think she would have sided with Cooper had an argument developed. But the mood of the evening would definitely have been soured by my public castigation of her friend, and the momentum of our flirtations would have been quite irreparably derailed. And so, I said, 'That's OK'. I learnt an uncomfortable truth about myself that night: sometimes I am hornier than I am anti-racist.

Just so that you can rest assured that my dereliction of civic duty did not go rewarded, this is how the rest of the evening went: I recovered as best I could from my shock at Cooper's outburst and tried to pretend that all was fine when we caught up with the others at the next bar. Upon which it turned out that everyone had suddenly become tired and had called taxis to go home. *Don't let Cooper sit in front!* I wanted to shout. Twiggy, too, was tumbling into a car now, saying it was nice to meet me and to make sure I tried the local cheese before I left town. And before I knew it, I was standing alone on the pavement. I also really needed a wee.

How quickly an evening can turn, I mused, peeing against a wall in an abandoned lot on the way back to my bed and breakfast. The night had started with such triumph and promise, and now here I was: alone, drunk, committing a minor act of public indecency, and having sold out my South Asian brothers and sisters, all for a tumble in the Herefordshire hay that didn't even end up happening. All I had achieved out of finally conquering Hereford – it dawned on me – was a quick kiss and the gentle encouragement of a provincial xenophobe.

The next day, when the alcohol had dissipated and the blood had been decanted back from my penis into my brain, I began to think more clearly about Cooper and his Freudian slip. It was a social blunder that encapsulated British racism, i.e. racism followed by an apology. I don't think it was the first time he had used that word in front of someone. He said it too easily, too readily, too casually. I think it *was* the first time he'd ever said it to someone non-White, though. And I think, between the beer and the pleasant conversation, he had forgotten that I wasn't White for a moment. When he remembered I was Asian, and had performed forty-five minutes of stand-up largely about *being* Asian, he realised his mistake and was embarrassed.

I wouldn't be surprised if that was his first night out *with* an actual Asian person. The areas of the country with the strongest anti-immigrant sentiment are also the ones with the fewest number of immigrants actually in them. And Hereford is extremely White; 98 per cent White, in fact, according to the national census. So the chances that Cooper had ever had a prolonged conversation with an Asian person of any kind before me were low. When he did, however, that night when we'd hung out, he found that he had a good time. He was so comfortable in my presence that he forgot about my race altogether, regarded me simply as another human being, and that, ironically, led him to say something racist out of comfort.

I often wonder what Cooper is doing now. Whether or not he remembers saying what he said. I hope that he does. And I hope that it got him to consider the way he thinks and speaks about people. It might sound strange, but I look back on that night with more hope than despair. If he could feel a moment of guilt and embarrassment about a word he regularly used, because he'd met (and spent an evening of pleasant company with) me, perhaps all that is required for him to review and rehabilitate his feelings on Indian and Pakistani people is just to actually speak to one.

Dress for the Culture You Want

Not all resistance to the assimilation of non-White people comes from the far right or the openly xenophobic. People on the left, people who consider themselves progressive, can slow the stirring of our glorious melting pot too. Though they may not be aware they are doing so. In fact, they often think – as they tend to do about everything – that they are helping. Over the last decade or so, 'cultural appropriation' has become household terminology. And the relentless demonisation of cultural appropriation by people on the left of society has made it both common and fashionable to believe that it is a Bad Thing that must be avoided in every instance for the sake of social justice. But, if you ask me, it's an own goal. An impediment to the integration of minority cultures, not a help. And an often silly – if well-intentioned – anxiety.

* * *

In 2018, Keziah Daum of Salt Lake City, Utah, attended her high-school prom wearing a *cheongsam* – a traditional Chinese dress. It's a lovely thing, form-fitting, finely embroidered with delicate patterns, seductive, confident, and tasteful all at once. Problem was, Keziah wasn't Chinese. She was White. Photos of her in the dress, posing alongside her even Whiter friends, began circulating on online nuance hub, Twitter, and in an instant, she was the Internet's villain *du jour*. 'My culture is not your prom dress' was the first – and fastest spreading – condemnation to accompany her photos, and soon Keziah was branded a racist for wearing a dress that was – according to her critics – not hers to wear because she was not Chinese.

Soon she was on American news programmes defending her choice, insisting the whole time that far from wanting to mock or cheapen the *cheongsam*, she had chosen it because 'It's beautiful'. And it was! She wasn't pulling her eyes apart and screaming 'Me love you long time'. She was wearing a dress she found in a vintage shop that she thought was beautiful enough for – if American movies are anything to go by – the most significant event of her life: senior prom. Presumably with a 'cute boy' who had just got a 'baseball scholarship' to play 'quarterback' for 'the 'Utah Dogcats', right after a delicious diner dinner of yam jerky and candied beef and a ride in his Mustang Sally so that he wouldn't dirty his tuxedo pants on the sidewalk.

Despite the enormous pile-on, Keziah Daum stood firm. She refused to take down the photos, refused to apologise, and reiterated her appreciation of the dress and the Chinese culture. And you know what? Good for her. She had nothing to apologise for and I found it genuinely encouraging to see her stand her ground. She had done nothing wrong, knew it, and wasn't going to be bullied into accepting guilt for a fabricated crime.

At eighteen she showed greater self-knowledge, strength of character, and courage than many twice her age.

Cultural appropriation – in its most popular interpretation – is the idea that a person of one race, nationality, or identity should not adopt, engage in, or emulate the cultural markers of another race, nationality, or identity to which they do not belong. Be it clothing, food, music, or dance, the originators of those traditions hold the exclusive right to them, and only they can bestow the permission required to take part in them. By this definition, cultural appropriation is – in a phrase – the theft of culture.

To use the term 'cultural appropriation' in such a way is to misunderstand the nature of culture itself. It presumes a rather unpleasant world in which we are all expected to be possessive of our cultures and police how others interact with them. But no culture really belongs to any one person or any one group of people. Cultures are themselves derived from other cultures. Cultures don't come into being out of nowhere, but emerge through the convergence, adoption, and modification of other cultures that preceded them. Culture *is* appropriation. So the idea that appropriation *hurts* culture doesn't make sense.

My friend Isabelle loves *cheongsams* and I'm always chuffed to see her in one. But being a White English girl, she often tells me of her hesitation in wearing them, for fear of being accused of cultural appropriation. I always reiterate my support, and assure her that she can refer any detractors personally to me, so I can tell them she has my approval. Sensationalising the idea of cultural ownership and getting off on high-profile take-downs of supposed cultural appropriators will only make decent people like Isabelle more hesitant to engage genuinely with other cultures. It will make those cultures appear untouchable, distant, and segregated from 'normal' society. And in the case of the Chinese, make us an even more alien people in the West than we already feel. Cultural protectionism, special treatment, and the fencing off of 'people of colour' to be protected from the corrupting influence of our majority White fellow citizens, all disrupt – not assist – true assimilation.

In the UK, accusations of cultural appropriation are usually to do with something a White woman has worn to a music festival or something Jamie Oliver has cooked. In the same year as Keziah Daum's fateful prom, Oliver released a bag of flavoured microwaveable rice called 'Punchy Jerk Rice' even though there is no such thing as jerk rice. In Jamaican cooking, jerk is something you do to meat, not rice. Some British Jamaicans were irritated by Jamie's misuse of the terminology and accused him of disrespecting Jamaican cuisine in order to make a quick buck, and of generally being a bit of a punchy jerk himself.

It is worth being aware that the demonisation of cultural appropriation is a Western phenomenon. The original countries of the cultures supposedly being insulted are often left perplexed by the controversies that make the news here. When the debate over Keziah Daum's dress blew up, observers in China – where the *cheongsam* is from – were scratching their heads. Many online commentators thought the criticism was absurd, saying they were proud to have the Chinese culture represented overseas and that anyone who thinks they look good in a *cheongsam* should absolutely wear one, because that's what *cheongsams* are for. Many also pointed out that the *cheongsam* was itself adapted by the majority Han Chinese from a traditional garment of the Manchu ethnic minority from the country's North East. Culture *is* appropriation.

In my chat with the Chinese Malaysian comedian Jason Leong for this book's COMEDY chapter, he brought up the topic of cultural appropriation, and specifically the viral story of Keziah Daum's prom dress. He was bewildered by it. 'In Malaysia, it's the *total* opposite,' he exclaims, perplexed and amused, 'If another race wears a *cheongsam* to an event, that person is celebrated! "Oh, thank you for embracing my culture – that's so nice. One Malaysia."* Or if a Chinese guy wears a *Baju Melayu*† or a *songkok*‡ to a Malay wedding: "Oh man, you look good! This is what Malaysia's about!" It's totally different. *Totally* different.'

The backlash Keziah Daum faced for her choice of dress was particularly baffling to Jason, as an ethnically Chinese man himself. 'To me that was *weird* . . . the lady just wants to wear a *cheongsam* and she gets flame for it.' As someone who grew up in a truly multicultural society, the idea that cultural appropriation should be a bad thing is inconceivable to him.

Appropriation does not have to be a bad word, and it serves none of us to condemn each other unthinkingly for revelling in the bounty of humankind's variations. As Keziah Daum put it herself, exasperated in a TV interview, 'I wore it to show my cultural *appreciation* of the Chinese culture'.

This is not to say that care and respect for other cultures are not important, of course. I'm not calling open season on

* The name for the concept of Malaysia's cross-cultural national unity.
† Traditional Malay dress.
‡ The traditional cap for Muslim men in Southeast Asia.

whatever interpretation of a minority culture you want. Some cases of cultural appropriation are certainly deserving of criticism. A posh White girl from Hertfordshire raving at a music festival out of her mind on MDMA whilst wearing a bikini and a feathered Native American headdress should give you an instinctive bout of indigestion. It's hard to shake the suspicion that 'Flora' has never actually *met* a Native American, let alone led enough Apache war parties to victory to be bestowed one of their sacred bonnets. Flora has most likely only decided to buy and wear that headdress to dance around a campfire in Somerset because dancing naked around a campfire is all she thinks Native Americans do. Add to that the fact that millions of Native American people have been killed and displaced, predominantly by White Europeans and their descendants, and her choice of dress should be clear to anyone to be unambiguously distasteful. So in such a case, derision would be right.

Have I had negative experiences with the appropriation of Chinese culture and people? Absolutely! At Glastonbury Festival once, I wandered around the hippie field (technically all of Glastonbury is a hippie field, but this part is where the real card-carrying beatniks are), admiring the teepees (honestly, the poor Native Americans really are everywhere at a British music festival, except in person). As people milled around, nursing hangovers in the West Country sun, I noticed by the entrance to one of the teepees a large canvas painting of a smiling old Chinese lady wearing a traditional Chinese shirt covered in embroidery so Oriental that had Keziah Daum been there she would have ripped the painting off its struts and draped it over herself for the rest of the weekend. Underneath the painting were the words 'Chung Fu'. *Yep. Definitely meant to be Chinese, then*, I thought. I wanted to move on, knowing there was some hippie nonsense about that I wanted no part in. But the friend I was with was somewhat more appreciative of the spiritual arts (or as I call them, fraud with crystals) and wanted to have a look. Before I could protest and suggest we move on to a part of the field that smelt less of incense, the teepee flap opened and to my surprise, out came . . . a ginger guy. A topless White man with bright ginger hair, just like Chinese people don't have.

'Hello,' Ginger Topless said, 'Please, sit'. He patted a patch of grass next to him.

'You don't look much like your picture,' I said. For one, he was a man, and Chung Fu looked like a cheeky grandmother from a Studio Ghibli film.

He explained that he was not Chung Fu, much to my shock. It was in fact his mother who occasionally channelled a trans-dimensional spiritual entity called Chung Fu. Chung Fu has lived for many thousands of years, Ginger Topless went on to explain, and has taken on many different forms. Currently Chung Fu was Chinese (which was lucky with that name) and – to my surprise, looking up at a painting of what was without doubt that of an old Chinese woman – a man. Here were folks so unfamiliar with Chinese people, I thought, that they can't even tell a man one from a woman one.

'Would you like to see my stone sack?' said Ginger Topless. And before I could say, 'Woah, we've only just met,' he crawled back into his teepee and returned with a small felt bag full of smooth black rocks. *I knew it*, I thought, *Fraud with crystals.* He started telling us about his special rocks and how they were cure-alls for anything that ailed you. Anxiety? Depression? Heartache? Hold the rocks. They will fix you. Diabetes?

Melanoma? A railway spike through the leg? Just hold the rocks and prepare to be healed.

As we held his stones he remarked on their weight. *Wasn't it incredible how they pushed down ever so slightly on your hand*? I felt that I didn't have the energy to explain the theory of gravity to a grown man, and began to make 'let's go' eyes to my friend. I had started to become annoyed about Chung Fu. The Chinese are often used as props for mystic nonsense. And it had become obvious to me that that was happening here. Especially when Ginger Topless began to tell us how much his rocks cost in case we'd like to take one home with us. It was at that point that I simply got up and walked away.

Here's my rule for how to treat other people's cultures. Forget about 'cultural appropriation'. Just don't be rude. That's my rule: Don't Be Rude. Before appropriating a bit of culture. Have a think. Is what you're doing disrespectful, exploitative, or inconsiderate? If it is, don't do it. Consider each case separately. Appropriate responsibly. Don't Be Rude.

Was it rude of Keziah Daum to wear a nice Chinese dress she liked? No. Is it rude of Flora to wear a Native American war bonnet and go 'OWOWOWOWOWOWO' with her hand over her mouth to a remix of 'Tubthumping' by Chumbawamba in a muddy field? Yes, it is. Flora is being rude, isn't she? Questions about which bits of culture belong to whom aside, it's just plain rude to dress up as a historically devastated people and fanny around like it's a joke. Stop being rude, Flora. Is it rude of Jamie Oliver to make jerk rice? A little. But it's mainly bad cooking, which is a heinous crime too, but we shouldn't revel in disproportionate cultural outrage about what is mainly bad cooking simply because

Jamie Oliver is, to be fair, quite annoying. Is it rude for Ginger Topless and other crystal-waving draft dodgers to use a Chinese name to give credit to their hippie scams? Yes. Don't Be Rude, Ginger Topless.

If you're a White person and are about to have a Mexican-themed dinner party, or you're wondering how experimental to be with your hair at Notting Hill Carnival, just think: Don't Be Rude. It doesn't mean you can't do what you want to do. What you want to do may very well not be rude. It may be a delicious plate of tacos or a killer hairdo. Just ask yourself before you do anything you're worried might be condemned as cultural appropriation: *Is this rude?* If the answer is an honest and considered 'No', then tuck in, enjoy. We mustn't punish curiosity. And we mustn't punish our fascination with one another; with each other's customs, clothes and cooking. Appropriate. Just make sure to appropriate *well*. Give it thought. Be respectful.

Appropriate, appreciate, assimilate, and be a part of the culture of the world.

NATURE

Kinabalu

I had never seen it before. Half of my life spent in the shadow of Mount Kinabalu and I had never actually *seen* it before, you know? But there it was now, looming in the sky ahead of us, enormous and ancient, keeping watch over Sabah's west coast. It looked just like the photographs; the drawings; the post-cards, its peak bursting up through the clouds. A giant peering lazily over the foam of his bubble bath. Had I really never seen it before? I was twenty-seven years old and I had taken this flight into Kota Kinabalu countless times and yet this felt like the first time I'd seen the mountain. Which seemed impossible in this moment, with it framed so starkly, as if by design, in the plane's window.

Of course, I had seen it before. Many times, I'm sure. But I'd never actually noticed it. I had grown up with Mount Kinabalu standing over me, and after time it had faded into the background. I took its presence for granted, and I got on with my little life.

But now, it had been years since I'd seen it. I was flying back to Malaysia from the UK with my girlfriend of the time. I was taking her to Sabah to meet my Malaysian family and to introduce her to the place where I grew up. *West, meet East.* Without realising it, I had taken on her fresh eyes. Even before the plane had hit the tarmac. When you introduce someone to something familiar, you are enveloped in the freshness of their perspective, and to a degree, you feel new to it too. Kinabalu hung bold and proud, high in the distant air, as the plane began its descent.

'Yes, I am still here, little Phil,' it seemed to say, 'Always have been. Always will.' Though I wouldn't have heard it. Flying always bungs up my ears.

Mount Kinabalu is what gave Kota Kinabalu (literally 'Kinabalu City') its name when the British left and its old name, Jesselton, no longer felt appropriate. At over thirteen thousand feet it is officially the highest mountain in Southeast Asia*. It has a handsome craggy top, with a twin peak known as the 'Donkey's Ears' – two pointy pillars of rock that together look like, well, the ears of a donkey. The distinctive profile of Kinabalu's summit is the iconic symbol of Sabah. Its silhouette is emblazoned on the state flag where other flags have boring stars or violent swords. People climb it all year round (the mountain not the flag), but I had never done so. Not in sixteen years of living in Borneo. When you live in a place, you do not partake in its attractions. If you live in New York, you're probably not

* There were rumours during my childhood of a taller one somewhere in Indonesia. How a mountain could be just a *rumour* I don't know. It's a difficult thing to keep a secret. I doubt that all of a sudden, some hot new mountain somewhere in Sumatra had hit the scene and was ready to turn the tired old mountain industry on its head. It was almost certainly poppycock. The Indonesians are always trying to claim one thing or another over Malaysia. Better sambal, nicer hats, taller mountains. All nonsense.

going to go up the Statue of Liberty. Parisians are on the whole not bothered with the Eiffel Tower. And if you're London born and bred, you've probably never even seen the inside of M&M World.

It took having a British girlfriend who was actually into climbing to get me to do it. This climb was the focal point of our trip around Southeast Asia – a trip that was in part to show her where I was from and in part for me to get to see and do the things in Malaysia that I felt only tourists were allowed to. She was an active sort, loved the outdoors and hiking and awful things like that, and she'd convinced me that we should attempt the climb of Kinabalu. Now, it's going to get tiresome to constantly refer to my girlfriend of the time as 'my girlfriend of the time', but I also don't want to use her real name out of respect for her privacy. So let's call her . . . I don't know . . . Lara Croft Tomb Raider. I find books like this often waste opportunities to choose fun pseudonyms for the people in their lives. So why not. Lara Croft Tomb Raider. My girlfriend of the time was Lara Croft Tomb Raider. On account of the fact that she was English and liked the outdoors. And a decent movie about her has yet to be made.*

* As a kid in Malaysia, *Tomb Raider* was mistakenly pronounced 'Tom Rider' by us boys because 'tomb' and 'raider' were too uncommon a pair of English words for most Malaysians to be familiar with. And to be fair, a 'b' turning an 'o' into an 'oo' sound is absurd. Anyway, the effect was that *Tomb Raider* sounded less like it was about raiding tombs and more like it was about Lara Croft riding some guy called Tom. Which has actually been a common fantasy of nerds worldwide since the game's release in 1996.

Nature Boy

If I had an aversion to climbing Kinabalu, it was because I was sick to the teeth of 'nature'. Having spent my entire childhood in the thick of it, I had grown to be jaded by Borneo's lush landscapes and throbbing biodiversity. Bored; often annoyed by it. I wasn't always this way. I had had wonderful times when I was young in Sabah's natural bounty. Happy memories of bright light and quiet joy – running along sandy beaches as the sun cast its red spell over the fading horizon; slapping my chubby palms against the slimy-slick, glistening rocks of untouched inland streams, the stones rounded by centuries of current; splashing belly-first in water so clear it had the appearance of flowing quartz. As a boy I was anxious at bedtime, but the serenade of crickets, invisible but everywhere, soothed me to sleep with their steady violins, an orchestra of humble virtuosos hidden in the dark grass.

But after a while it all started to piss me off, to be honest. The bugs and the heat and the bites and the sweat. As year gave way to year, as my interests veered onto screens, and my commitments to study, nature became a crude and far-too-tangible thing. I was living in an abstract world now. Of books, and movies, and video games. And I began to find that nature got in the way of these things. Mosquitos would bite me as I started up the PlayStation. Lizards would dart crazily across the walls and ceilings to distract me with their threat while I was trying to read. Occasionally the rain would get so torrential it would block all signal to our satellite dish, and whatever show I was watching would flicker and stutter and turn black. And that was TV done for the day.

I also learnt to find nature dangerous, terrifying, and just plain gross. Malaysia is so hot that homes have to be open-air, which allows entry to any animal smaller than an ox. People in the UK have no idea how pleasant it is to not have to worry about snakes simply sliding into your living room whenever they please like The Fonz. Dogs in Malaysia have their work cut out for them, duty-bound to keep out not just human invaders but intruders with many more legs, and intruders with none.

I remember one day hearing our two dogs barking with great excitement in the garden at a snake that had found its way in. They had sandwiched it. One barking at its head, the other at its tail. Dog warnings, I imagine. Like 'Get out!' or 'We're not interested in Jehovah!' Eventually, the dogs decided this interloper had been given enough warnings, and almost as if they'd planned it, each grabbed one end of the snake in its mouth. They lifted it and pulled in opposite directions, like the snake had been found guilty of heresy by the Spanish Inquisition. They pulled it taut, and finding it all just too disgusting, too mad, too 'nature', I looked away. The sound that drew my eyes back I can still hear to this day. A juicy *snap*. A wet *pop*. I looked back and saw that the snake – now deposited on the ground – had become two shorter snakes. A snake with a head, and a snake that was just a tail. Incredibly, the head half of the snake was still alive. And even more incredibly, the tail half seemed to be as well, wriggling manically on the grass. The dogs barked at this wretched sight with fear and confusion, as if to say, 'What dark magic is this?! Foul is the curse that afflicts us this day! Woof!' What happened next was a rare live demonstration of natural selection in action. With the dogs distracted by the wriggling tail, the head half of the snake slithered away out of the garden to safety in the most cartoonish 'That's all folks!' skidaddle I've ever seen in the animal kingdom.

I feel sick just typing that out. Do you see what I had to live with? We were lucky to only get relatively small snakes in our house. Sabah is also home to the king cobra, which does not run away, and is instead known to *chase after people* and usually *catch them*. They have a terrifying appetite too. Mother once heard the story of a dead king cobra, which had been found on a patch of land that was being turned into a golf course. It had died choking to death. On what? Another snake. That was still in its mouth. Also dead. Its head poking out of the cobra's. Like a snake wearing a snake costume for Halloween. Hole in one.

The UK's natural mildness is one of its greatest unsung qualities. Walks in the British countryside are *relaxing* affairs. A safe and wholesome activity for all the family, adults and children alike. On a walk in the British countryside, you might chance upon a lovely pinecone, a handsome red fox, or if you're lucky, a deer will wander into the path ahead and allow you a moment's glance; a minute's admiration, before he shyly bounds away, leaving you to your day and him to his. The only dangerous animals in Britain are the lions on its coats of arms. And even then, they couldn't find enough and had to throw in a couple of unicorns to fill the ranks.

In Borneo, you will die. There are many, many, many, many, many animals that want to kill you. Snakes, crocodiles, boars, wasps. There are even bears. Bears! Little black bears that look cute, but only so that you get close enough for them to rip open your throat with their claws like they're checking your neck for mail. The advice I got about black bears: remember – they can climb trees. So, if you're running away from one and want to climb a tree to escape them, make sure to check how thick the trunk is (all while you're running for your life, remember). If the trunk is thick, *don't climb it.* The bear can get its claws into the bark and shimmy its way up to you to snack on your toes. Wait. Is that it? Or is it *thin* trees that you mustn't climb, because the bear can wrap a single paw around the trunk, and bend the tree down and pop you directly into its mouth like a grape? . . . See?! I've been *given* the advice and I still stand a fifty-fifty chance of being turned into a pulled dork sandwich out there.

Country walks in the UK, however, are marked with signs to accompany widely available maps, with public footpaths set aside for ramblers to enjoy England's green hills, Wales' lush valleys, and Scotland's majestic glens. Forests are spacious and your field of view is at all times wide enough to keep an eye out for the British wild's more dangerous inhabitants, like rabbits and fairies.

In Borneo, you will die. Half the battle is just finding a path to begin with. Because odds are there are none. You will have to make your own. Tropical foliage grows and grows and grows. There are no 'clearings'. There are no 'meadows'. There are just trees and trees and trees, bunched together like smelly men at a rock concert, and between the trees, vines (although some of them are in fact tree snakes in disguise so do keep an eye out), roots, mulch, anthills, and the rotting skeletons of White people who wouldn't shell out for a tour guide. You need a machete to make your way through, so it feels less like you're exploring the jungle and more like you're trying to dispose of its body before the feds arrive.

You can't move for nature in Borneo. It's everywhere. Borneo is so wild it beggars belief that human beings have managed to live there at all. Being mixed-race, I felt like an intruder in Sabah at times. But I also felt like we were *all* intruders for being humans in an environment that obviously didn't want us there. The mosquitoes, the malaria, the humidity, the rain, the spiders, the snakes. The whole island is a dog trying to shake people off it like fleas.

You aren't even safe in your own home! Nature will get you there too. From the ground, from the air, from the water. From time to time, the basement of our house would fill with muddy water after the monsoon rains, which would flood the adjacent river (that was also an enormous storm drain and supposed to prevent such an incident) and cause it to overflow into our home. For days afterwards, we would not be allowed downstairs. It was now the territory of centipedes and other crawly demons, who had come in with the water and had taken over like venomous gatecrashers at a soggy house party.

In the UK, going downstairs is a routine and safe affair. In Borneo, you will die.

Don't Have a Cow

I have only ever had one experience in the UK countryside that I would consider dangerous. And the threat wasn't one I had ever considered before. Cows.

My friend Fin was getting married. A stag weekend had been arranged in the West Country, and against my usual form, I had been invited.* This wasn't the stag weekend of unhinged

* For any readers outside the UK, a 'stag' is the British term for a man who is soon to be married. The stag party is the event that he and his friends organise to celebrate his final days of freedom from his wife, before his wedding day, when he will celebrate his first day of freedom from his friends. In Australia it

depravity you might have in your head. A weekend of inconceivable drinking, humiliation, property destruction, and arrests. We were a genteel group of young middle-class millennial softies to say the least. Each of us the kind of man you can tell subscribes to a vegetable-box delivery service, just from the grain of his knitwear. At least two were professional-level cooks (the only thing 'shotgunned' all weekend was who got the honour of making the meals), and up until the cows my main source of anxiety was whether or not the magnum of red wine I'd brought specially would go with the marinated spatchcock chicken they were preparing (it did). We of course had our psychopath. Every stag do has a psychopath – the guy who never seems to blink and wants the kind of weekend that will get him in the news – but even his appeals to get Fin wasted were met with relative disinterest from the others, who didn't want our groom to reach a stage of intoxication at which he would miss out on our Scotch's subtler floral notes. What's more, the family who owned the cottage seemed very nice and we didn't want to damage anything. And we *certainly* didn't want to get the best man a bad review on the booking website after all the hard work he'd put in finding such a lovely place at such a reasonable price for everyone.

Lads! Lads! Lads!

We'd booked a tour of a brewery in a nearby village on the Saturday (to really put our ability to not have a piss-up to the test) and decided it would be a nice idea to walk there and take in the life-affirming country air. It was an extremely pleasant

---

is called a 'buck's party', because they are all cowboys, and in America it is just called a 'bachelor party' because Americans are a literal and earnest people who go for the first word that comes to mind, too busy having fun and enjoying life to waste their time with synonyms. It is their gift/asset/blessing and their curse/bane/affliction.

stroll – at least at first. Down country roads, over babbling brooks, and past old stone inns.

Eventually, we came to a field, beyond which was another field. We knew the brewery was on the other side of these two fields, so we decided to take the straight line through them. The walk began pleasantly enough with a pebble path that took us up a hill. Soon, a cow came into view on the low side across from us. *Sweet*, we thought. *Truly, this is the countryside. Britain's beef basket.* But then another cow came into view, and then another, and another, and pretty soon we realised that we were sharing the field with a small herd.

Still, we thought nothing of it. These were cows, after all. Famously docile. Walking meat tables. But then the cows started lifting their heads, one by one, to look at us. This was starting to feel a bit weird, but we continued along the path. Then the mood changed. The cows instantly fell into – and I'm not being overdramatic when I use this word – formation. Like Roman soldiers, they formed a square block and began walking up the hill in front of us as if to intercept us.

We laughed, only a little nervously. 'Imagine,' we said. 'Imagine if these cows got aggressive.' And just as we said that, they did. They got up to the path and turned – all at once, as if synchronised by some hive brain – to face us. At this point we started to worry. Still not ready to believe we were going to be attacked by cows, we made a precautionary note of a gate next to us that led into a small side field as a possible escape route. 'Let's go over that if we need to,' someone said. 'Don't be ridiculous, they're cows!' said another. And as if taking that as an insult, the herd began to charge directly at us.

'Go! Go! Go!' We clambered over the gate one by one and ran into the side field. When we'd created enough distance, we turned back to look at the gate we'd just jumped. From behind the cover of the hedge, like in a horror movie, the herd swung into view. They were now staring us down over the gate's metal bars. 'You know we can't open this latch,' they seemed to say, 'and we know you know we can't open this latch. On account of our lack of fingers. But these are our fields, boys. We know them like the backs of our hooves and we're going to get you. You rambling, liberal, metropolitan elite fucks.' In my memory, one of them lifted a front hoof and made a threatening throat-cutting gesture. Though I know this is impossible.

We were now in an unplanned field, but it had a gate at one end that led back into our original field at a point further along the path where we'd be hidden from the cows by some trees. We could go through it and bypass the hellish heifers and rejoin our planned route. We had to be quiet, though, lest those bovine bastards hear us. We went through the gate, taking care not to make any noise, but no sooner had we made five paces did the cows reappear. How did they know?! There was no time to find out. We ran again. This part of the field descended in the direction of the brewery, so half of us tumbled down it in fear of the cows, while the other half shouted at us not to, as this would only anger the cows further, before giving up on that argument and running themselves.

We made it to the end of the field, but found no gate into the next (and final) one. The cows were still on the top of the hill, looking down on us, gloating over their high ground. Then they started slowly advancing again. We were running out of time.

'We need to go!' someone begged.

'There's no gate!' wailed another.

We followed the hedges towards a corner, finding no escape, certain the cows had us trapped. And then: a gate emerged from amongst the green. 'Quick!' We climbed over and at last found ourselves in the final field before the brewery, with a closed gate behind us to keep us safe from the herd.

We patted each other on the back in joyous relief. We'd made it. It was scary, it was close, but we'd made it. And then, right in front of us, another herd of cows appeared. *This* field's cows. This was the end. We were finished. Ah well. At least that wine went with that chicken.

'Fuck this,' said the psychopath. He had had enough. To our horror, he began walking directly at them, and as the rest of us hung back and drafted his eulogy ('He was a psychopath so there's no point grieving, he wouldn't understand the emotion'), the cows simply . . . parted. They stepped out of his way and he just walked right through them like Moses through the Red Meat Sea. It turns out that cows, like all of life's bullies, are cowards deep down, and give up intimidating you immediately if you just walk at them.*

The brewery was fine.

Base Camp

Back in Sabah, I have been unable to feign an illness compelling enough to cancel the climb. So it looks like it's happening.

The day comes and my father drives Lara Croft and me to base camp. Getting dropped off by my dad isn't exactly the

* I just want to say: do be careful with cows. I looked up 'cow attacks' on the Internet after our brush with dairy death and it turns out they do happen, and if confronted with an aggressive cow, the official advice is to – and I'm not making this up – punch it in the face.

confidence boost I need in preparation for the first mountain climb of my life, but it will have to do.

Watching the car creep its way back to the road, I already miss its air conditioning. Beyond the wood-carved welcome sign and an expanse of jungle, Kinabalu soars up into the misty sky. It had looked tall even from the plane's window. Looking up at it now from the ground, up close and personal, it is greater still, and its peak somehow even further away.

Lara is excited and I put on a happy face for her benefit, but I am not looking forward to this. It seems inconceivable that in a mere thirty-six hours I will be (or am meant to be) on Kinabalu's peak; that lofty horizon; a far-off landscape I had always dismissed as a desktop background, purely for decorative purposes, impossible to actually reach. The idea that I will get there by the strength and will of my body alone seems preposterous. The same body that failed a lifetime of PE classes and sports days. The same body that lags and reddens with heat going up the stairs too fast. The same body that gets tired after some shits.

Too late. The car is gone now.

The first thing to do is to find our guide. All climbers must hire a Sherpa to take them up the path. The Malaysian outdoors is not for ramblers, after all. Step off the beaten track and you may never be seen again.

The Kinabalu mountain guides are for the most part local Kadazan-Dusun men, whose eyes have known the mountain since birth and whose blood has known it for centuries longer. Ours is called Francis*, and greets us with a polite smile. He's

* Colonialism.

in his mid-thirties, I'd say, with the high cheekbones of a runway model and the rough, strong skin of a mountain goat. He's about a foot shorter than me but a mile more capable in this, his element.

We are to have a night's sleep in preparation for an early start to our day's climb and are taken to our cabin, nestled amongst the trees and in Kinabalu's shadow, which watches over our night, protector and challenger. I savour the evening's comforts of a good mattress and little to do. This is *my* element, I think: bed and idleness. Lara is out like a light, but I take my time to fall asleep, avoid the fast-forward to a day I don't feel ready for.

The Climb: Day One (of Two)

We're up the next morning and Kinabalu greets us in the sunshine. Towering happily overhead in the brightness like an eccentric host at a Titan's bed and breakfast. 'Good morning, Phil,' it says, 'Today you will climb my face.'

Francis greets us with a gentle cheeriness, a genuine enthusiasm subdued pleasantly by professionalism and routine. He does this climb twice a week and it shows in his calm. He asks if we're ready. 'Yes,' I lie.

Timopohon Gate sees us off – built in the simple native style with a two-tier roof, spanning the breadth of the path, with the words '*SELAMAT MENDAKI*' emblazoned across its arch. Literally, 'SAFE CLIMBING'. All Malay greetings and well wishes begin with 'safe', whether it's 'safe arrival' for welcome, or 'safe night' for goodnight. But this time the translation feels particularly foreboding. Safe from what? What does this gate know that I don't?

The start of the climb is a walk in the park. Literally. We are technically in a national park, and for now the journey is relatively flat. So, our first forty-five minutes or so is a pleasant stroll through the green brush and under small waterfalls. It's all very picturesque and already I feel wild. Before I know it, my hair is matted with sweat to my forehead, and my clothes hang heavy with moisture. Barely minutes from '*SELAMAT MENDAKI*' and already the cicadas are drowning our ears with their screeching and moaning, taking the day shift while the crickets sleep. They are relentless, leaving no moment without noise, and I wonder how my ancestors ever got any damn sleep out here. Lara Croft is thrilled, of course. She's never been anywhere like this.

The hike soon becomes steeper as we begin the true work of the climb. Most of the vertical progress is made on man-made steps built into the path, their shape held with a combination of wood planks and conveniently placed roots. These require bursts of effort that are beginning to take their toll on me already. But you can only feel so tired about man-made steps in the jungle. Left by people who climbed the mountain *and* built steps as they went along to make the journey easier for the likes of me. The gall to feel exhausted when I'm not leaving anything in my wake except a mild stench.

Other guides pass us, going up and down. They all know Francis and exchange words with him in laughing Dusun – presumably, I think, about how much I'm struggling. But no, Francis is too nice for that. It strikes me that I'd never actually heard the Dusun language spoken before. It's strange and comforting at once. Like being introduced to a relative you've never met but have always heard about; foreign and familiar. It has the rhythms and sounds of something I should understand, but I don't.

We are making consistent progress (at the very least I haven't started climbing back down yet or soiled myself), although I do have to take regular breaks to catch my breath and re-energise my legs. Occasionally, Lara Croft does too. Francis never does – he climbs Kinabalu with the casualness of someone walking from their bedroom to their kitchen – but is polite enough to pretend to be tired every time we are. He'll turn around to see us panting, then instantly sit on his haunches and wipe fake sweat off his brow, exhaling deeply, even though he was absolutely fine a moment ago. It's kind of him. And well-practised from his many unfit tourists, I'm sure.

Occasionally, our rests are too long for him to keep up his charade without arousing suspicion, so he takes the opportunity to photograph the scenery with his phone. It's funny to watch someone who does this hike so often still want to take photos of it. But he really does love this mountain. The shine has not worn off. He tells us the photos are for his Facebook page, and he asks to add us as friends. I look at my phone and see that we still have full signal, which makes me wonder how far we've even gotten.*

A few hours in and we're still climbing. There's no noticeable difference in our surroundings except that I am seeing them through a thicker and thicker lens of sweat. I am reminded of

* It turns out there are phone towers on Mount Kinabalu, which makes sense as the highest point on the island. So mobile signal is perfect the whole way up. Checking Francis's Facebook profile afterwards I was amazed to find he wasn't kidding. All his photos are of the flowers and vistas along the hike he does for a living. His profile picture is of him standing, looking down proudly over the park. Some people are blessed to love their jobs and Francis is one of them. His Facebook page is a shrine to climbing Kinabalu. I can't imagine how much targeted advertising he must get for guy rope.

why I have never enjoyed the outdoors: the interminable *sameness* of it. Megajoules of energy and hours of time spent on a view you could pick up in a second. Trees, rocks, steps. Trees, rocks, steps. Steps, rocks, trees. Rocks, trees, steps. Steps, steps, rocks. Rocks, rocks, trees. Trees, rocks, trees. Steps, steps, steps. We would have had the same experience if we'd turned back half an hour in and Francis had said, 'It's just that, really.'

We've passed a few *pondoks* now – small open-air huts for climbers to sit and rest in, with maps of the trail showing our progress with an encouraging 'YOU ARE HERE' pin. There are also diagrams and displays about the flora and fauna you might chance upon, and general histories about the mountain and the people who have climbed it. At one *pondok*, there is a display about Kinabalu's summit: Low's Peak. Named after Hugh Low, a British colonial administrator with a flair for the outdoors and an ironic name for the top of a mountain. In 1851, Low became the first person to ever scale Kinabalu's heights, and so the peak was named after him.

I find this difficult to believe. There have been people living on this island for millennia, and none of them thought to climb the largest thing in sight? I interrogate Francis, who seems to have no problem with the display's claims.

'Hugh Low was the first person to climb Kinabalu?' I ask.

'Yes,' he says.

'Really?'

'That is correct.'

I'm still sceptical. 'But what about the Dusuns? Did none of them climb it before him?'

Francis gives me a perplexed look.

'Well, of course they did. Hugh Low had a guide.' And he walks away, on up the path, as if he hadn't said anything confusing at all.

There is a passive ease about colonialism among many Malaysians, I find. People who have always gone with the flow of history as a survival instinct, surviving the events and rulers that come upon them as they would any other natural element: just another storm to weather; just another tide to ride. It requires a separation of two conflicting but somehow concurrent histories and belief systems that would seem to others to be completely contradictory. My father and his siblings did it with believing both Christianity and Chinese paganism at once, and Francis does it with the mountain. He sees no conflict between the official history giving Hugh Low the honour of pioneering Kinabalu, and his own knowledge that his people had done it before Low. One was the official history, and the other was the history he knew. No problem. Perhaps this disinterest in who named what is why the British found so many things unclaimed in the first place.

Hugh Low's guide was a Kadazan-Dusun man called Gunting Lagadan. Hailed in the official records as the first Kadazan-Dusun to climb Kinabalu, but most likely in truth, simply the first to be photographed doing so. History is sometimes run by the same rules that run the social media that Francis so loves. Pics or it didn't happen.

The peak is not the only thing on the mountain to carry a White man's name. There are various species of plants and animals named after Low as well as Stamford Raffles, the British founder of modern Singapore, who gave his name to the famous Raffles Hotel, but also to the iconic *Rafflesia*: an enormous flower with a stinky centre that lures and dissolves curious insects.*

I ask Francis how he feels about it. About how all these Sabahan treasures have British names. Again, he doesn't understand the purpose of my question. Their names are either completely fair to him or totally unimportant. His name is Francis, after all. Why shouldn't the birds and the flowers have similar names too? He can see I'm unsatisfied and presents an olive branch to my apparent desire for nominative justice. 'One of the *pondoks* is named after Gunting Lagadan,' he offers, 'It's broken, though. You can't use it.' And he walks away, on up the path.

From time to time we are passed, going both ways, by porters. Very, very old Kadazan-Dusun men, backs laden with cartoonishly large loads of food, supplies, and building materials. It's hard to tell if their backs are hunched under the weight of their cargo or just because they are so damn old. Their pace is steady, their thin legs rippling with muscle and sinew, and although they don't seem to be moving quickly, I realise the ones going up the mountain are all overtaking us. Their steps are methodical, clockwork, almost bored. They are heading to, and returning from, the Laban Rata Resthouse, where we are heading ourselves for a *very* short sleep before making for the summit in the earliest hours of the morning. *Great*, I think, *an entire day of this interminable hiking in the baking heat, but at least I get to recover tonight with an indulgent THREE HOURS of shut-eye. What a refreshing holiday!*

* * *

* At one point, Francis took us off the path to show us a cluster of pitcher plants, which employ a similar technique to the *Rafflesia*, but in the shape of, well, a pitcher. Hence the name. To be honest, at that point I was just relieved it wasn't named after some guy from Kent called Jeremy Pitcher or something.

All of a sudden, at about ten thousand feet above sea level, the landscape changes. The trees thin out and then fall away entirely, revealing a strange new tundra. Barren and cool and rocky. The earthy path turns into grey rock, and there are no more steps. There are alien plants here. Tall, thin flowers and wispy, dry grass that appears to be hay already. Plants I have never seen before. *This is what I expect from a walk – change*, I think. Francis is snapping away. His Facebook is going to love this. Who knew? Another beautiful day on the mountain.

Turning around and looking back at where we've come from, we can at last, as it were, see the wood for the trees. Well, the jungle. For the first time all day we are out of the cover of greenery, and the air flows crisp and cool like someone's just opened a really big window.

It isn't long before we're at the rest house. A delightful wooden lodge overlooking the foothills below. Here we are treated to an incredibly good buffet of local food. Especially considering how remote and high up we are. Those porters do good work. I wonder how many of these eggs sailed slowly past me on the back of a septuagenarian while I sat panting in a *pondok*.

After dinner, I notice how thin the air is up here. It is impossible to take a satisfying breath no matter how much you inhale. Going up the lodge's stairs feels like a mountain climb in itself. How on earth am I going to make it to the peak?

Later that night, we are shown to our bunkbeds. I'm worried about their comfort. We need to be up at 2am to get to the summit in time for sunrise and I'm not the easiest sleeper. But then again, I'm not usually this tired. I go to the men's washroom to brush my teeth. One of the sinks is full to the brim with vomit. I guess someone else is nervous too. Or doesn't have the stomach for *nasi goreng* at altitude.

Full Affrontal Nudity

On 12 June 2015, Eleanor Hawkins, a twenty-three-year-old from Derbyshire, was bundled into Kota Kinabalu Magistrates' Court, her hands holding on to the guard in front of her, her head bowed down to avoid the flashing cameras and clattering reporters. She had been arrested and charged with public indecency.

Photos had emerged on social media of Eleanor stripping naked on the peak of Mount Kinabalu. She was not alone. Eight others are in the photos with her, taking their clothes off and looking down triumphant over their conquered ascent. Three of them ended up arrested along with Eleanor. The other five got out of Malaysia in time and are presumably still on the run, streaking naked from country to country, nude outlaws living off the land.

Malaysia is a socially conservative nation, so getting naked in public is a fast ticket to Sing Sing (jail, not Singapore) in any case. But the backpackers' choice of spot elevated public outrage to a fever pitch. To the native people of Sabah, Kinabalu is not just a mountain but actual Heaven. My grandmother Po Po's own Kadazan-Dusuns believe that the mountain is the home of souls, where the spirits of the dead go for their final resting place once their earthly vessels have expired. So, what Eleanor and Co saw as a cheeky challenge, many locals saw as akin to walking up to the pearly gates and lifting up Saint Peter's toga for everyone to see his gatey pearls. They demanded to see justice done.

A few days after the nudes were taken, Sabah was hit by an earthquake. A big one. It shook Mount Kinabalu, breaking one of the summit's beloved Donkey's Ears in half. This couldn't have happened at a worse time for Eleanor and the rest of the Fool Monty. For many in Sabah, that the earthquake happened so soon after the backpackers had given Kinabalu an unwanted lap dance was no coincidence. They had disrespected the mountain, angered the spirits and – with that bit of peak shaved off – given those damned Indonesian mountains a leg-up.

Eleanor and the rest of Ass Club 7 were in trouble. They were far from popular with the locals. They had defiled a sacred mountain, caused an earthquake, and – the worst crime of all to an Asian parent – taken a gap year between A levels and university, disrupting their academic momentum.

They pleaded guilty and were each fined £860 and sentenced to three days in jail. Backpackers really will always manage to find the worst accommodation possible, won't they? And at £287 a night, not even at a good price! Still, probably more comfortable than a hostel.

The UK's tabloids had a field day with Eleanor's field trip. A story about a young British woman abroad and her blasphemous boobs was too good to turn down. For a week, she was notorious. The living embodiment of Western depravity and neo-imperialist entitlement. And only twenty-three years old, fellas!

She served her time and got on the next plane back home. Expressing to news cameras when she was reunited with her parents how happy she was to be back in Derbyshire, not something often said, and how sorry she was to the people of Sabah for the offence she and her cohorts had caused.

* * *

The poignancy of the whole episode was hard to miss. Here were nine White Westerners – people from countries that had long lost touch with their animism – suddenly in a country where nature was still sacred. And not sacred in a bullshit 'our annual family camping trip to the New Forest is sacred – only two hours of screen time allowed a day!' kind of sacred. *Actual* sacred. Literally 'that mountain you just showed your hoo-ha to is God' sacred.

The backpackers obviously didn't see things that way. To them a mountain was just a mountain. A geographical feature with great views. Nature's The Shard. The mountain would not care about their nakedness because mountains don't care about anything. They're mountains.

I wondered which side I related to more. With almost a decade of British life under my belt by that point, was I on the side of the backpackers? Had I become like them? Had Kinabalu become just a rock to me? I felt that maybe it had. I had never really had a spiritual relationship with nature, and prided myself on my scientific perspective on things. As a kid in Malaysia I had fallen in love with science and European rationalism. It was a rebellion against the religious and superstitious society I was growing up in.

In particular, it was a rejection of the especially literal and devout strain of Christianity that had become dominant in Sabah. The work started by Father Groot and all those other missionaries all those years ago had really taken root (well, 'Groot'), and the Christianity I grew up around preached an especially watchful, judgemental God, which I found suffocating, oppressive, and nonsensical.

In my late childhood and early teens I became a bit of a

problem child to teachers and even a couple of aunts, who took Mother aside to express their worries about my burgeoning atheism and offer a guiding hand back into the arms of the Lord. At school, my religious education teacher, Miss Jetti* – who took her duties beyond mere teaching and into conversion where necessary – asked me into her office one day.

'Philip,' she said, with concern in her eyes, 'who would you say is your best friend?'

'Bryan,' I replied, without hesitation (Bryan was brilliant).

'Oh, Bryan. I see. I see.' Miss Jetti trailed off.

I had no idea where this was going. Was she going to ask if she could hang out with me and Bryan? Because if so, tough luck! We didn't have enough PlayStation controllers. Eventually she picked her head up and got to the point.

'Well, God is a lot like your best friend.'

'Oh Jesus Christ.'

'Yeah, that's the guy.'

I should have seen it coming, really. What else could the meeting have been about? This was the same woman who'd made our class of thirteen-year-olds watch the entirety of a bootleg copy of Mel Gibson's *The Passion of the Christ* – a gruesome (and grainy) blow-by-blow (by whip, by stab, by nail, by cross) portrayal of the torture and execution of Jesus – so that we would 'understand how he suffered for us'. All it actually

* In Malaysia we show respect to our teachers by addressing them with the usual prefixes – Mr, Miss, Mrs, or simply 'Teacher' – but then their first names. So, I'd be Mr Philip, for example. And you'd be Teacher Gemma. Presuming your name is Gemma. I hope it is and that you just leapt out of your fucking skin.

did was plant a seed of anti-semitism in a class of kids who had never even heard of Jews before then.*

What I'm trying to say is, I've always been suspicious of religion, and, for that matter, any belief in anything that science can't back up. So, I found the Eleanor Hawkins story not just embarrassing for her and the other backpackers, but for the angry Sabahans too, who were being irrational and superstitious in blaming the tourists' nakedness for the earthquake. No one came off well in the whole affair. Just the backpackers' clothes.

The Summit: Day Two (of Two)

I am woken by Lara Croft Tomb Raider at 2am. My alarm went off but I didn't hear it through my earplugs and deep sleep. She is more excited than anyone has any right to be at 2am. We get dressed and set off. Francis leads us with his head torch through the pitch dark. The idea is to get to Low's Peak by five o'clock, when sunrise is due, and take in the view of an island awaking. We have 2,700 feet to climb.

This leg of the journey also begins with wooden steps. But they soon disappear and then it's just rock. Cold rock. The air is cold too. Freezing. Colder and colder the higher we go. It is weird to feel this cold in Malaysia. It doesn't seem right. I think back on all my sweltering childhood nights and can't comprehend that they shared a landmass with this cold.

* Miss Jetti was a good sort, really. Funny, kind, and genuinely caring for her students. Her judgement was just occasionally impaired by the fact that she was really, really, really, really, really, really, really, really, really, really, really, really, really, REALLY into God.

The hike goes on and on. We are surrounded by a thick mist, so we can't see more than six feet in front of us, which makes the trek feel all the more endless. Like we've been condemned in a Greek myth. We just keep climbing blindly in the hope that the end will eventually arrive.

An hour in and I am exhausted. My legs want to give way, and I'm begging for the security of steps. I can't catch my breath no matter how hard I try, and the cold is paralysing. The cold has really gotten to Lara Croft, whose enthusiasm for the outdoors has abated. 'Told you so,' I want to say. But fortunately I don't. Suddenly Lara cries in agony and has to sit down on the ground. She has bad circulation to her hands, which is causing her excruciating pain. She is wailing and inconsolable through her tears. Francis fortunately has an extra pair of gloves (I had offered mine and am secretly thrilled not to have to see my generosity through) and we get them on her hands through the shivers. She improves and gets back up and we continue through the fog.

With Lara taken care of, my own despair takes its opportunity to indulge itself and I start moaning and cursing with the pain and exhaustion. 'Fuck! Fuck! Aaaaaargh!' I suddenly understand why my ancestors believed this is where the dead go – dead is sure how I feel. 'How much longer??'

'Soon. Not long,' Francis says. For another hour and a half.

The fog has warped my sense of space, and now I've lost my sense of time. I am convinced we are never going to get there. I am now guiltily grateful that the Birthday Suit Backpackers' striptease broke the summit with that earthquake and took a few metres off our hike. Every step less is a gift. My mouth is dry and full of froth. I spit it out angrily onto the ground, and

I realise this doesn't look good accompanied by my swearing. I turn and ask Francis if what I've done is disrespectful, but he doesn't answer. Either my chattering Malay is incomprehensible or he'd rather just pretend it didn't happen. In any case, I hope no one has taken a photo. I haven't factored a prison stay into Lara's and my itinerary for 'Southeast Asian Getaway 2017!! <3'.

Eventually, the ground underfoot begins to level out, though it is now smoother, more slippery, and more dangerous. There are no steps to help us along the way, but instead, cables nailed into the mountain's surface. We grab on and pull our way up, like proper mountain climbers.

We can begin to hear the voices of others congregating ahead of us. A few final steps into the unknown and we are amongst them. It is still impossible to tell where we are beyond our fishbowl of vision. The air clears only a little, but it's enough to feel our way to the signpost that marks the top of the mountain: 'Low's Peak – 4,095.2 m, Mount Kinabalu'. It's a photo opportunity that Lara isn't interested in. She says it's too touristy but I know it's because she's exhausted and embarrassed that she cried. I assure her it's the done thing and someone takes our photo in front of it, hunched over, still freezing, but relieved.

I look down now for the first time in what feels like an eternity, and there's not much to see. It's certainly different from what I'd expected. Just mist and rock. Still, we did it. I climbed a mountain. I can say that now. And I never have to climb one again. That's the important thing.

Then comes the sun. I'd somehow forgotten about the sunrise. Streaks of gold pierce the fog like arrows and it disappears like an army of ghosts dispelled. In an instant, Borneo opens up beneath us. Green and gleaming, and bursting with life. The trees and hills and the sea beyond unfurl at Kinabalu's feet, and our mist has settled now into a thin white bed of resting spirits between us and the island below. We are not *in* the clouds, I realise. We are above them. And in this moment, I understand Heaven.

All around us is the usual happy quiet of an early morning – the other climbers taking in what they can, congratulating one another, our odyssey seemingly forgotten in the warmth of a new day. Francis is off on his own, catching up with Kinabalu like an old friend. He fishes his phone out of his pocket one more time and takes photos of Sabah. He is still not over it. I realise for the first time that neither am I.

HOME

MH4

MH4. That's the flight number for Malaysia Airlines, Kuala Lumpur to London Heathrow. The flight that connected my two selves: Malaysian and British. I sometimes wonder how many hours in total I have accumulated over the years in Kuala Lumpur International Airport (or KLIA, as it's affectionately known), waiting for the familiar chimes of the announcement that MH4 was ready for boarding. The cumulative days of my life spent on the floaty monorail between the domestic and international terminals, wandering the shops, squeaking along the shiny floors, shivering unnaturally in the conditioned air, waiting for that ding-ding-dong-ding, '*Tuan-tuan dan puan-puan* . . . Ladies and gentlemen . . .'

I feel peculiarly at home in airports, where everyone is between worlds. Aside from the obvious exception of differently classed tickets and exclusive lounges, there is a unique egalitarianism in airports. All are equal in their alienness. The airport is a transient place, home to no one. Like a filthy United Nations, its travellers all unwitting ambassadors, all brought down to the same level – shopping in the same duty-free, peeing in the same toilets, gasping in disbelief at the same currency exchange rates, having emotional breakdowns at the same check-in staff.

I saw an airport before I saw Malaysia. That first journey home when I was three weeks old must have instilled a lifelong familiarity with departure lounges and baggage carousels. Flying was one of the first experiences I ever had, I suppose. The first of many identical trips between Britain and Borneo, the two islands of my life.

England is about as far away as you can get from Malaysia before you start coming back around. The flight from Kuala Lumpur to London is thirteen hours long. To get to Kuala Lumpur from Kota Kinabalu, my hometown, is itself an additional two and a half hours in the air. With transit times and travel to and from airports, the overall journey is about twenty-four hours. Twenty-four hours. Seven thousand miles.

My whole life is marked by this routine odyssey, from one world to the other. From the country I grew up in, to the country I'll probably grow old in. From one of the youngest nations in the world to one of the longest standing. From the world of my childhood to the world of my adulthood.

Those were exciting hours as a child, the hours in KLIA before the flight to Heathrow. On the other end were not just my grandparents, but a different world. The *Western* World. A world I had seen on TV, and read in books, and could feel in my blood. It was a magical world where the air was cold, even when you were outside in the sun, and people built fires indoors. Dad once brought a friend to the UK who was so astonished by the gas fireplace in our living room that he took a photo of it with his phone to show everybody back home. You have to remember he had spent his entire life in Malaysia, where an open fire in the house only ever meant a terrible disaster. Cold outside and hot inside? British life was inside out.

This was the English-speaking, season-having West that I had been told so much about. The only world I had ever seen documented in any cultural artefact that seemed to matter. A world of pop stars and power and history. It was the world I was born in. The world I was meant for. My Malaysian life was simply an exercise in biding time, Sabah the chrysalis in which my chubby grub was growing slowly into the butterfly that would one day soar alongside MH4 to the glittering West.

Growing up, I referred to the UK as 'the real world'. 'Malaysia is the real world too,' Mum would try to argue, a little concerned by my outlook. But I ignored her. What did she know? She had lived in the UK. She was from there. She had been in the real world, but chose a strange, hot one on the other side of the planet instead. That was her choice. She didn't understand. When I visited the UK, the people looked like the people in the movies I watched, if much lumpier. How was this not the real world?

Britain was an older, more powerful world. A world that once owned Malaysia's; that had caused Malaysia to come to be in the first place. Planet Earth had been Britain's. Malaysia just lived in it. Britain was rich and strong enough to build itself in its own image. Malaysia was put together unnaturally, with an identity borrowed from others. From China, from India, from Britain. I felt like I was equally unnatural. A chance fluke of genetics; the result of two cross-cultural horndogs who for some reason did not follow the normal order of things, and made a child who was out of place everywhere.

I thought myself lucky to be connected to the West, to have a claim to Western and White identity. Why wouldn't I? Even in Malaysia I could feel Western domination; Europe's claim to the world. My name was Philip. My Chinese father's was Benny. Adverts for skin-whitener abounded on television and billboards. *Look prettier, look Whiter, look how you are supposed to.* Imagine my surprise and confusion when I moved to the UK and found out about tanning salons. *Tanning* salons? To look *darker*? Don't you know that halfway around the world people spend all their money trying to achieve the exact opposite? I guess the grass is always paler (or more tanned) on the other side.

And so, I grew up feeling defined by what separated me from the rest of Malaysia – my Whiteness, partial though it was. I held onto that Whiteness as something that made me special; that marked me out. And aside from my mother, and the handful of expats in town, the only other place I saw that Whiteness was on TV, in movies, and in books, all from the West.

Let's Get Up to Business

In 2016 I became that which I swore I never would. I started collecting frequent-flyer miles. I'd always considered the idea laughable; pathetic. The slow, arduous collection of a virtual currency devised by airlines solely to keep you flying. The points held only a pretend value. Like the money in *The Sims* or the British pound post-Brexit.

Of course, the only reason anyone collects air miles is because you can theoretically use them to upgrade to Business Class. Airlines offer other uses for their points too – discounts on bills at participating businesses, an ugly pen from their gift shop, or – get this – charity. Ahahahaha you can donate your points to charity! Imagine. What am I? Charles Dickens? No thanks. I'd rather take the pen than be the kind of rube who helps his fellow man when there's stationery up for grabs. No, the only reason anyone collects points is to chase that elusive bump up to Business Class; an upgrade to a seat worth taking selfies in.

For most of my life, I didn't care about Business Class. I thought it was an ostentatious waste of money on an experience barely distinguishable from Economy and for the price of a wedding. I mean, how much could it improve the experience, really? You're still on a plane, aren't you? However much you paid for your ticket, you're still trapped in the same flying fart corridor in the sky for hours on end. I would have understood the appeal if buying a Business Class ticket shortened the journey somehow. Now *that* would be worth paying extra for. When the plane arrives at its destination, Business Class passengers would be parachuted out like James Bond along with their luggage directly into the taxi rank, while Economy Class have to remain on board as the plane does doughnuts above the airport for another three hours.

I opposed the names of the classes themselves. Like all marketing terms, 'Business' and 'Economy' only have the illusion of meaning – specific and vague at once – just enough to imply the hierarchy of customers without hurting anyone's feelings explicitly enough to warrant complaints. But think about them for a moment. What class of people would a 'Business' class even refer to? What, like, a merchant class? Like in the fifteenth century? Sorry is this a Lufthansa flight to Cape Town or Renaissance Milan? Am I about to tuck into a microwaved beef stroganoff or help finance the next war in Lombardy?

Aren't 'business' and 'the economy' essentially the same thing anyway? 'Businesses' make up 'the economy'. 'Economy' is the term for the group, 'businesses' are the individual elements within that group. Ah! That must be it. Business Class is for *individuals*. Lives with value. *Persons*. Economy Class is for the hordes. Society at large. *People*. A plane is about as heavy-handed an analogy for capitalism as you could ask for. Business at the front, seated first, served first, considered first, and the economy they feed off in the back, a forgotten mass of despair, worth only the small extras they're able to pay for.

Business Class was an insult to the promise of an equal society. It was a posturing, arrogant waste of money, and I felt it had to be abolished for the sake of all humankind.

And then, of course, I flew Business Class, and it was the best thing in the world. I was hired to be in an advert for a hostel-booking app which was filming in Indonesia. Hostels are big money apparently, so I was booked on a flight to Jakarta, *Business Class*. And now I wish I was in Business Class all the time. Even when I'm not flying. Hell, I wish I were in Business Class right now, instead of writing this.

Of course, there's better booze and more leg room, but that's not what makes Business Class so magnificent. It's the mere *humaneness* of it. What's amazing about the flying experience is how the things we expect as standard in our everyday life become the height of luxury when we're on a plane. You're denied things in Economy, like space, basic comfort, and privacy, so that creating luxury in Business is a piece of piss for the airline. You have a seat that reclines *all* the way back so you can lie down *flat* to sleep. Wow. I haven't had a sleep like that except for every other sleep I've ever had in my life. No sleeping standing like a cow for me tonight! What's this? Food on actual plates instead of tweezered out of an astronaut's takeaway box? *Metal* knives? What trust! They don't expect me to storm the cockpit at all! Why would I? I'm in Business Class. What issue could I possibly have with the world? How could I hold any grievances in such luxury? An actual terrorist could probably muster together the money for a one-way Business Class ticket for access to the deadly silverware. But so confident are the airlines in the comfort of Business Class, they know he would change his mind about the decadent West, halfway through his third complimentary Kir royale.

However, as wonderful as all that is, the *true* reward of Business Class is the quality it provides in the central charade of commercial flight: that you, the passenger, are in charge, and the flight attendants serve you. In actuality, this is of course not true. Not for any of the passengers, no matter what class they're in. The flight attendants are there to make sure you don't crash the plane. They're the experts who have to keep you and your pig hands from opening the cabin door mid-flight and getting sucked out over Kashmir you fucking idiot. They're there to keep you in your seat and keep you alive. Flight attendants are security guards in disguise as waiters. And the best ones wear that disguise well enough to convince passengers that the customer is the boss.

Now, in the majority of my flying experience, that particular play gets one star. Flight attendants in Economy Class let you know you're a slug with their dead-eyed smiles and barely concealed contempt. A contempt that is fair, by the way. We are like dumb children to them. With our demands and our questions and our stink.

In Business Class, however, are the flight attendants who can act. Air travel's Oscar winners. Professionals at the top of their field who can actually convincingly play the role of someone who is happy to see you. Of course, they aren't. They don't care. It's their job. They're as happy to see you as a postman is happy to see an envelope. But by Buddha they make such a good show of it even someone as cynical as myself can't help but get sucked into the privileged pantomime. When I stepped onto that Business Class flight to Jakarta, they smiled at me like I was their long-lost son. I was assigned a specific attendant who knew my name, and looked at me every time I dropped a fork like I'd just cured cancer.

This was a game changer. Had this been going on up here this whole time? I felt like a worm for ever having travelled any other way. I began wondering if all those times I'd flown Economy Class I was even a customer. Was I actually just a part of the plane? Were we fuel? Do the shits we take in Economy power the plane? Is that why we aren't allowed in the toilets up front? Because those are the real toilets and not the vacuum-powered methane extractors *in disguise* as toilets that we have in the back? It would certainly explain why all the food seems designed to give you diarrhoea.

That flight to Jakarta marked a change in my life. After that flight (and the return flight, of course – equally delightful) I was no longer just some nobody who flew Economy. I was some nobody who flew Economy but was spending every other waking moment collecting frequent-flyer miles to maybe at some point stand a chance of upgrading a flight to Business Class, where I belonged.

Get to the Points

I've always had an eye for a freebie. Every Malaysian does. All shopping in Malaysia is open to a haggle – no matter the shop. No purchase is beyond negotiation, no product too highfalutin to be accompanied by a discount or offer. Many offers in Malaysia include a 'Free Gift' to entice customers – a pencil case, a lamp, a small animatronic dog – nothing anyone would actually want, but which was absolutely necessary to stand any chance of selling that house. Regularly going around town with my father as he shopped, I grew up thinking 'Diskaun' and 'Free giff' were traditional Malaysian greetings.

Haggling is so deeply ingrained into Malaysian culture that even if you don't haggle with a shopkeeper they'll often just do it for you, dropping the price of whatever you're trying to buy without you even asking. Once, when I was about eight years old, I was given some money to buy a new motor for my Tamiya car from a hobbies shop.* I pointed at the motor that I wanted in the display case, the price next to it: 50 Ringgit. 'OK,' said the man behind the counter. He then stood still, and looked at me through his round spectacles, as if waiting for me

* Tamiya cars were a phenomenon in Malaysia during the nineties. They were a Japanese brand of battery-powered toy car that came unassembled in a box. It was up to you – the child – to follow the instructions and put them together, wheels, gears, chassis and all. Bringing the famous Asian sweatshop into the comfort of your own home. There were many different models of Tamiya car, and you could tinker with the performance of yours by buying faster motors or stickier tyres. It was more of a lifestyle than a toy, really. A calling. There was even an accompanying anime series about the cars and their heroic owners, who raced them against . . . I don't know . . . evil cars? Tamiya was essentially Pokémon but for the kids most likely to grow up to be arrested for building a bomb in their garage.

to say more. I didn't, and just held out a fifty Ringgit note. Eventually, he said, 'I'll give it to you for forty-five.'

'OK,' I said, a little confused.

He went into the back room to pack it up, and when he returned with it continued, 'Fine, thirty-five, but that's the best I can do.'

'O . . . K . . .' I said, again. I handed him the money and he gave me back my change. Change, remember, that I was only due because of *his* efforts. He smiled and nodded as I left, chuffed to bits with the great deal he'd struck. For me.

Haggling is noticeably less common in the UK. It's just not a part of the culture in the same way. I've never seen anyone sweet-talking thirty pence off their carrot sticks in Waitrose. In the country of due process and fair play, the assumption is that everything is already at its correct price. Father always got frustrated with Mother's willingness to pay the asking price on everything in Malaysia. A gullible European paying too much, getting rinsed everywhere she went. In response, she adapted. Hardened. Years later, having internalised the Malaysian mercantile spirit, Mother found herself back in England at a charity fair in Staffordshire. At one of the stalls she found some earrings she liked for £5 a pair. Forgetting where she was, she instinctively asked the man behind the trestle table, 'How about £12 for three?' He was shocked, and slowly looking for words he had not expected to need that day, said, 'But we're raising money for the children'. It was at that moment that Mother remembered she was at a fundraising fair at a school for children with learning difficulties.

£5 a pair *is* a lot, though.

Now, Business Class was quite the 'free giff' so I set about planning how I was going to get it.

I already had a credit card that got me frequent-flyer miles. One point for every £2 spent on it. Or, for the mathematical among you, half a point for every pound spent. Better than nothing, but it simply was not going to do. I was a Business Class flyer now, and at this rate I wasn't going to have enough points for a Business Class flight until I was well into my eighties. I don't plan on living that long. And between the melting ice caps, the burning forests, and the vanishing species, neither is the planet. Time was of the essence.

I spent days researching credit cards online, looking for the one that would optimise my point collection. Writing this in a COVID-19 lockdown, looking at a glowing screen, alone, stuck at home for so many days that I've lost count, it is incredible that in a time of freedom I willingly spent hours on my laptop, sat alone at home looking up credit cards on a glowing screen in order to earn the chance to sit in a flying metal tube, alone, looking at a glowing screen. But life's a prankster like that.

Eventually I found it. A credit card that would earn me one whole point for every £1 spent. I had doubled my earning potential. Sure, the card had an annual charge of £140 just to *have*, but the benefit of getting to that Business Class flight twice as quickly would more than make up for it. Now all I had to do to get there was simply spend as much money on it as possible! It was official. I was a financial genius. I felt like the Wolf of Wall Street, buying extra groceries, making up excuses to go to restaurants. It was your birthday last month? Let me take you out to dinner. Your football team avoided relegation? Let me treat you to dinner, where you can explain to me what that means. You got all the way to the end of a bar of soap? Why this calls for a spot of dinner. On me!

It turned me into something else, collecting these points. A different man. Purchases were no longer an exchange in which I surrendered money, but an opportunity for me to earn points! Why, I was basically *making* money when I bought that smart coffee-bean grinder with the LCD display. Does the coffee taste better than pre-ground coffee from the shop? Not really! But how else was I going to make those 159.95 points?? Well, 159 points. They round down. Which is fine! Completely fair, actually!

One day my sister told me she'd got the same card. I was overjoyed. *Wonderful, sister! Together we will be lords of the sky. Sat upon our rightful, reclinable thrones in the clouds.* And then my heart skipped a beat. She'd already got it. I could have referred her. She could have made an extra 2,000 points for nothing. And, more importantly, *I* could have made *6,000* points! For nothing! I was irate.

'Why didn't you tell me you were getting the card?' I seethed, froth tumbling from my lips.

'I don't know. I forgot. Whatever.'

Whatever? *Whatever?* I didn't talk to her for weeks.

MH3

When I moved to the UK at sixteen, I thought, *At last, the end of the flights. The end of the odysseys. The end of MH4.* I quickly realised that it was of course not the end of the flights. I had moved to England, but the rest of my Malaysian family hadn't. And I would now have to get on a flight going the opposite direction to see *them*. Gone were the days of MH4. Now were my years of MH3 – Malaysia Airlines, London Heathrow to Kuala Lumpur. This was the curse of my family. Wherever I was, half of them would be at the other end of a trek of check-in queues, security pat-downs, and long waits. The latter was partly because when it comes to getting to airports early, my parents are the biggest dorks around. Getting us there five hours before the flight. What were they worried about? That one of us would step in a bear trap in duty-free? That customs would make us sit a surprise exam about aeroplanes? That we might lose our tickets and need enough time to work a full career in the control tower to earn them back?

I suppose those trips in my youth were when I first learnt my unparalleled skill in killing time. Sitting in departure lounges and riding in suitcase trolleys made me the adult I am today – someone who can spend an hour sat on the toilet perfectly content, long after he's finished his business; who can whittle away an entire afternoon closing and then opening the same app on his phone; who can lie in bed awake all night just thinking about Batman, and what he might do in various situations. Because of my training in the airports of Asia and Europe, I am a world-class procrastinator. Look upon me, idle time, and despair. Your hours melt like fresh snow in the hot yellow stream of my unrivalled dithering. I learnt these skills waiting to board delayed flights across the world, for families who needed to see how tall I had gotten since they last saw me.

Family reunions are just a fact of life for us all. And I'm not saying that they're particularly easy for anyone. At least I know where my family *is*. That's not a luxury all enjoy. In Sabah we have a family friend called Fagap, a native of the state of Sarawak and a member of the Penan tribe. The Penan are a remarkable people who have lived in the jungles of Borneo for thousands of years. Fagap is one of many native Borneans who have left the jungle over the last century or so for the towns and cities that have risen since the British arrived and the missionaries came. But Fagap, like all of us, has to go home every now and then to see his parents. However, because the Penan are nomads, he never knows where they are. All he knows is that they are in the jungle somewhere. So, whenever Fagap wants to see his folks, he has to track them through the rainforest. This takes days, as he scours the jungle floor and the barks of trees for signs of Ma and Pa. When night falls, he will sling a hammock up wherever he can, to stay off the ground and away from snakes and centipedes. Sometimes he never finds them, and has to give up and go home, and hope for clearer tracks next time. And here I am complaining about check-in queues.

Fortunately for Fagap, the Penan employ an extraordinary communication system, using what the jungle offers. Signs built out of sticks, twigs and leaves, left to give directions or pass on a message to whoever is tracking the messenger. A long branch stuck in the ground points in the direction they have gone. If its sides are shaven, the journey is long. A folded leaf means the traveller has no food, a sharp stick pointed at arse height means hurry the hell up.

Without knowing it, my own family have also always used a similar system of signs throughout the house. A bare cardboard cylinder on the toilet roll holder means 'we need more toilet paper'. And the TV on at 11:30 pm with no one in the room except for an unconscious middle-aged woman on the sofa means 'Mum's been on the brandy again'.

There's No Phrase Like 'Home'

Home. What a word. It's hard to think of any other that can rouse so much in the heart so quickly. As a species we are obsessed with home. Our entire lives revolve around it. From the moment we're born, we just want to be home. What does a child cry when they're tired and fed up? 'I WANNA GO HOME!' What does a commuter say when they want to be left alone by a lunatic on the train? 'Look, I'm just trying to get home.' How do you entice a room of people to do a little extra work? 'Look, let's just get this done, and then we can all go home!'

From the moment we're out of the womb we spend the rest of our lives trying to build a new one for ourselves with bricks and mortar. Home is the best thing in the world, no matter who you are. And this love of home is reflected in our language. Any phrase with the word 'home' in it is a positive one.

You're home free. Homeward bound. When you find yourself in a place that you like, it's homely. A home away from home where you've got some home comforts. Home is where the heart is, after all.

Keep going! You can do it! You're almost there! This is the home stretch. Let's bring it home! Just a couple more hours and we'll be home and dry.

Even sports people – who you'd expect to be more outgoing than the rest of us – just want to go home. Where do football teams prefer to play? At home. Because that's where they're on home ground with their home fans and have a home-field advantage. What's the best thing you can do in baseball? A home run. That's when you run all the way around and get back to home plate. If a team is underperforming, then their coach bursts into their dressing room and gives them some home truths to really bring home the message that they suck.

Home is important. It shapes who we are, gives us our grounding in life. Without it we feel adrift, destitute. You're lucky if you come from a good home. If someone seems depressed or not their usual self, we ask 'Is everything alright at home?' Home is precious, irreplaceable, sacred. What's one of the worst things a person can be? A homewrecker. What's one of the scariest things that can happen? A home invasion.

Nothing like a home-cooked meal. And if you're nowhere near home, don't worry. Restaurants will offer 'good home cooking'. Even though that's impossible, because they're a restaurant. Still, just £3 for a plate of home fries!

Don't want to go out to eat? Well then let's stay home! I'm a real homebody anyway. And that restaurant does home delivery so we are home safe on the food front. Home alone? That's a great movie! You've homed in on one of my absolute favourites there. Pop it on the home cinema. Put your legs up, get comfortable, make yourself at home.

Ah. Home sweet home.

A home is not to be confused with a house, of course. A house is not always a home. You might live in many houses over your life, but not every one will earn the honour of 'home'. However, a house sufficiently loved can be imbued with the spirit of home. A spirit that, with enough time, can grow; can radiate, extending outwards beyond those four walls, to engulf the town your house is in, the county your town is in, and the country your county is in. The further away you are from it, the wider the radius grows, the broader your idea of 'home' becomes. After a long trip away, you might think, upon arriving back at Heathrow, and falling once more into the calm, comfortable order of a British queue, *Ahhh, it's good to be back in Britain*. Then on the train, as the green of the Dales dashes past the window, *Ahhh, it's good to be back in Yorkshire*. Then when the train doors open at Edinburgh, *Ahhh, I think I missed my stop*.

I have not had this feeling for a while. I feel happy and relieved when I return to Britain now. Back from a holiday or work abroad. But I'm not sure that it's a feeling of coming home. Not yet. It isn't the feeling I used to have as a child, flying back *from* Britain. That was the last time I had it. Landing in Kuala Lumpur, the humid air rushing to engulf me like an impatient friend kept waiting, I would think in my high little voice, *Ahhh, it's good to be back in Malaysia*. Then, as the coastline of Borneo broke over the horizon after two hours of sea, *Ahhh, it's good to be back in Sabah*. Then, as the car rolled away from the airport, and the familiar coffee shops dashed by glowing in the night, *Ahhh, it's good to be back in Kota Kinabalu*. Then, as the car slowed, and the iron gate of our house shuddered awake, rolled squeaking along its narrow rail and clattered open, *Ahhh, it's good to be home*.

That was the last time I had that feeling.

No-stalgia

Like Fagap, I too left the jungle for the wider world. A world of cities and noise and opportunity and dirt. Trading trees for towers, and soil for grime.

I like to leave things behind. I always have. It is cleaner and simpler than holding on to people and places, and I'm well practised in it. I have never been in a single school for more than two years. I learnt to make and drop friends as I went from school to school, from country to country.

I am not a nostalgic person. I don't have a wistful affection for my childhood or past in the way many people seem to – a luxury of the grounded life. People who still live in the country of their childhood, among the friends of their earliest years, with the two sides of their family close enough to see them both at Christmas. Nostalgia is for those lucky enough to still live among reminders of their past. Carved branches stuck in the ground of their lives, pointing back in time.

I have no nostalgia. As I said at the start of this book, I have a clear memory only for embarrassment; mistakes. I can't remember the face or name of my first childhood friend, but I *can* remember the time I shat myself in the library at kindergarten. We were all sat around in a ring on the floor as the librarian talked to us about how the place worked. A pressure grumbled in the pit of my belly, but I did not want to miss out on the finer points of the Dewey Decimal system.* So, I just did it in my pants. I thought I had gotten away with it until I saw the nostrils of the kid next to me dance their telltale twitch. He turned to me, eyebrows furrowed. *I'm finished*, I thought, then feeling the lump between my butt cheeks and the floor, *in more ways than one*.

'Did you fart?' he asked, clearly disgusted.

I thought about this for a while, and weighed up my options. *OK, Philip. Think. I have done a shit. But my classmate here thinks I have only done a fart. Ideally, he wouldn't think I had done either. But at this point, with this much stink so clearly centring around me,*

* Knowledge I would one day need to troll a friend's librarian father in my book. Got you again, David!

the idea that I haven't even done a fart is – let's face it – ludicrous. I know what I have to do.

'Yes,' I whispered back, 'I farted.'

The boy gave me one more look of disapproval, then turned back to hear about borrowing limits. And that? That was my first lesson in damage limitation. And an introduction to the idea that there is sometimes a 'lesser of two evils'.

I remember the first time I called a teacher 'Mum'.

I remember being caned at Chinese school. And fearing my Malay teacher's thin cane (short sharp pain) less than my Mandarin teacher's thick one (an explosive sting followed by a deep, lingering ache), and so prioritising Mandarin homework over Malay if I only had time to finish one. Again, the lesser of two evils.

I remember one of the cool girls at school turning around on the bus to catch me with my hand down my pants gleefully scratching my groin. '. . . Itchy,' was all I could think to say, with a dumb chuckle.

The past is a humiliating place. I have always been happy to leave it.

It was with as much ease that I was able to leave Malaysia behind when we moved to the UK. I felt no sadness, no loss. Only excitement. Excitement about England – this new, and yet old, home of mine – and the life of unlimited possibility before me in the cold, crisp, relevant West. My life in the real world had begun.

Over the years I grew resistant about going back to Malaysia. For holidays; to see family. Anything. It felt like a backwards step to a part of my life that I was done with. I wanted to move on, focus on British life, focus on my future. The past would always be there waiting for me in Malaysia, where time is slow. Here in the UK, I had A levels to ace, university to get into, comedy to take by storm! Malaysian Phil was done. Here came British Wang.

Every year or two, Mother and Father would tell us it was time to go back to Malaysia for a few weeks. To catch up with the family, to celebrate Chinese New Year, to see a new baby. And every time I would curse the inconvenience under my breath. *I don't have time for this! I've got things to do. Girls to try to kiss. Comedy to write. A career! I don't have time for my extended family!*

My family years were done. I had my own path to furrow. A path away from Sabah. I was living in the real world now. A world with deadlines and expectations and competition. A world that requires constant attention to keep up with. A world that isn't going to wait for you to lie around in Borneo meeting babies that aren't even going to remember it anyway.

Should Auld Acquaintance Be Forgot

By the final third of 2019, life was good. I had just finished a sold-out run at the Edinburgh Fringe Festival, and was playing to full rooms around the country on my second national tour. But most importantly, through hard work, perseverance, ingenuity, and travel, I had collected over sixty-thousand frequent-flyer points. I was on top of the world.

This was what I had moved to Britain for. I was in the entertainment industry. I was successful. I was appearing on comedy panel shows, I was guesting in sitcoms. I was on TV and radio. People I'd been at school with would say, 'I'm seeing you all over the place!' and I would feign humility. I was going to parties, I was dating, I was debating politics heatedly with smart friends in smoking areas. I had been right. This was the real world – the West – and this was where I belonged.

And then a message appeared on the Wang family WhatsApp. Our cousin Gina was getting married at Christmastime. And we were all going back to Malaysia for a big family reunion, a wedding, and a Malaysian Christmas, just like old times.

For. God's. Sake. This annoyed me no end. Not that my cousin was getting married, of course. I am very pro-Wang procreation. You can't have too much of a good thing, I say. But we had to fly back to Malaysia for a wedding? I've heard English friends of mine make excuses to avoid weddings in *Wales*. But I was going to have to disrupt my brilliant Western life for two weeks to fly back to Malaysia for a *wedding*? How selfish, I thought, of Gina to have her wedding in Malaysia just because she 'lived' there. Why couldn't they do it in London where I was? Where I could easily drop in for an hour or two? And we had to go back at Christmastime, no less. A time of year when the UK really comes into its own. I've always found Britain the most beautiful in the winter, and Christmas makes so much more sense in the cold. That's its natural habitat. Now I was going to have another humid, false-feeling Yuletide on the equator in Malaysia, where frost-dappled decorations and carols about snow are cruel taunts as I sweat in shorts.

And then I remembered: New Year's. No! The wedding was only a couple of days before New Year's Eve, and I'd be damned if I was going to spend it in Malaysia with my *family*. Ew. How pathetic would that be? New Year's Eve isn't for your *family*. Christmas is, sure. It's wholesome, and centred around a big meal, and seeing your parents, and nodding politely at something your uncle mumbled. But New Year's Eve is a sexy night. Not for family at all. It's for friends and kissing and dirty dancing. It's meant to be a hedonistic night that marks your annual return from the family world back into your social life, your personal life, and, for me, my Western life.

Well it wouldn't do. I decided I would fly to Kota Kinabalu for Christmas and the wedding, but I would then fly back to London earlier than the others on December 30 – New Year's Eve's Eve – so that I could see in 2020 – sure to be my best year yet – back in the real world with my London friends. Not that I had actually *been* invited to a party. Yet! But New Year's plans are always a last-minute affair, and an invite was due any moment. Of this, I was sure.

Then an epiphany. Heathrow to Kuala Lumpur is a pretty long flight. And the perfect opportunity to use those hard-earned points for my first ever upgrade. An upside to this whole disruptive affair! I called the airline to see if it was possible. Surely not? Thirteen hours of pure opulence at no extra cost? Could it be? This was what all those credit cards and unnecessary purchases and short flights and hours spent deal hunting had been building up to. Had I done it?

The lady on the phone had a check and a one-way upgrade to Business Class would cost . . . 35,000 points. I had enough! Enough to upgrade my trip one way.

I chose to upgrade the return flight – something to look forward to while I was over there, and just the sort of confidence boost that was sure to make me a hit at whichever New Year's Eve party I was definitely going to be invited to by someone at some point very, *very* soon. All was set. Now I just had the journey over to Kota Kinabalu, Christmas and the wedding to get through.

The flight to Kuala Lumpur was an evening one so I managed to sleep through the main body of it. Not that that would be the case on my Business Class return, of course. I was going to stay awake for *all* of that. Watching all the movies, moving the chair up and down, and side to side just because I can, ordering wine until they have to give me some of the captain's personal stash, smoking cigars with the crew in the alarm-free toilet cubicle they reserve for legends. But for this leg of the journey, I would sleep.

At Kuala Lumpur, Southeast Asia's humidity hit me like a bus. And with the sense of warm moisture on my skin, and the smell of rain either passed or imminent tickling my nose, I was surprised to feel an old self return. A Malaysian self that seems to stay in KLIA whenever I leave for England, and wait for me to return, when he will jump back into my skin once again. The shuttle train took me over to the domestic terminal and I got on the smaller plane that would take me to Kota Kinabalu.

When I arrived in Borneo, the air felt even thicker. I bathed in moisture and memory with every step out of the airport. Dad was there to pick me up, phone in a case on his belt in the way that all Chinese fathers apparently agreed to do. It was on this car ride that he told me the story of 'Chong Are You', which I laughed at maniacally. We drove to a *kopitiam* to meet Mum and my sisters, who had already arrived. It was there that I made him tell the story again, this time, him falling into hysterics. The food was perfect, and the rich night air enveloped me like a blanket.

Every evening that week we spent with our extended family. Our uncles and aunts and cousins. Cousins who had come back from their own new homes abroad, with their own young children. Children who were babies the last I had seen them, but who had grown to be beautiful and clever and funny little people. Children who were Chinese Malaysian, and others who were half German, and others who were half Bosnian, but all with those same Wang eyes that were in Gong Gong and Po Po's black-and-white photograph.

Christmas was just like it used to be. Kids running up and down the house's hard tiled steps like I used to. The uncles doing wrist locks on each other in the corner like they used to. My Uncle Ricky asking me how my 'comedy speeches' were going. And as always, no one touching the alcoholic punch. Presents were passed from the youngest child to Uncle David to read out. Still, in his advanced years, hardier, stronger, and more athletic than me.

The wedding was wonderful. Both the Christian service in the morning, and the Chinese tea ceremony in the afternoon. My sisters and I watched and laughed as our mother (the only White person to receive the honour) was presented by the happy couple with a cup of tea – a mark of respect from the newlyweds that is repeated for all the elders of the family. Naturally, the ceremony took all afternoon. That evening at the reception dinner, Gina and her husband entered the banquet hall singing a karaoke of 'A Whole New World' from *Aladdin*. In the video I took of the moment, Dad closes his eyes and sways his head in rapture like it's Rachmaninov at the Royal Albert Hall. Everyone applauds and whoops, then an unlikely MC takes the stage: Edin, my cousin's eccentric young son. Half Bosnian and all attitude. He hosts a quiz about the couple, and is so funny about it, and out of place, and the situation is so wonderfully absurd, that I collapse into fits of laughter at our table.

The next day the cousins are talking about a trip out to the islands on the thirtieth, and the uncles and aunts are talking about a quiet New Year's Eve for us all at the old family home in Tuaran. I'll be gone by then, I tell them. I'll be missing it all. I realise then that I want to stay. But the flight back is booked. And to reschedule is one thing. To reschedule and keep the upgrade? Forget about it.

The family smile and nod and say, 'Ah you must have a lot to be getting back to. You must be busy.' I say yeah. I say there's a lot to be getting back to. The comedy speeches have been going very well.

I check my phone. I still don't have a New Year's invite. My London friends are having quiet ones with their families. Of course they are. Why wouldn't they? That sounds nice.

The cousins say goodbye. I hug the kids. They'll never be this small again. Dad drives me to the airport.

At KLIA, my Malaysian ghost steps out of me and waves goodbye, off to peruse the souvenirs and watch the departure boards until I'm back. He can't get on the plane. The cabin crew smile as I approach, and then smile slightly harder at the sight of my ticket. I'm guided to my private pod by a window just over the wing. I did it. All on points. I'm handed a glass of champagne, the plane takes off, and I cry all the way to London.

Epilogue

'Where are you from?' I still get asked, after over a decade of life in Britain. My answer to the question (as I have a few) changes depending on my mood, who is asking, and where I am. If I'm travelling around the UK, I say London, which has been my home for eight years. Sometimes this doesn't satisfy the inquisitor, who still needs me to explain away my accent and my face. 'Right . . .' they offer, a little nervous, before pressing on with – and this is the infamous bit, 'But where are you *originally* from?'*

It's a question every non-White Brit is familiar with. But I have to say, it is a question that I have never really minded. People are almost always asking out of genuine curiosity. And I would never punish curiosity. If anything, when I had just moved to the UK, I relished the opportunity to display a little exoticism and say, 'Deepest Borneo, where the orangutans swing and men are named Chong Are You'. But not everyone likes the question. If you grew up in Britain, went to school in Britain, consider yourself as British as anyone else,

* I used to do a stand-up bit about being asked this, and every time I began the question 'No, where are you . . .', every non-White person in the audience would say along with me 'ORIGINALLY FROM!' Singing along like it was 'Angels' at a Robbie Williams concert. Must be a specialty of us Stoke boys.

I can understand the frustration. While visiting Pakistan, Sadiq Khan was asked by a BBC reporter 'Does it feel like coming home?' 'Home is South London, mate', the Mayor of London replied, barely hiding his annoyance. *I became the Mayor of London for fuck's sake, what more do I have to do?*

Khan was born and raised in Tooting, and grew up to be mayor of the nation's capital, so I can understand his disbelief at still having his Britishness questioned. But I don't have the same right to anger. When someone asks me where I'm originally from, having assumed that I didn't grow up here, I'm afraid they're bang on. What can I do but answer honestly?

'I'm originally from Malaysia,' I say happily and proudly, but hoping they don't ask me where I was born so that I don't then have to say, 'Oh, Stoke-on-Trent' and watch their face melt with confusion. Does the question make me feel less British? Yes, it does. But the truth is, I *am* less British. Less British than someone who grew up here, less British than someone who has always said 'trousers' instead of 'pants'. But that's fine. I'm no less Phil for being less British.

I get the question in Malaysia too. When I throw out a bit of fluent Malay, and shocked faces ask me 'Where are you from?' 'Here!' I say happily and proudly. Before offering the explanation they're desperate for: 'But my mother is English.' Does the question make me feel less Malaysian? Yes, it does. But the truth is, I *am* less Malaysian. Less Malaysian than them. Less Malaysian than someone who has continued to spend their life in Malaysia. Less Malaysian than someone who continues to laugh at *Mind Your Language* without hesitation. Less Malaysian than someone still blessed to have never seen a bag of microwaveable rice. And that's fine too. I'm no less Wang for being less Malaysian.

However, sometimes my answer is less assured. There are times when I am asked 'Where are you from?' and the honest answer is, I don't know. I am from two places and nowhere at once. I am from however I feel that day. I am from whatever I last ate. I am from whichever accent I last used in conversation. I am from the last book I read and the last joke I told. I am from the last hurt I felt and the last victory I won. I am from the last parent I texted. I am from the last language I wrote in.

I am lucky that I came to the realisation, early on in my British life, that I may not – and probably never will – fit in. Not completely. I have too much lost time on my fellow Brits. I will never feel at home as much as someone completely British does in Britain, or wholly Malaysian does in Malaysia. I have come to terms with that. Not every life can expect every joy. And what I've lost in the comfort and certainty of a single point of origin, I have gained in a wider perspective; a more global life. A strong sense of belonging, friends of a lifetime, a football club I feel qualified to support, are all joys that I simply will never know. But I will know the joys of both Christmas and Chinese New Year. I will know the limber beauty of English, the majesty of Mandarin, and the calm friendliness of Malay. I will never know the familiar embrace of a Yorkshire pudding, or understand Marmite. But I will know both the homely thrill of hot noodles in cheap plastic bowls and the underrated salty-sweet genius of a sticky toffee pudding in winter. I will never know the intense beacon of a single, clear ancestry, and its radiating pull wherever I am in the world. But I will know the gentle pulse of two familiar islands, on opposite ends of the earth, beating softly across Eurasia. Each in my possession. Each possessing me. Each the other's completing half. Each home.

Acknowledgements

First of all, it would be remiss of me not to thank Cai Lun, the Han dynasty Chinese court official who invented paper, without whom none of this would have been possible.

Now that Lun's dealt with, a big thank you to Mum (aka Mother) who furnished me with most of the family history I needed, her memories of Borneo, and a lot of my own that I'd forgotten or was too young to remember. Thank you to Dad and Uncle David, who helped me with the history of Sabah and the Wangs therein.

Thank you to Myfanwy Moore and Izzy Everington at Hodder Studio, whose guidance and patience have been invaluable in the development of this book. Thank you to Julien Matthews and Katie McKay at Avalon who kicked my ass into gear (very nicely).

Thank you to Mum, Myfanwy, Julien, and Pierre Novellie for reading through early versions of this book and letting me know what was misspelt/untrue/crap. Without them, this thing would have been littered with errorrs.

Thank you to the marvellous NHS. Thank you to the people who made the COVID vaccines and the people who put them into our arms. Thank you to the supermarket staff, delivery people, security guards, drivers, postmen and women, computer programmers, and volunteers who have kept life going this past year and a half.

And a huge, enormous, colossal, giant, immense, humongous, gargantuan, mammoth, massive, gigantic thank you to Thesaurus.com.

Notes

p.53 https://www.dw.com/en/uk-fishing-industry-or-brexits-red-herrings/a-51418061#:~:text=The%20UK%20catch%20is%205,and%20decent%20quotas%20for%20cod

p.60 https://www.bbc.com/worklife/article/20161216-why-japan-celebrates-christmas-with-kfc

p.89 According to a 2015 estimate

p.89 According to the 2011 census

p.105 https://www.vice.com/en_uk/article/mba49a/all-your-favourite-old-british-sitcoms-are-racist-as-hell

p.164 https://yougov.co.uk/topics/politics/articles-reports/2014/07/26/britain-proud-its-empire

p.165 https://yougov.co.uk/topics/international/articles-reports/2020/03/11/how-unique-are-british-attitudes-empire